MORE

THAN YOU EVER WANTED TO KNOW

ABOUT

GLASS

BEADMAKING

by James Kervin
GlassWear Studios
1197 Sherry Way
Livermore, CA 94550-5745
(510) 443-9139

© 1996 James Kervin

More Than You Ever Wanted To Know About
Glass Beadmaking

by James E. Kervin

Published by:
GlassWear Studios
1197 Sherry Way
Livermore, CA 94550
(510)443 9139

All rights reserved. No part of this work covered by copyright hereon may be reproduced or used in any form or by any means - graphic, electronic, or mechanical, including photocopying, recording, taping, or information storage and retrieval systems - without permission of the publisher, except for the inclusion of brief quotations in a review.

Copyright © 1994, 1995
First Printing 1994
Second Printing 1995, completely revised.
Third Printing 1996, completely revised.

Library Cataloging Data

Kervin, James E., 1950-
     Glass beadmaking: more than you ever wanted to know about
        by James E. Kervin 254p
     Includes bibliographical references
     ISBN 0-9651458-0-8
     1. Glass blowing and working. 1. Title
748--dc20

Library of Congress Catalog Card Number 96-94284

Preface

Beadmaking is rapidly becoming one of the hottest new trends in glass and with good reason. It is relatively cheap to get started making beads. For $50 you can get started using a small handheld torch. With it you will be able to wind, shape and decorate beads of your own design. But because these torches are not as hot as a fuel-oxygen system, the glass can be difficult to manipulate and slow to respond. To really get control and provide flexibility in beadmaking, you can move on to a fuel-oxygen system. A good fuel-oxygen system starter kit with torch, regulators and tools can be purchased for about $500. The control possible with one of these systems will allow you to start making real works of art (with a little bit of practice, of course).

I was first introduced to the potential of wound glass beadmaking by Brian Kerkvliet of Gossamer Glass Studios at a beadmaking class that he presented at Fenton Glass Studio in 1992. Dan Fenton continues to sponsor classes by talented beadmakers. If you are interested in one of these classes or one of the many classes on kilnworked glass technique, call or write Dan at Fenton Glass Studio, 4001 San Leandro St. #8, Oakland CA 94601, (510)533-5515. There are also classes in beadmaking springing up all over the place. Before you sign up for one of these classes, check out the artist's work and compare it to some of the gorgeous work now advertised in Ornament magazine to get a feeling for their skill level. You want to learn from someone who knows their stuff. Also ask previous students whether they felt that they got what they wanted out of that artist's class.

Anyway, once I took that class from Brian, I was hooked and came back again the next year when he taught to learn more. I examined others' work ideas for technique as well as content and really fell in love with beadmaking. One of the really nice features about wound glass beadmaking is that you have product relatively quickly. You can make a number of beads an hour, rather than the one piece in a number of days, as I had been used to with other glassworking techniques. Then I started seeing some of the books that were coming out on the subject, and boy was I disappointed. As I read them, I felt like that old lady in the hamburger commercial, "Where's the beef?" I decided that what was needed was a more complete guide to glass beadmaking techniques, equipment and tools. That served to start me on the long and difficult journey of compiling the information for this book. As I researched the

© 1996 James Kervin

4   Glass Beadmaking

glass bead scene, I realized that there was more out there than just wound beads and decided to expand this work to include other glass beadmaking techniques. The work you see before you continues to grow and may never be complete, because the art form itself continues to develop. Since the first edition of this book, it has been updated with techniques received from many of today's hottest glass bead artists. The current edition for example has a much expanded section on millefiori and mosaic cane based on information from Loren Stump.

This is my first attempt at writing a how-to manual and I encourage you, the reader, to provide feedback. I have chosen to publish it in a spiral bound format because it allows you to have it open on your bench for reference as you work. I have tried to include exhaustive details on the techniques and equipment involved in glass beadmaking – thus the name of this manual. If there are things that you do not understand because I have not explained them well enough, let me know. If you think that there are other areas that should be covered or more figures are needed, again let me know. If you think something is wrong, I would very much appreciate hearing your opinion. This third revision of this book incorporates suggestions that I have already received from other readers. You too can help. At the same time, I hope that you will find this effort and the 14 months that were initially spent preparing it will be of some benefit in helping you learn the exciting art of glass beadmaking.

This book was designed to provide information in regard to the subject of glass beadmaking. Although this topic is presented in great depth, it is impossible to cover everything. You are urged to read all available material on the subject. Check out the many references listed herein to supplement this text. Be aware that, even though I have attempted to provide as complete and accurate a sourcebook as possible, **there may be some mistakes** present both typographical and in content. Therefore use it as a guide and if something seems wrong, realize that it might just be. This manual was written to educate and entertain. The author shall have neither liability nor responsibility to any person or entity with respect to any loss or damage cause, or alleged to be caused, directly or indirectly by the information contained in this book. **If you do not wish to be bound by these and the following restrictions, you may return this book with a copy of your receipt to the publisher for a full refund.**

It should also be mentioned that discussion of particular equipment or supplies in this book does not constitute a recommendation. They are just some of those used by or known by me. Results will vary among individuals depending on their skill level, so no warranty is implied for these products. Instead this information is supplied so that you, as an educated consumer, can make your own choices. Because of the nature of this art form, injuries can occur and you as user of these products have sole responsibility for your safety as well as for that of other individuals who could be injured by your actions. Neither I nor the equipment are responsible for injury resulting from equipment misuse. You need to learn as much as you can about how your equipment is operated, follow manufacturer recommendations and take classes from qualified instructors. With this attitude, you will be able to safely enjoy the fascinating world of glass beadmaking.

© 1996 James Kervin

Table of Contents

PREFACE **3**

TABLE OF CONTENTS **5**

TABLE OF FIGURES **11**

TABLE OF TABLES **15**

INTRODUCTION TO GLASS BEADMAKING **17**
BEAD TERMS.. 17
BEAD SHAPES... 18
GLASS BEADMAKING TECHNIQUES 19
SUGGESTED FURTHER READING... 20

EQUIPMENT **21**
WORK AREA 21
    Workbench.. 22
    Lighting... 23
    Marver 24
    Vermiculite pan... 24
TORCH GASES... 25
    Oxygen.. 25
    Fuel gases... 26
    Propane 28
    Acetylene... 29
    Propylene.. 30
    Natural gas 30
    MAPP Gas® 30
    Chem-o-lene.. 31
HANDHELD TORCHES 32
    Disposable fuel gas tanks 32
    Handheld torch head 34
    Torch stand for handheld torch 35
FUEL-OXYGEN SYSTEMS 36
    Propane tanks.. 37
    Oxygen cylinders 41
    Propane regulators... 43
    Oxygen regulators.. 46
    Check valves and flashback arrestors.. 48
    Tubing and fittings.. 49
FUEL-OXYGEN TORCHES... 51
    Premixed torch 51
    Surface mixed torch... 52
    Hybrid torches 53
    Stands 53
    Lighters... 54

© 1996 James Kervin

6   Glass Beadmaking

LAMPWORKING HAND TOOLS 55
    Glass cutters.. 55
    Nippers 56
    Triangular file 56
    Paddles.. 56
    Tweezers.. 57
    Pliers and pinchers 58
    Reamers and shapers 59
    Tungsten Pick.. 59
    Scissors 60
    Hot fingers 60
    Winding mandrels 61
GLORY HOLES... 62
    Glory hole construction 62
    Glory hole operation.. 63
KILNS AND ANNEALERS 64
    How kilns work 65
    Measuring kiln temperature... 66
    Setting up your kiln 71
    Kiln care 72
    Kiln safety 73
SUGGESTED FURTHER READING 74

GLASS **75**

GLASS CHEMISTRY... 75
TYPES OF GLASS 76
    Quartz 76
    Soda-lime glass... 76
    Borosilicate glass (Pyrex) 77
    Lead glass 77
COLORANTS.. 77
    Blending colored rods.. 80
COATINGS... 80
    Iridized coatings.. 81
    Dichroic coatings... 81
TEMPERATURE REGIMES OF GLASS 82
    The brittle solid regime.. 82
    The non-brittle solid regime... 82
    The flexible regime.. 83
    The fluid regime.. 83
GLASS COMPATIBILITY... 83
SUGGESTED FURTHER READING 85

FLAMEWORKING TECHNIQUES **87**

HANDHELD TORCH OPERATION 87
FUEL-OXYGEN TORCH OPERATION 88
    Turning on the gas 88
    Lighting the torch.. 89
    Adjusting the flame 91
    Shutting off your equipment... 93
    General torch care tips 93
GLASS MANIPULATION BASICS 93
    Holding the glass 93
    Heating the glass... 95

© 1996 James Kervin

Gathering	96
Fusing rods	96
Drawing a point	97
Flame cutting	98
Punty use	99
Compatibility testing	100
Flame annealing	101
General glass manipulation comments	102

COMPONENT CONSTRUCTION 102

Latticino or twisted canes	102
Ribbons	106
Cased rods	107
Loops	108
Button holes and loops	109

SUGGESTED FURTHER READING 110

MILLEFIORI AND MOSAIC CANE 111

OPTIC MOLDS 112
RIBBED CANE 112
BUNDLED CANE TECHNIQUES 113
LAMPWORKED MOSAIC CANE 114

Mosaic cane construction principles	114
Beginning mosaic images — block letters	116
Complex mosaic images — faces	117
Advanced cane techniques	122

OTHER MOSAIC CANE IDEAS 123
SUGGESTED FURTHER READING 124

WOUND BEADS 125

BASIC TECHNIQUES FOR WOUND BEADMAKING 125

Preparing for winding	125
Winding a bead	127
Shaping a bead	129
Finishing the bead	131

DECORATING WOUND BEADS 132

Frit and enamels	132
Dots	132
Trailing	133
Distorting the bead surface (raking and twisting)	134
Major distortions of the surface	137
Pressing shapes into the beads	137

APPLYING CONSTRUCTIONS 137

Canes	137
Latticino	138
Ribbed cane floral decorations	139
Ribbons	139
Murrine	140
Casing constructions	141

INCLUSIONS 142

Foil and leaf	142
Mica	143
Wires and screen	143
Dichroic coatings	143
Bubbles and cracks	144

8   Glass Beadmaking

EXAMPLES OF MORE COMPLEX WOUND BEADS 145
    Tableau beads 145
    Hollow wound beads 146
    Sculptural beads (fish, heads) 147
SUGGESTED FURTHER READING 149

BLOWN BEADS **151**

TUBING SKILLS 151
    Cutting tubing 152
    Gathering or shrinking 153
    Pulling out points 154
    Inflation/reinflation 155
    Blowing it out 155
BOROSILICATE TUBE BEADS 156
BLOWING BEADS 157
    Basic blown bead 157
    Shaping blown beads 158
    Decorating blown beads 159
SUGGESTED FURTHER READING 161

DRAWN BEADS **163**

PREPARATION 163
FORMING AND DECORATING THE BUBBLE 164
DRAWING OUT THE TUBE 167
FINISHING THE BEAD 167
SUGGESTED FURTHER READING 168

PRESSED AND PIERCED BEADS **169**

BASIC TECHNIQUES OF PRESSED AND PIERCED BEADS 169
EQUIPMENT USED IN PRESSING BEADS 170
DECORATING PRESSED AND PIERCED BEADS 172
SUGGESTED FURTHER READING 173

FUSED BEADS **175**

CHOOSING YOUR GLASS 175
    Measuring glass compatibility for fusing 176
    Color stability 177
FUSING GLASS WITH YOUR KILN 178
    Preparing for a firing 178
    Phase one of the firing cycle: heating 182
    Phase two of the firing cycle: fusing 183
    Phase three of the firing cycle cooling down 184
FUSING CONSIDERATIONS 185
    Slumping 185
    Volume control 187
WHAT HAPPENED 187
    Cracking 187
    Bubbles 188
    Shelf marks and wash sticking 189
MAKING FUSED BEADS 190
    Simple layered beads 190
    Decorating your simple fused beads 191
    Making tubular bead stock 192
    Individual mold beads 193

© 1996 James Kervin

Table of Contents

SUGGESTED FURTHER READING 193

PÂTE DE VERRE BEADS 195

FRIT MAKING 196
BEAD MOLD CONSTRUCTION 197
    Simple brick molds 197
    Plaster based molds 198
FILLING YOUR MOLD 201
FIRING YOUR MOLD 202
SUGGESTED FURTHER READING 203

FINISHING BEADS 205

CUTTING BEADS TO LENGTH 205
    Chipping hammer and anvil 205
    Glass rod cutter of nipper 205
    Sawing to length 206
KILN ANNEALING YOUR BEADS 207
GRINDING AND SHAPING YOUR BEADS 209
POLISHING BEADS 209
    The theory behind tumble polishing 209
    The practice of tumble polishing 211
SUGGESTED FURTHER READING 213

SAFETY 215

FIRES 215
    Positioning your equipment to avoid fires 215
    Proper operation of your equipment to avoid fires 216
    Pressurized gas equipment 216
    What to do in case of a fire 217
BURNS 218
    What to wear to avoid thermal burns 218
    Proper equipment operation to avoid thermal burns 218
    What to wear to avoid chemical burns 219
    What to do if you get a burn 219
TOXIC MATERIALS 221
    Good work practices to avoid toxicity problems 222
    Ventilation 224
    Carbon monoxide detectors 225
    Respirators 226
OPTICAL CONSIDERATIONS 228
    Electromagnetic spectrum 228
    Electromagnetic radiation damage mechanisms 229
    Eye protection 232
HEARING RISKS 235
ERGONOMIC RISKS 236
    Risk factors 236
    Cumulative trauma disorders 237
SUGGESTED FURTHER READING 238

APPENDIXES 239

GLOSSARY 241
BEAD SHAPES 243
SUPPLIERS AND MANUFACTURER SOURCES 249
RELATED PERIODICALS AND RESOURCES 253

© 1996 James Kervin

10   Glass Beadmaking

© 1996 James Kervin

Table of Figures

FIGURE 1. SOME GENERAL BEAD TERMS 18

FIGURE 2. STANDARD BEAD SHAPES DEFINED BY BECK 18

FIGURE 3. EXAMPLE WORKBENCH LAYOUT 23

FIGURE 4. DISPOSABLE FUEL GAS TANK FOR HANDHELD TORCH 33

FIGURE 5. AVAILABLE HANDHELD TORCH HEADS 34

FIGURE 6. A SIMPLE HOME-MADE STAND FOR A HAND HELD TORCH 36

FIGURE 7. PROPANE-OXYGEN TORCH SYSTEM SETUP 37

FIGURE 8. CROSS SECTIONAL VIEW OF A TYPICAL PROPANE CYLINDER 38

FIGURE 9. COMPONENTS OF A TYPICAL OXYGEN CYLINDER 43

FIGURE 10. CROSS SECTIONAL VIEW OF A PROPANE REGULATOR 44

FIGURE 11. CROSS SECTIONAL VIEW OF AN OXYGEN REGULATOR 47

FIGURE 12. CHECK VALVE AND FLASHBACK ARRESTOR 48

FIGURE 13. OXYGEN AND PROPANE HOSE FITTINGS 49

FIGURE 14. USE OF HOSE CLAMP TO HOLD NOSE ON NIPPLE 50

FIGURE 15. ILLUSTRATION OF INDUSTRIAL HIGH PRESSURE HOSE AND FITTINGS 50

FIGURE 16. NATIONAL 3A TORCH AND ASSOCIATED TORCH TIPS 52

FIGURE 17. SURFACE-MIXED MINOR BENCH BURNER 53

FIGURE 18. DIFFERENT TYPES OF LIGHTERS USED FOR TORCHES 54

FIGURE 19. SOME OF THE TOOLS USED FOR CUTTING GLASS RODS 55

FIGURE 20. SOME OF THE TYPES OF PADDLES AVAILABLE 57

FIGURE 21. SOME TYPES OF TWEEZERS AVAILABLE 57

FIGURE 22. DIFFERENT TYPES OF GLASS PLIERS 58

FIGURE 23. REAMERS FOR SHAPING BEADS 59

FIGURE 24. TUNGSTEN PICKS AVAILABLE 60

FIGURE 25. HOT FINGER TOOL 61

FIGURE 26. CROSS SECTIONAL VIEW OF A TYPICAL GLORY HOLE 62

FIGURE 27. CROSS SECTIONAL VIEW OF A KILN 67

FIGURE 28. SET OF THREE CONES 70

FIGURE 29. VARIATION OF COE WITH TEMPERATURE 84

FIGURE 30. DIFFERENT FLAME ADJUSTMENTS POSSIBLE WITH YOUR TORCH 91

FIGURE 31. WHERE TO WORK IN THE FLAME FOR DIFFERENT PROCESSES 92

FIGURE 32. PENCIL GRIP FOR GLASS 94

FIGURE 33. THE TENNIS GRIP FOR HOLDING GLASS ROD 94

FIGURE 34. MAKING A GATHER ON THE END OF A ROD 96

FIGURE 35. JOINING TWO RODS TOGETHER 97

FIGURE 36. DRAWING CANE USING PULL AS GO TECHNIQUE 98

FIGURE 37. FLAME CUTTING A GLASS ROD 98

FIGURE 38. ATTACHING A PUNTY 99

FIGURE 39. BASIC LATTICINO MANUFACTURING PROCESS 103

FIGURE 40. THE FOLD AND TWIST LATTICINO MANUFACTURING TECHNIQUE 104

FIGURE 41. MAKING CENTRAL CORE LATTICINO 105

FIGURE 42. FABRICATING CENTRAL RIBBON LATTICINO 105

FIGURE 43. RIBBON FABRICATION TECHNIQUE 106

FIGURE 44. FABRICATING CASED CANE WITH CIRCUMFERENTIAL WRAPS ... 107

FIGURE 45. APPLYING THIN CASINGS LENGTHWISE 108

FIGURE 46. MAKING PENDANT BEADS 109

FIGURE 47. ATTACHING A LOOP-LIKE BUTTON SHANK 110

FIGURE 48. ALTERNATE BUTTON SHANK CONSTRUCTION TECHNIQUES 110

FIGURE 49. SOME EXAMPLES OF MORETTI MURRINE SLICES 111

FIGURE 50. USING OPTIC MOLDS TO MAKE CHEVRON MILLEFIORI 112

FIGURE 51. MAKING MILLEFIORI BY BUNDLING CANE 113

© 1996 James Kervin

12 Glass Beadmaking

FIGURE 52. MAKING STRAIGHT SIDED LETTER CANE 116
FIGURE 53. MAKING A PARTIAL CURVE LETTER CANE 117
FIGURE 54. DIFFERENT BASIC EYE SHAPES 118
FIGURE 55. SOME BASIC EYELASH TREATMENTS 119
FIGURE 56. CONSTRUCTING A MOSAIC NOSE 120
FIGURE 57. MAKING A MOSAIC MOUTH 121
FIGURE 58. ASSEMBLING THE FINAL MOSAIC FACE CANE 122
FIGURE 59. USING COLOR GRADATION 123
FIGURE 60. OTHER MOSAIC CANE IDEAS 124
FIGURE 61. WINDING A BEAD ON A MANDREL 127
FIGURE 62. OTHER WAYS TO WIND BEADS 129
FIGURE 63. SHAPING A TORPEDO BEAD ON THE MARVER 130
FIGURE 64. INTRODUCING RIDGES IN A WOUND BEAD 131
FIGURE 65. DECORATING WOUND BEADS WITH DOTS 133
FIGURE 66. TRAILING COLOR ONTO A WOUND BEAD 134
FIGURE 67. SOME VARIATIONS POSSIBLE WITH RAKING 135
FIGURE 68. MORE EXAMPLES OF RAKING AND SURFACE TWISTING 136
FIGURE 69. POSSIBLE ORIENTATIONS IN WHICH CANE MAY BE APPLIED 138
FIGURE 70. HOT APPLICATION TECHNIQUES OF RIBBED CANE 139
FIGURE 71. APPLYING DECORATIVE FOIL DESIGNS 142
FIGURE 72. MAKING A TABLEAU EYE BEAD 146
FIGURE 73. MAKING A HOLLOW WOUND BEAD 146
FIGURE 74. THE STEPS IN MAKING A SCULPTURAL FISH BEAD 147
FIGURE 75. MAKING A WOUND HEAD BEAD 148
FIGURE 76. GATHERING TUBING 153
FIGURE 77. PULLING POINTS WITH TUBING 154
FIGURE 78. BLOWING A HOLE OUT THE SIDE OF A BLOWN BEAD 155
FIGURE 79. BASIC STEPS IN MAKING BLOWN BEADS 157
FIGURE 80. SHAPING IDEAS FOR BLOWN BEADS 158
FIGURE 81. RAKING-LIKE TECHNIQUE FOR BLOWN BEADS 160
FIGURE 82. THE STEPS IN MAKING DRAWN BEADS 164
FIGURE 83. ALTERNATE DRAWN BEADS TECHNIQUE 166
FIGURE 84. SIMPLE CABOCHON PRESSING TOOL 170
FIGURE 85. BEAD PRESSING TOOL FOR HOLES PARALLEL TO BEAD SURFACE 171
FIGURE 86. BEAD PRESSING TOOL FOR BEADS WITH PERPENDICULAR HOLES 172
FIGURE 87. EFFECT OF FUSING TEMPERATURE ON FINAL WORK 175
FIGURE 88. STRIP TEST RESULTS WITH VARYING AMOUNTS OF STRESS 177
FIGURE 89. LAYING UP GLASS FOR A SIMPLE FUSED BEAD 180
FIGURE 90. TYPICAL FIRING SCHEDULE FOR FUSING 180
FIGURE 91. A SAMPLE KILN RECORD SHEET 181
FIGURE 92. PLOTS OF TEMPERATURE VERSUS TIME FOR A CRESS C-20-H 183
FIGURE 93. TWO BASIC SLUMPING MOLD TYPES 186
FIGURE 94. FIRING OF SQUARES TO ILLUSTRATE VOLUME CONTROL 187
FIGURE 95. EFFECT OF VARYING LAYER SIZE IN FUSED BEADS 190
FIGURE 96. SIMPLE FIREBRICK MOLD 197
FIGURE 97. BASIC STEPS TO PLASTER MOLD MAKING 198
FIGURE 98. BASIC PÂTE DE VERRE FIRING SCHEDULE 202
FIGURE 99. SOME OF THE DIFFERENT WAYS TO CUT TUBULAR BEAD STOCK 206
FIGURE 100. TYPICAL KILN TEMPERATURE CYCLE DURING AN ANNEALING RUN 207
FIGURE 101. SMALL HOME-MADE GLOVEBOX 223
FIGURE 102. SIMPLE STUDIO VENTILATION SYSTEM 225
FIGURE 103. ELECTROMAGNETIC SPECTRUM 229
FIGURE 104. CROSS SECTIONAL VIEW OF AN EYE 230
FIGURE 105. BLACKBODY MODEL OF THE ELECTROMAGNETIC RADIATION FROM HOT GLASS 232

© 1996 James Kervin

Table of Figures

FIGURE 106. IR RADIATION REACHING THE EYE DURING WINDING OF BEADS 233
FIGURE 107. LOUDNESS OF COMMON SOUNDS 234
FIGURE 108. MAXIMUM RECOMMENDED SOUND EXPOSURE LEVELS 235
FIGURE 109. EXPECTED HEARING LOSS FROM WORKING NOISE EXPOSURES 236
FIGURE 110. FAMILY OF DISK BEAD SHAPES 245
FIGURE 111. FAMILY OF SHORT BEAD SHAPES 246
FIGURE 112. FAMILY OF STANDARD BEAD SHAPES 247
FIGURE 113. FAMILY OF LONG BEAD SHAPES 248

© 1996 James Kervin

14   Glass Beadmaking

© 1996 James Kervin

Table of Tables

TABLE 1. PHYSICAL PROPERTIES OF OXYGEN 26
TABLE 2. SOME PHYSICAL PROPERTIES OF TYPICAL FUEL GASES 27
TABLE 3. SOME SAFETY PROPERTIES OF TYPICAL FUEL GASES 28
TABLE 4. TYPICAL PROPANE CYLINDER SIZES.. 29
TABLE 5. TYPICAL ACETYLENE CYLINDER SIZES 30
TABLE 6. TYPICAL MAPP GAS CYLINDER SIZES 31
TABLE 7. TEMPERATURE VARIATION OF VAPOR PRESSURE OF PROPANE............................ 39
TABLE 8. DATA ON COMMON OXYGEN CYLINDER SIZES 41
TABLE 9. TEMPERATURE RANGES FOR VARIOUS KILNWORKING PROCESSES 65
TABLE 10. AVERAGE PROPERTIES OF SOME BASIC GLASS TYPES...................................... 76
TABLE 11. GLASS COLORANTS AND THE COLORS THAT THEY PRODUCE 79
TABLE 12. COEFFICIENT OF EXPANSION (COE) OF SOME COMMON ART GLASSES 84
TABLE 13. COE DIFFERENCE VALUES FROM THREAD TESTING.. 101
TABLE 14. COMMON GLASS TUBING SIZES.. 152
TABLE 15. MAXIMUM KILN HEATING RATES FOR VARIOUS GLASS THICKNESSES............... 182
TABLE 16. FUSING PROCESS TEMPERATURE RANGES FOR DIFFERENT GLASSES................. 183
TABLE 17. ANNEALING ZONE TEMPERATURES FOR COMMON GLASSES 185
TABLE 18. ANNEALING SCHEDULE TIMES AND RAMPS FOR BULLSEYE GLASS................... 185
TABLE 19. ANNEALING HEATING AND COOLING RATES FOR MORETTI BEADS 208
TABLE 20. SYMPTOMS OF CARBON MONOXIDE POISONING.. 226
TABLE 21. NEW UL STANDARDS FOR CARBON MONOXIDE DETECTORS 226
TABLE 22. FAMILIES AND SUB-GROUPS OF REGULAR-ROUNDED BEAD SHAPES.............. 243

© 1996 James Kervin

16   Glass Beadmaking

© 1996 James Kervin

Introduction to Glass Beadmaking

The history of the use of beads for decoration is almost as old as that of man himself. Prehistoric beads were made from teeth, bones, seeds, wood and other pierceable objects. They may have originally been used more as amulets with sympathetic magic powers rather than as ornaments. As such they may have been thought to possess attributes of other creatures, such as the strength of a bear, or the courage of a vanquished foe. The oldest recorded objects which appear to have been pierced and used as adornment consist of small marine mollusks that are dated to be 100,000 years old. As a rule, those types of objects are generally not considered to be beads, unless they have been worked into a regular form. Glass beads obviously, came until much later.

The exact origin of glass is unknown but it is believed to have occurred in Egypt around 1400 BC. It probably developed from some ceramic artisan's understanding of and experimentation with glazes. They were already making faience beads from powdered sand, clay and limestone that were packed into small balls around a stick and then coated with a glazing solution of soda. In the firing, the sticks would be consumed leaving a hole in the bead. The limestone would combine with the sand to form the body of the bead. If there was a little copper or iron oxide in the mix, the bead would end up being beautifully colored . Through experimentation, the artist may have observed that if he added more soda he ended up with a shiny clear surface that was a crude glass.

These new glass artisans must have been struck by the resemblance of this material to naturally occurring gemstones and found themselves trying to duplicate the colors they saw in nature. As they got more accomplished, they learned to make batches of glass in thick earthware crucibles. They could then form vessels by dipping clay forms into the glass and soon learned to make beads by dipping a metal rod into the crucible and winding the glass clinging to it around a stick. This stick was later removed by burning it out. With that the glass bead adventure began.

Bead terms

There are a number of terms that describe the parts of a bead and their shapes that should be defined to facilitate subsequent discussion of beads and beadmaking techniques. An imaginary line drawn down the

© 1996 James Kervin

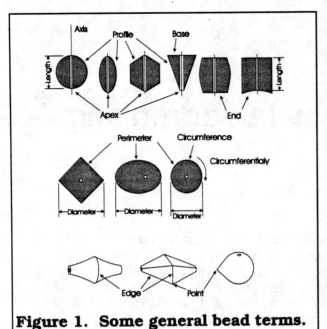

Figure 1. Some general bead terms.

center of the hole in a bead is referred to as the axis of the bead. Going up or down this line is referred to as moving down the axis or moving axially. The largest distance across the bead when looking down that axis is called the diameter of the bead. The edge of the cross section perpendicular to the axis is called the perimeter or, if round, the circumference of the bead. Moving around this perimeter or circumference is referred to as moving circumferentially. If one end of the axis of the bead ends in a point, that point is referred to as the apex of the bead. If the end of an axis ends in a flat or semi-flat surface, this is called an end of the bead unless the other end of the bead ends in an apex in which case it is called the base of the bead. The shortest distance from one end or apex of the bead to the other is called its length. The contour of the bead along its length is referred to as its profile. A sharp meeting of surfaces on a bead is referred to as an edge. Edges may have any orientation to the axis. A sharp meeting of three or more surfaces or the tip of a cone that is not an apex is referred to as a point. All of these general terms are illustrated in Figure 1.

Bead shapes

A whole naming system was developed for bead shapes by Beck. He defines the standard bead as one whose diameter is equal to its width. Figure 2 shows the shapes that he has defined for standard beads. A bead that has a length greater than its diameter is referred to as a long bead, and one with its length shorter than its diameter as a short bead. If the length of the bead is a third or less of its diameter, it is called a disk bead. Beck also has names for how beads are faceted and ornamented. For more

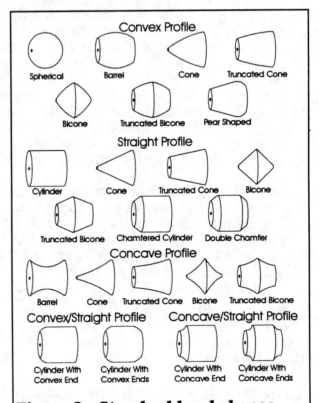

Figure 2. Standard bead shapes defined by Beck.

© 1996 James Kervin

Introduction To Glass Beadmaking   19

information on bead shapes look to appendix A.

Glass beadmaking techniques

Glass beads are also categorized by the technique used in their manufacture. It is many of these processes that you will learn about in this book.

The first of such processes is that of core **winding** softened glass upon a mandrel. By working the glass with tools and decorating with glass of other colors, the variations are endless. Winding is probably the most wide spread beadmaking technique.

The next process, that of **blowing** beads, is where small bubbles of glass are blown, decorated and shaped without the help of a mandrel to stabilize the process.

If a still larger bubble is blown and decorated, it can be stretched out to form a long tube that can be cut up into small individual beads. This is the basis for the process of **drawn** beadmaking.

The next technique, called **pressing**, was traditionally performed by taking two blobs of glass and sandwiching them in a mold around a hole former to make a bead. The pressing mold was often decorated with designs. A variation of this technique, called folding, used a single blob of glass that was folded over the mandrel in the mold. We will not discuss this technique.

We will briefly discuss a variation of the pressing technique known as **pressing and piercing**. In this technique, a blob of glass is put into a mold and formed into shape by pressing a second half of the mold down on top of the blob. The second half of the mold incorporates a needle that pierces the blob to form the hole.

Cold glass casting will be the last traditional technique that will be discussed in this book. It will be referred to here as **Pâte de Verre** beadmaking. It involves filling a small mold with broken glass frit and heating it up in a kiln. The mold has material incorporated into the mold to form the hole. Then, when the mold is broken away after firing it in the kiln you have your bead.

A non-traditional variation of cold casting is what I refer to as **fused** beads. It involves heating up larger pieces of cold glass in a kiln to form your bead (or bead stock to cut up into beads). This technique may or may not include the use of a mold to help shape the beads.

Another variation of casting that we do not discuss in this book is hot glass **casting**. Here you have a mold with pore former that is filled with molten rather than cold glass. The only advantage of this technique over that of Pate de Verre beadmaking is in the clarity of the glass in the final bead.

© 1996 James Kervin

20   Glass Beadmaking

Thus in this book, we will discuss wound, blown, drawn, pressed and pierced, Pate de Verre, and fused glass beadmaking. Before we go into a discussion of these techniques, you need to learn about the equipment that you will use to make them. That is what we will do next.

Suggested further reading

Dubin, Lois Sherr. The History of Beads, Harry N. Abrams Inc., 1987

Francis, Peter Jr. Beads of the World, Schiffer Publishing Ltd. 1994

Karklins, Karlis. Glass Beads, The 19th Century Levin Catalogue and Venetian Bead Book and Guide to Description of Glass Beads, National Historic Parks and Sites Branch Parks Canada, 1985

Kucukerman, Prof. Onder. Glass Beads - Anatoliann Glass Beadmaking, Turkish Touring and Automobile Association, 1988

Liese, Gabrielle Liese. The Work of Contemporary Glass Beadmakers, The Bead Museum, 1993

Liu, Robert K. Ph.D. Collectible Beads, Ornament Magazine, 1994

Erikson, Joan Mowat. The Universal Bead, W. W. Norton & Company, 1993

van der Sleen, W. G. N. A Handbook on Beads, George Shumway Publisher

Equipment

Our first area of discussion is on the equipment used in glass beadmaking. This is one area that does not always get covered as well as it should in classes or video lectures, and it is hoped that if this book serves no other purpose, it will provide you the knowledge that you should have about your equipment, the principles behind its operation, the dangers involved in its use, and how to operate it safely. For that reason, this chapter is the longest one in this book and should receive detailed attention by any potential beadmaker. In your first reading of this book, you may want to skim through this section and go on to find out more about beadmaking and then come back to it later when you start setting up equipment in your studio.

Work area

In developing a workspace for beadmaking, you should keep at least two factors in mind: safety and convenience. Safety is utmost because there is nothing more precious than your own well being and that of your loved ones. Convenience is considered second because a well organized work area helps make everything easier. The space doesn't have to be very big, a small portion of your garage or basement is more than sufficient.

The kind of things that you should consider for safety in a work area are those that are required to prevent fires, material toxicities, ventilation, etc. These things are so important, that they will also have their own chapter at the end of the book for easier reference later. The minimum required safety items necessary for your work area are covered in this section. First, your work area should have a non combustible flooring. If not cement, then some other protective covering should be used. Molten glass can start fires when dropped on a combustible floor if not handled immediately. Also have a metal waste container reserved exclusively for any hot glass you might have to get rid of in a hurry. Never put any combustibles like paper in it. This points out the need for your second required piece of safety equipment, a fire extinguisher. Your fire extinguisher should be prominently displayed in some easy to reach place and not buried away.

Since you will be working with open flames, you should move all combustible materials away from your work area. All flammable liquids should be kept in tightly capped containers and stored in a flammable liquids cabinet that prevent vapors from leaking out into your work area. Check all natural gas lines, if any, to make sure that none are leaking. If

© 1996 James Kervin

22   Glass Beadmaking

working in your garage, pull your car out of the garage while you are working.

Another thing to consider is that your beadmaking torch can give off carbon monoxide or unburned hydrocarbons during use. Breathing these gases and fumes are unhealthy. For this reason make sure that you have proper ventilation in your work area. If you don't have an industrial ventilation system, at the very least have a window and a fan to exchange your air. Don't have the fan blowing at your work area, instead have it in the window blowing air out of your work area. This is because sudden drafts can thermal shock your work and may result in cracked beads.

Make a storage rack to hold your oxygen bottles. This rack should allow for easy addition and removal of bottles, but at the same time should ensure that no bottle can be accidentally knocked over. The bottles should be securely held in place by stringing chains around them attached to hooks in the rack. It should be located in shady dry location. If you keep more than one tank of oxygen at a time have them tied down so that they do not bang against each other. Your oxygen tank and your propane tank should not be located near furnaces, hot water heaters or other sources of ignition.

To make your work area an easier place in which to work, you should construct an easy to reach rack for your glass where you can keep glass rods already cut to working length. Have individual bins for different colors and types of glass with which you will be working.

Workbench

Your workbench should be large enough to fit all your equipment comfortably. I use a 2' x 6' one that I got cheap a school auction. Some flame workers use inexpensive 6' banquet tables. Another alternative is to build your own bench from plywood and 2" x 4" studs. Modify it to fit you and your work style. Hooks can be added underneath the table to keep the torch hoses from being under foot.

The workbench should be at a comfortable working height both while seated and while standing. When standing, the ideal workbench would be about waist high. You will want it to be about mid abdomen level when seated so that you can rest your elbows on it. You may even want to mount cushions on the workbench for your elbows. A stool or swivel chair is preferred to a normal chair because it is much easier to back off from a stool than from a chair if you should accidentally drop some molten glass into your lap. An example layout of a workbench and immediate area is illustrated in Figure 3.

The flame working area of your workbench should be covered with a fire resistant material. A number of such materials are available: sheet metal, asbestos board, non-asbestos board, etc. Sheet metal is not the best material because it transmits the heat to the bench below and because it can rapidly chill any hot glass and possibly cause it to crack. Asbestos board is not desirable because of the cancer risk. Both Wale Apparatus Company and Ed Hoy's carry rigid non-asbestos work

© 1996 James Kervin

Equipment 23

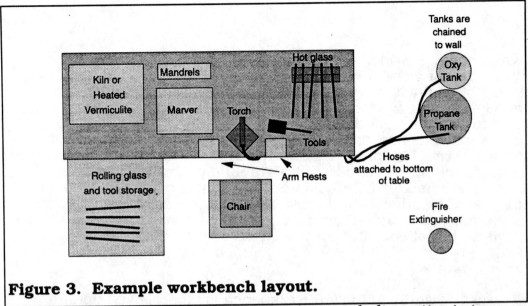

Figure 3. Example workbench layout.

surfaces that are a good choice. Another good alternative is to use Wonder Board or Dura Rock. These are some of the brand names for concrete board that is resistant to moisture and used in construction of showers. It is also noncombustible. It usually has a rough side to which tile is glued and a smooth side to go against the studs in the wall. A sheet of Wonder Board can be cut to fit your work table using a carbide scribe and installed smooth side up.

If your bench is to be up against a wall, you should also cover the wall behind your work area with the same board. Space the board off the wall about 1/2" with noncombustible fittings and allow air to circulate behind the board to carry away any heat that might build up. Your flame should not be directed directly on the board but should be at least a foot away.

Lighting

Lighting is important for a couple of reasons. The first is probably fairly obvious, to see your work. Lighting from above and behind you will avoid light shining in your eyes or getting reflections off your glass. Diffuse lighting such as fluorescent lighting is recommended because it is easier on the eyes. It is also useful to use as full a spectra a bulb as possible so you can see the true colors of the glass that you are working with. Use Chromolux incandescent bulbs or daylight balanced florescent bulbs.

Lighting is also important in being able to see the torch flame. When making beads or any flameworked item, control of how much you heat the item or different parts of the item is very critical to the final results. Sometimes you want the bead in the flame, sometimes beneath the flame, sometimes off to the side of the flame, etc. To be able to control this, you have to be able to see the flame. This requires good lighting. Almost as important as the lighting in being able to see the flame is the background behind it. The flame is most visible if your background is flat black. Against a light background the flame is nearly invisible. If you want to paint your background darker, use of a heat resistant wood stove paint is recommended.

© 1996 James Kervin

24   Glass Beadmaking

Marver

Often when making beads, you will need a bench surface on which to work them. In hot glass shops, this working surface is called a marver because traditionally it was made of marble. You will use it primarily to help shape and work air out of your beads. The marver also has a secondary function as a surface off of which to pick up surface decorations, such as fine glass frit. The preferred material for this purpose is a sheet of graphite because it can withstand high temperature and hot glass will not stick to it. With graphite you can also preheat your decorations using a handheld torch without problems. If you can not get a graphite pad, you could resort to a thick piece of iron or brass. Make sure that you clean off any rust or other surface corrosion as much as possible so that it does not get picked up by your beads.

Vermiculite pan

An indispensable addition to your workbench is a pan of vermiculite. Vermiculite is a clay mineral which has been expanded 10-15 times its original size by a high temperature process into light airy pellets (resembling mica). It is an inert material often used for insulation or for providing loft to planting soil. One thing that you should be aware of is that vermiculite as purchased from the hardware store or nursery may not be completely dry. So it is recommended that you heat it up to about 350°F for about an hour in your annealing oven before you use it. Otherwise the moisture in the vermiculite may cause your beads to cool too quickly and crack.

In glass beadmaking, the vermiculite is used to slow down the cooling of your beads. This prevents immediate thermal shocking of a bead and reduces the risk of subsequent cracking. A pan of vermiculite several inches deep should be kept on a hot plate in an easy to reach portion of your workbench. Some bead artists use an old crock pot or electric skillet instead of a hot plate but that may not be hot enough. A hot plate allows reaching much warmer temperatures in your pan and if large enough allows an area on which to preheat some of your glass rods. As soon as the bead is flame annealed, it is buried in the vermiculite. This slows down the heat loss from the surface of the bead, allowing the temperature distribution throughout your bead to remain more uniform as it cools. Slower, more uniform cooling reduces the stress introduced into the bead. This does not completely alleviate all stress, though, or the requirement to kiln anneal your beads later.

A good container for your vermiculite is an old roasting pan or one of those disposable roasting pans for turkey found in most supermarkets. This pan of vermiculite closely resembles a cat litter box, so if you have a studio cat you may want to keep your pan covered when not in use.

A different method to slow cool your beads that is used by some glass beadmakers is to have a fold of ceramic fiber blanket, such as Fiberfrax®, on their workbench instead of vermiculite. This ceramic blanket material is what is used as the insulation liner on many of the newer glass kilns. After finishing work on a bead, they tuck the bead

© 1996 James Kervin

Equipment   25

into the fold of the blanket to slow cool. Like the pan of vermiculite, this fiber blanket can be kept warm on a hot plate to further slow cooling of the beads. Some artists have reported to me that they were getting a lot of cracked beads using this technique but others say it works just fine for them.

Recently some glass bead artists have been advocating using a small annealing kiln that you keep on your bench, instead of vermiculite, because of concern about possible health hazards of using either vermiculite or ceramic blanket. These materials apparently have a physical structure similar to asbestos and might lead to similar health problems. Therefore you may want to consider adding an annealer as you expand your operation to avoid any possible health hazards.

Torch gases

Before discussing different torches, equipment and torch setups, it is probably worthwhile to learn something about the various gases that can be used by them. They vary in properties, cost and availability. You may have reasons for preferring one over another. We will first discuss oxygen which supports fuel gas combustion and follow that with a discussion of the various fuel gases.

Oxygen

Oxygen is the gas that living things metabolize to stay alive. It makes up 21% of the air we breathe. If that value is reduce to 15% or below then the air can no longer support a candle flame. Increase that value to 25% and cotton fabric will burn eight times faster than normal. This in fact is one of the hazards of working with oxygen. Fabrics in a near pure oxygen atmosphere, will burn with almost an explosive force. Oxygen enrichment allows all materials to burn faster and hotter. This is why we use it with most of our torches to make beads. Depending upon the adjustment of your torch, not all of the oxygen may be consumed by your flame and it may build up in a confined work area. Thus the purpose of workspace ventilation is not only to remove combustion fumes but also to vent excess oxygen.

Another danger of using oxygen is its reaction to the presence of oil or grease. A violent spontaneous combustion may result. This response is particularly dangerous if it occurs in the confined space of a regulator when a cylinder valve is opened. Therefore only equipment "cleaned for oxygen service" should be used with it. Never-never use oil or organic lubricants on oxygen valves or regulators. In fact, use clean gloves or freshly washed hands free of any oils or grease when handling oxygen equipment. Cloth that may have become saturated with oxygen needs to be aired out for at least a half hour before it is considered safe to wear.

Pure oxygen is generally considered to be nontoxic, but long exposures to high concentrations may damage your respiratory track. This is not so much a danger to we beadmakers as it is to those of you who may be "technical" scuba divers or respiratory patients on oxygen. Some people are more susceptible to this than others, and I had to pass a oxygen

© 1996 James Kervin

26   Glass Beadmaking

tolerance test before being admitted to hard hat diving school back in my old Navy days.

Oxygen is the most abundant element on earth. It is a colorless, odorless and tasteless gas. (Unless of course you are somewhere where the temperature is below approximately -300°F when it is a transparent, pale blue liquid slightly denser than water. If you know of such a place, let me know where it is so that I can stay away from there.) Without oxygen, combustion or life as we know it would not be possible. It reacts with all elements, excepts the inert gases, to form oxides. Table 1 presents more information on many of its properties.

Table 1. Physical properties of oxygen

Physical Property	Value
Chemical formula	O_2
Molecular weight	31.9988
Specific gravity (relative to air) at 70°F, 1 atm	1.105
Specific volume (cu ft/lb) at 70°F, 1 atm	12.08
(cu m/kg)	0.6996
Density, saturated vapor (lb/cu ft) 1 atm	0.27876

Fuel gases

A number of different fuel gases can be used in torch work. They may be mixed either with air or for better performance with oxygen. The most common of these are: propane, acetylene, propylene, natural gas and methylacetylene-propadiene stabilized (MAPP® gas.) Because of their flammability, all fuel gases should be considered potentially hazardous. They should be used, handled and stored in accordance with the recognized safety practices that I will try to summarize in this manual. If you want more information, I suggest consulting some of the following recognized standards for welding:

ANSI 249.1   Safety in Welding and Cutting
NFPA 51   Oxygen-Fuel Gas System for Welding and Cutting

Some of the physical properties of the fuel gases are summarized in Table 2. One of the first things of readily visible importance to beadmaking is the flame temperatures of the different fuel gases. Acetylene, propylene and MAPP Gas burn much hotter than either natural gas or propane, although pound per pound, they all provide about the same amount of heat. The low vapor pressures at 70° F and the higher boiling temperatures for propane, propylene and MAPP Gas mean that these fuels can be provided in liquid form and which allows their cylinders to be of much thinner wall construction. This makes these cylinders lighter. (For those of you not familiar with the term psig which appears in the table, it means pounds per square inch as read on a gauge. This means the pressure over that of the surrounding air pressure – which at sea level is 14.7 psi.)

Looking at the specific gravity of the vapor relative to that of air, we see that propane, propylene and MAPP Gas are heavier than air and that

Equipment 27

acetylene and natural gas are lighter than air. Those gases heavier than air will sink and collect on the floor of your work area. So if you use them, you need to consider ventilation down near the floor to prevent their vapors from building up. For the ones that are lighter than air, the vapors will get stirred up and dispersed much quicker and won't need floor ventilation.

Table 2. Some physical properties of typical fuel gases.

Physical Property	Fuel Gas				
	Propane	Acetylene	Propylene	Natural Gas	MAPP Gas
Chemical formula	C_3H_8	C_2H_2	C_3H_6	CH_4	C_3H_4
Specific gravity of gas relative to air at 60° F	1.55	0.906	1.476	0.554	1.48
Vapor pressure at 70° F (psig)	120	635	133	NA	100
Specific gravity of liquid relative to water at 60°F	0.507	NA	0.522	NA	0.573
Specific gas volume at 70° F (cu ft/lb)	8.6	14.7	9.05	23.6	9.0
Liquid density at 60° F (lb/gal)	4.22	NA	5.0	NA	4.77
Boiling range (°F) for liquid at 1 atm	-44	-84	-54	-259	-36 to -4
Flame temperature in oxygen (°F)	4579	5589	5193	4600	5301
Heat of vaporization at 25° C (Btu/lb)	184	NA	188	NA	227
Total heating value (after vaporization) (Btu/lb)	21,800	21,500	21,100	23,900	21,000
Total heat value of vapor (Btu/cu ft)	2498	1470	2371	900-1000	2404

Besides physical properties, you should also consider safety properties in choosing a fuel gas. Table 3 lists some of the safety properties of common fuel gases. As you can see, they are all fairly nontoxic and most do not backfire much. One major consideration is the operating pressure restriction for acetylene. In concert with its shock sensitivity, this should convince you to avoid its use. The shock sensitivity of natural gas is not as much of a concern because we tend to pipe that into our studio. We also see that acetylene has a much larger explosive range than the other fuel gases. This equates to more chance of possible explosions, most likely in the fuel gas line.

© 1996 James Kervin

28   Glass Beadmaking

Another property of interest to a flameworker is that of reactivity with other materials. Looking at the table we see that both acetylene and MAPP Gas react with alloys (usually brasses) that have a copper composition greater than 67%. What this means is that you can not necessarily use all torches with these two gases. You have to check to see that the torches are rated for use with these gases. On the other hand, you can use any torch rated for one of these fuel gases with all of the other gases. (Both the Turbo Torch® and the Hot Head® as we will see later are rated for MAPP Gas. In other words, they are constructed of an alloy with a copper content less than 67%.) A safety concern not seen in the table is the danger of frostbite from the fuel gases that are in liquid form. For this you have to look back into the physical property table to see that propane, propylene and MAPP Gas are so provided.

Table 3. Some safety properties of typical fuel gases.

Safety Property	Fuel Gas				
	Propane	Acetylene	Propylene	Natural Gas	MAPP Gas
Shock sensitivity	Stable	Unstable	Stable	Unstable	Stable
Explosive limits in oxygen (%)	2.4-57	3.0-93	2.3-55	5.0-59	2.5-60
Explosive limits in air (%)	2.2-9.5	2.5-80	1.9-11	5-15	3.0-11.0
Max allowable working pressure (psig)	Cylinder	15	Cylinder	Line	Cylinder
Burn velocity in oxygen (ft / sec)	12.2	22.7	15.4	15.2	15.4
Tendency to backfire	Slight	Slight	Slight	Large	Slight
Toxicity	Low	Low	Low	Low	Low
Reactivity with common materials	None	Alloys with 67% Copper	None	None	Alloys with 67% Copper

Propane

Propane is a saturated hydrocarbon gas with three carbon atoms and eight hydrogen atoms on each molecule. It is the fuel gas most commonly used by glass beadmakers because of its ease of availability, handling, safety and cheapness. It is also a much cleaner fuel than one like acetylene. Propane is a single-component, liquefied fuel gas obtained from crude oil and gas mixtures emanating from oil and natural gas wells. In addition, it also produced in certain oil refining processes and in the recycle of natural gas. Propane itself is odorless, but for

© 1996 James Kervin

Equipment   29

safety's sake, a smelly oil is added to it that can be easily smelled by anyone. This oil is a derivative of garlic.

Propane is available in small one-pound disposable cylinders as well as in bulk quantities. The fact that it liquefies under pressure allows the bulk cylinders to be light and easy to handle. Dimensions and weights of typical refillable propane cylinders are listed in Table 4.

Table 4. Typical propane cylinder sizes

Feature	Dimension		
Size (lb)	20	33	100
Empty weight (lb)	26	36	77
Length (in)	19	27.3	48.9
Diameter (in)	12.2	12.2	14.5

Propane is generally considered to be nontoxic. Short exposures to its vapor is not harmful, although high concentrations may produce a slight anesthetic effect. Avoid contact with liquid propane because it will cause frostbite-like burns. Propane has relatively narrow explosive limits, 2.2 to 9.5% in air. Mixtures outside of this range are safe.

Acetylene

This is the most common fuel gas used for oxygen-fuel gas welding and cutting. It is not used much for beadmaking because it is more dangerous. It is colorless and tasteless, but has a garlic-like odor. Like any of the fuel gases, it is flammable and can asphyxiate you if released in enough volume to displace your breathing air. The garlic-like odor is easily apparent at levels well below those that are hazardous. Standard commercial grade acetylene (grade D) is 98% pure. Many manufacturers carry higher purity gas at increased cost.

The heat and flame temperature produced when burning any fuel gas depends upon the amount of oxygen with which it is mixed. Mixing acetylene with air at 21% oxygen produces a flame temperature of around 4000°F (2200°C.) This in itself is hot enough for most glass work. If it is burned in combination with pure oxygen, flame temperatures as high 5730° F (3166° C) are achievable. Varying the oxygen to acetylene ratio will vary both the flame temperature as well as the amount of heat you can transfer to your work. Acetylene can generate the full gamut of flame types to be discussed later from reducing to oxidizing.

Because acetylene is shock sensitive at pressures greater than 15 psig, it is not supplied as a liquid as propane is. Instead it is supplied dissolved in acetone. This is contained in heavy-walled cylinders filled with porous packing material to prevent sloshing. Acetylene cylinders should be handled carefully and not dropped in order to avoid damage to this packing material. This construction leads to much heavier cylinders as can be seen from the weights in Table 5. Acetylene should never be used at regulator pressures higher than 15 psig because of its shock sensitivity. It can react explosively to mechanical shock or ignition

© 1996 James Kervin

30   Glass Beadmaking

sources under such conditions. Acetylene can also react with copper, silver or mercury to form explosive compounds. Therefore gages tubing and fittings have to be steel, stainless steel or brass with copper content below 65%.

Table 5. Typical acetylene cylinder sizes.

Feature	Dimension					
Size (lb)	MC	B	3	4	4.5	5
Empty weight (lb)	8	25	43	70	120	168
Length (in) w/o cap	13	19.5	25.5	34.3	38	41
Diameter (in)	.4	6	7	8	10	12

Propylene

This is a single-component liquefied fuel gas like propane. It is produced as a by-product at petrochemical and oil refineries. Its main commercial use is in the production of plastics (polypropylene) and other chemicals. Propylene can serve as a fuel gas with outstanding performance, safety and economy. As you can see from Table 2 which compares the physical properties of different fuel gases, propylene has a flame temperature considerably higher than propane which may make it desirable for some applications such as pyrex work.

Propylene, like propane, is very stable. It is not shock sensitive nor will it react with copper. It can be stored for long periods of time as it will not decompose without oxygen. Short exposures to its vapor are not harmful, but high concentrations may produce an anesthetic effect. Direct contact with the liquid can cause frostbite-like burns.

Natural gas

Natural gas is a fuel gas readily available in most urban areas. The primary combustible component of natural gas is methane, but because it is a natural product its chemical composition varies wildly depending on the location from which it is mined. It is obtained from wells and is trapped in the rock above petroleum. After bringing it to the surface, it is purified and piped to our homes. The flame temperature achievable with natural gas is approximately the same as you can get with propane but much cheaper. Because of its wide availability, it is a good fuel gas to use in beadmaking and the convenience of not having to go out and get tank refills are appreciated.

Natural gas and it prime constituent, methane, are generally considered to be nontoxic. Breathing high concentrations of it can cause a feeling of pressure in the forehead or sinuses. Natural gas is relatively odor-free so a smelly hydrocarbon is added to it to make it more apparent when leaks have occurred.

MAPP Gas®

MAPP Gas is a mixture of methylacetylene and propadiene stabilized. It is a stable high-energy fuel gas offering excellent performance. A neutral

© 1996 James Kervin

Equipment   31

MAPP Gas-oxygen flame has a flame temperature of 5301° F (2927°C.) It is insensitive to shock and a cylinder will not detonate even if dented, dropped, hammered or even incinerated (although I would not suggest trying this at home). MAPP Gas can be used safely even up to full cylinder pressures of 100 psig at 70°F, although some regulations may still limit its use to the traditional 15 psig required for acetylene.

MAPP Gas is available in the small one-pound disposable cylinders as well as in bulk quantities. The refillable cylinders are easy to handle because they, as shown in Table 6, are light like propane cylinders. Like acetylene it reacts with copper, silver or mercury to form explosive compounds. Therefore gages tubing and fittings have to be steel, stainless steel or brass with copper content below 65%. Because of this, any torch usable for MAPP Gas will be so marked. If not so marked, don't use it for MAPP Gas.

Table 6. Typical MAPP Gas cylinder sizes

Feature	Dimension			
Size (lb)	7.5	30	70	115
Empty weight (lb)	7.5	25.5	56	72
Length (in)	22	35	44	48.5
Diameter (in)	6	9	12	14.75

MAPP Gas is nontoxic, but exposure to higher concentrations may produce a slight anesthetic effect. Contact with liquid MAPP Gas can cause frostbite-like burns. It has narrow explosive limits in air. Unlike some of the fuel gases, MAPP Gas has a natural distinctive odor that smells just terrible if any leaks are present. This odor is detectable in concentrations as low as 100 ppm (parts per million) which is a concentration 1/300th that of its lower explosive limit.

Chem-o-lene

This is a additive that is being marketed to be mixed with propane which increases the flame temperature for an propane-oxygen system from about 4300°F to about 5800°F. It was originally designed for industrial use around oil fields as an alternative to acetylene. It is being packaged in a proprietary bottle for use in lampworking by a company in Georgia called Chemweld and is being distributed by Ricky Charles Dodson. It is a sticky, oily, transparent yellowish liquid, about the consistency of motor oil, that comes in a five pound bottle that gets hooked up in the propane line between the regulator and the torch. As the propane flows through the bottle, it picks up some of the Chem-o-lene into the flow. When burned in the torch, things do not appear any different but the heat transfer is much greater than normal. It has been reported that you can work twice as fast or with half the flame as usual. Of course, this may not be right for everyone, especially those of you who like to work with a low flame. For those that work in large borosilicate beads though, it may be a major boon.

A five pound bottle filled with Chem-o-lene currently sells for about $300 and will treat about 800 pounds of propane. When the chemical runs

© 1996 James Kervin

32   Glass Beadmaking

out, the bottle can be refilled for about $225. This price can easily be recovered in fuel savings to do your work. When done for the night make sure that the additive bottle gets closed or it can get into your system. This will require be draining it back out before you can get to work.

Handheld torches

Several videos and booklets have popularized the use of small, normally handheld torches for use in glass beadmaking. These torches are not as desirable for a number of reasons. First and foremost of which is that the lower flame temperature which they provide makes working of the glass harder than with a propane-oxygen systems. Secondly, they provide a very reducing atmosphere that may reduce many of the metal oxides used to color glasses – resulting in undesired color changes. They also tend to be much noisier than surface mixed, propane-oxygen torches. Lastly not all of these torches have not been manufactured with flame adjustability in mind and this can prove frustrating when you want a small pin point flame for use in detail work. I provide some introduction in their use as a way to get you started into glass beadmaking cheaply, but urge you to think about quickly moving on to a more sophisticated although unfortunately a more expensive torch system. (Note that some beadmakers, notably those working in dichroic glass, may like these torches and work with them hooked up to larger refillable tanks.)

Disposable fuel gas tanks

Handheld torches are mainly used with the liquefied fuel gases stored in small disposable cylindrical tanks weighing about a pound. These cylinders are constructed with a thin metal wall sufficient to contain the pressure of the liquid fuel inside. These walls are not thick enough to contain the fuel if the tank is heated up. As will be explained in greater detail as we discuss propane tanks for propane-oxygen system, the pressure inside a tank of any fuel gas increases when heated. This is the result of more and more liquid fuel gas boiling off as the temperature rises. Eventually the pressure can get so high that the cylinders could burst. To prevent this from happening, the cylinder manufacturers put a small pressure relief valve recessed into the top of the tank as seen in Figure 4. This pressure relief valve has been set to bleed off fuel gas vapor at pressures substantially below the burst pressure of the tank. Of course bleed-off fuel gas vapors are very flammable, so this poses a different type of risk, fires. For this reason always store these tanks in a cool place. You also want to ensure that the storage area is dry so that the cylinders are not weakened by rusting.

The connection between the disposable fuel gas tank and the torch is made by way of a threaded joint on the top of the tank. If you look down inside the threaded joint, you will see an opening down into the tank. At the top of the opening, you can see a short taper in the throat leading to a white hollow Teflon cylinder and beneath that you see a small valve like on a bicycle tire. The way that this joint works is that the torch head has a shaft that sticks down into the Teflon cylinder. As you screw it onto the tank, the shaft pushes in the bicycle valve to let fuel gas out of the

© 1996 James Kervin

Equipment 33

tank. The Teflon washer seals around the shaft to reduce leakage of fuel gas around it.

The torch head also has a washer that seats against a flat on the top of the tank as you screw the two together finger tight. The washer on the torch is the final and most important seal to prevent fuel gas from leaking out the joint between them. If you ding the flat on the top of a disposable tank, it can cut into the washer as you screw the torch onto the tank. This can ruin the torch washer and allow the joint to leak fuel gas. For that reason, you need to protect the flat on the top of the tank when in storage. When you get the tank from the hardware store, it should have a protective plastic cover on it. Store the tank with that cover in place to protect the flat.

From the description of the tank, it sounds pretty simple and seems like nothing could go wrong with it. Well that is almost true. I have read of situations, where after use, a person was removing a camping stove from a disposable propane tank for storage and the bicycle valve got stuck open. So here is this person holding the stove in one hand and the disposable propane tank spewing propane in the other. To make matters worse, as propane or any of the liquefied fuel gases evaporate, they suck heat out of their surroundings to give them that little bit of extra energy needed to change from a liquid to a vapor. This causes the tank to cool and if the fuel gas is evaporating fast enough, cool can become freezing. Have you ever heard about children licking frozen sign posts. Yes, you guessed it, the tank can get frozen to you hand. Sobering thought isn't it.

Let's examine that situation for a second. How could it have happened? What could have caused that valve to get stuck open? The most likely scenario is that dirt somehow got stuck in the bicycle valve. So always make sure that the seat of the torch and the throat of the tank are clean before you screw them together. That's another reason for keeping the protective plastic cap on your disposable fuel tank during storage. Another possibility for what could have happened, is that the seat of the torch that pushes in the bicycle valve may have gotten a burr on it perhaps by dropping it or something. Then when it was screwed into the propane tank, the burr could have caught the top of the valve and bent it. This may have caused the valve plunger to get bound up when it was pushed in, making it unable to move back after removal of the torch head. So make sure that you check over your torch head before each use.

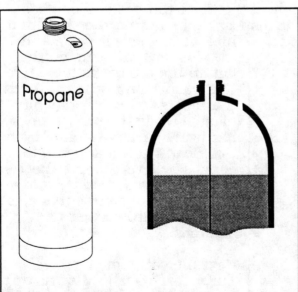

Figure 4. Disposable fuel gas tank for handheld torch.

© 1996 James Kervin

34   Glass Beadmaking

This also brings into question how should you store your disposable fuel tank and torch. Should you store them separately or connected? I believe that the joint between the torch and the tank is probably less reliable than the valve built into the propane tank; so I always store them separately as is recommended. You may also have small children around that may play with the torch if they find it. So it makes sense for you to disassemble the two after use and store them separately. Before you disassemble them, move to a more ventilated space and listen for leaks. After disassembly listen again for leaks, smell and hold your thumb over the top of the tank to feel if any fuel gas is leaking out. Remember to put the plastic protective cover back on the top of the tank.

Some general rules for the use of disposable fuel tanks are as follows: use them only in well ventilated areas, do not store them in living areas, do not store them near appliances with open flames (water heaters, furnaces or gas dryers), do not store them in direct sunlight or areas that get above 120°F (49°C), never puncture or burn tanks (even if you think they are empty), discard empty tanks in a safe place, do not try to refill tanks, detach cylinders when not in use and make sure to close the torch burner valve before detaching.

Handheld torch head

If you decide to try using a handheld torch for making beads, there are a number types of torch heads to choose from; the basic torch available in any hardware store or little more specialized ones, either a TurboTorch® and a new one called a Hot Head®. Two of these torch heads are illustrated in Figure 5. Basically the function of a torch head is to control the flow of the propane, mix it with air and to get the flame away from the tank. The TurboTorch® and the Hot Head® burn with a slightly hotter flame for reasons that will soon become apparent.

If you look at the bottom of main body of the three torches you can see the threads that screw down over the disposable fuel tank, the shaft that hits on the bicycle valve and the washer that seats on the flat on the top of the fuel tank. The washer on my TurboTorch ® appears to be Teflon (white plastic) while the one on my hardware variety torch and my Hot Head® torch appears to cork. I believe Teflon to be a better material because it is a little softer, of course this also makes it a little easier to scratch.

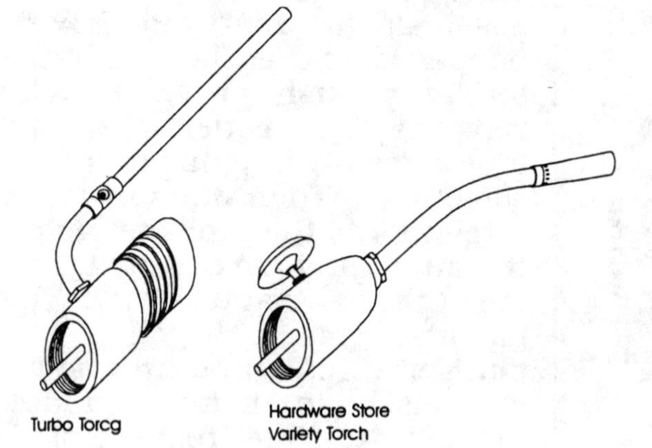

Next the valve for the TurboTorch® is located as an integral part of the top of the main body of the torch. This makes it a little less likely to

Turbo Torcg

Hardware Store
Variety Torch

Figure 5. Available handheld torch heads.

© 1996 James Kervin

Equipment   35

snag on your clothes or get damaged if dropped. The hardware torch has a plastic knob and the Hot Head® has a brass knob off to the side for turning the torch on and off. This makes them a little more vulnerable to snags and damage.

The next feature to compare between the three torches is the fuel gas/air mixing system. All three of these torches use venturi mixers to accomplish this. The venturi system with which most people are probably familiar is that on a perfume atomizer. The way that they operate is that as the jet of working liquid (air for the atomizer and fuel gas for the torch) goes by the suction hole at high speed, it pulls material through them. Thus when you squeeze the bulb on the perfume atomizer, you shoot a fast moving jet of air over the top of the tube that goes down into the perfume. This causes the perfume to be sucked up the tube and pulled into the air stream. The six small holes for accomplishing this on my hardware torch are on the bottom of the head. As you can see, they are not as big as the holes on the TurboTorch® or the Hot Head®. This restricts the amount of air that can be sucked into the torch. The other thing that you cannot see is that in the TurboTorch ® and the Hot Head® the fuel gas stream going through this mixing area is smaller in diameter. This causes it to flow faster and pull more air into the stream. This is what causes them to be noisier during operation with the TurboTorch® being the noisiest of all. The air and the fuel gas mix the rest of the way up the torch neck until they reach the tip. The longer path in the TurboTorch® allows better mixing.

So what do these differences mean. If you look at the flame from each of these torch heads, you would notice that the hardware torch has a softer and more yellow flame. The yellow color indicates a fuel rich flame which is both cooler and reducing (starved for oxygen.) The flame on the other torches is a little less blue and a lot hotter mainly because it allows better mixing of the fuel gas with the air.

One major advantage that I like about my TurboTorch® over the other two is the fact that the torch arm swings. This allows you to adjust the arm so that when it is in a holder on your workbench the torch tip can be adjusted to point perpendicular to the torch. This adjustablity gives you a lot of flexibility in how you set up your system and allows you not to have the tank as much in our lap when it is in its stand as we will discuss next.

Torch stand for handheld torch

Some beadmakers actually hold the handheld torch tank tightly between their legs while working, allowing the torch head to just stick up over the top of their fireproof work surface. I can not caution you strongly enough against this work practice. There will be times when you are beadmaking and you may drop some molten glass into your lap. If you are holding the tank in your lap, what are you going to do when you have to get up quickly to avoid getting burned? Also that tank gets pretty cold as the propane evaporates making holding it uncomfortable as well.

For these reasons, I suggest that you purchase or build a torch holder. Some suppliers are now offering a bracket which will hold the propane

© 1996 James Kervin

36 Glass Beadmaking

tank and can be clamped to your workbench. The problem I see with the clamp is that as I said it is holding the tank out over your lap. This can prevent quick egress from the bench and puts the torch in a very vulnerable position. But this is probably the best that can be done with the disposable tank. If you try to position it over your workbench, the torch gets too high to work with.

If you want, you can make a stand similar to the one currently on the market, as discussed above, using a right angle bracket purchased from the hardware store. I suggest using about a 3 or 4" bracket. One end can be screwed or clamped to your work table as is illustrated in Figure 6. The other end of the bracket can be fastened to the disposable fuel tank using two aeroseal clamps. These clamps are tightened to the fuel tank by screwing the screw head of the clamp clockwise. To get the angle of the torch right for your work, you can adjust the angle of the bend in the bracket.

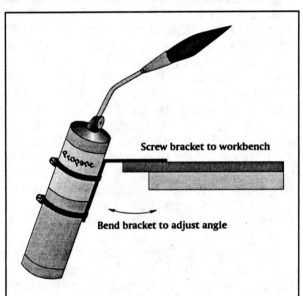

Figure 6. A simple home-made stand for a handheld torch.

Another easy kind of stand to make is one from plaster. Line a shoe box with plastic wrap and fill it about 1/2 full with wet plaster. Adding fillers like vermiculite will make it a little lighter and stronger. Wrap a disposable fuel tank in plastic wrap and set it about half way into the plaster mixture tilted at about a 30° angle with the full top of the tank exposed. Let the plaster completely set up (a couple of hours). Then when you remove the tank from the plaster and the plaster from the shoe box, you are ready to go. This kind of stand works well with the Turbo Torch® where we can adjust the angle of the torch arm.

Fuel-oxygen systems

To be able to make beads easily, really requires a mixed gas torch system. This means that both a fuel and an oxygen source are required. Without both, it is just not possible to provide enough heat to the glass. For a fuel, most beadmakers use propane. For this reason I will focus on the setup of a propane-oxygen system and then later go back and talk about variations from this.

Using oxygen, rather than air in your torch, provides a hotter flame. This is a result of two factors. First, since air is only 21% oxygen by volume, it does not provide as much oxygen per volume to burn in the flame and oxygen is the only gas consumed from the air. Second, when you use air as the source of oxygen for your torch, you are also heating up these other gases in the air. Both of these factors result in a cooler

Equipment 37

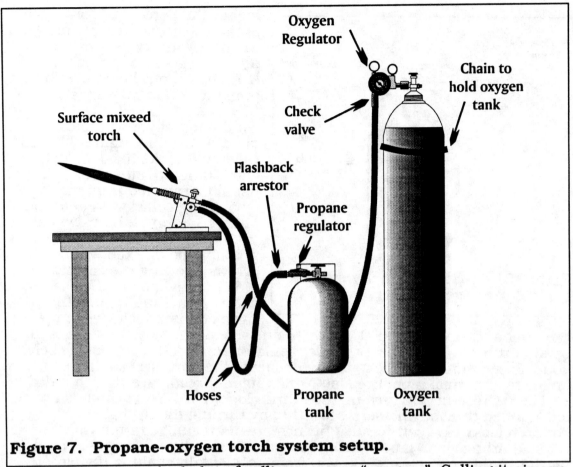

Figure 7. Propane-oxygen torch system setup.

flame. Also get in the habit of calling oxygen, "oxygen." Calling it air can cause a lot of confusion when trying to communicate with others.

The gas system that you will work with in making beads is probably the most dangerous part of the whole operation. It stores an awful lot of energy that could, if abused, do a great deal of harm. On the other hand, when handled properly, the risks are not unreasonable. For this reason, it is very important to understand how your equipment works and how to operate it safely. A completely assembled propane-oxygen torch system has the components illustrated in Figure 3. Let's now go over each of the components for the mixed gas torch system in detail.

Propane tanks

As mentioned earlier, propane provides a dense energy source. The mixed gas systems use propane stored in refillable containers. These tanks, as described back in Table , are typically available in 5, 20, 30 and 100 pound sizes from camping, hardware or recreational vehicle centers. The weight designator represents the approximate weight of propane when full. How big a tank you want, depends on how often you are going to make beads. A 5 lb. tank will last a fairly long time and is very portable but you may want to go to a 20 lb. size if you are going to be doing a lot of flameworking. You can get tanks refilled at many of the same places which sell them, as well as some gasoline stations. When getting your tank refilled, check to see how pure the propane is. The

© 1996 James Kervin

Glass Beadmaking

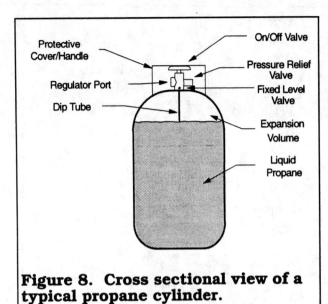

Figure 8. Cross sectional view of a typical propane cylinder.

higher the percentage of propane, the cleaner burning it will be. Not everyone carries the same grade of propane. Ask, to find out how pure the propane you are using is.

On the top of your propane tank, as seen in Figure 8, is a valve that looks like a "T". This is the tank on/off valve. It is usually protected from damage by a lifting collar welded to the tank. The top of the valve has a "roundish" handle that will probably be marked with arrows showing the correct direction to open and close the valve. You usually turn this valve counterclockwise to open the tank and clockwise to close it. To one side of the vertical shaft is an open port into which your propane regulator screws. If you look closely, you will see that the threads on the inside of the port are exactly the opposite of normal pipe threads. Normal pipe threads are right-handed and screw together by turning the fitting clockwise. These threads are left-handed threads and screw together by turning the fittings counterclockwise. Left-handed fittings are distinguished from right handed fittings by a groove notched in the fitting. The fittings are made left-handed to try and prevent you from accidentally making the wrong connection. Left-handed fittings are sometimes hard to get used to. If you are have trouble tightening or loosening them, double check to see that you are turning it in the correct direction.

The other appendage on the on/off valve, opposite to the regulator port, is the pressure relief valve. It is a safety feature that, like on the handheld propane tank, will vent pressure from the tank if the pressure were to rise too high for some reason. This prevents the tank from rupturing. This safety valve should only be adjusted by qualified personnel. It is usually set to release at 250 psig. In between the pressure relief valve and the pressure regulator port may be what looks like a brass screw with a hole in it. This fitting is called the fixed liquid level or 10% valve. Its function will be explained shortly, but in normal operation of the tank, this valve should always be closed (screwed in).

The propane in your tank is mostly a liquid, but propane has a very low boiling temperature, -43.8°F. Because you are usually working in an area that is warmer than this, you will always have propane vapor over the liquid; just as you get steam over the surface of water when you boil it. As the vapor evaporates off the surface of the propane, it cools the local area of the tank. You can often tell the level of the propane in your tank by looking for a sweat line (condensation ring) around your tank. This indicates the level of the propane. There are also liquid crystal strips available which change color with temperature that you can attach

Equipment   39

to your tank making the cooler region near the propane surface level more readily visible.

The pressure of the propane vapor in the tank and thus the pressure available to supply propane to your torch is a function of the bottle temperature. Table 7 lists this vapor pressure at selected temperatures. From the table we see that the pressure available at normal room temperature is about 110 psig. If instead, you kept your bottle outside and it is winter, you may only have 11 psig available. If on the other hand, you store your cylinder next to your hot water heater, your pressure may soar to over 250 psig in the heat of summer. Under such conditions your pressure relief valve may release some of the pressure rather than allow the tank to rupture. This presents a safety problem of another sort because now you have propane venting out into the room and it could cause an explosion. So try to keep your propane tank in a location where it will neither get too hot nor too cold.

Table 7. Temperature variation of vapor pressure of propane.

Temperature (°F)	Pressure (psig)	Temperature (°F)	Pressure (psig)
-44	0	70	110
-40	2	90	150
-20	11	100	172
0	24	110	197
20	41	120	225
32	54	130	257

The smelly garlic-derivative oil added to propane does not get completely volatilized during normal operation and thus gets concentrated in your tank over the usage of a fill. Therefore as you approach the bottom of the tank, it tends to get stinkier and you may be able to smell it in the torch combustion fumes. After a number of propane fills, more and more oil builds up in your tank and the smell gets worse. When it starts to get obnoxious, you may want to drain the oil out of your tank at the next opportune time. Do this only when your tank is empty. Vent the tank outside for a while first to get rid of any propane vapors that might still remain. Then lean the tank over a tray to catch the oil and drain it. After it is all drained, clean up the tank and dispose of the oil properly.

Another effect that heat has on propane is that it causes the volume of the liquid to increase. This is compensated for in the tank design by always having a vapor volume above the surface of the liquid. Tanks are never filled more than about 85% full to allow for this expansion region. This is so important, that propane tanks should never be filled except by qualified personnel. Since this factor is so important, you should also understand the filling procedures so that you can ensure that it is being done properly. When going back and forth to the fill station always screw the protector plug into your regulator fitting (the regulator has to be removed to fill the tank) to prevent any damage to the threads that might cause them to leak. Tanks are filled by one of two methods: by use of the fixed level valve or by weight.

© 1996 James Kervin

40   Glass Beadmaking

The fixed level valve is that fitting which looks like a screw with a hole in it that was discussed earlier. It is attached to a tube, called the dip tube. This tube extends down into the tank to the designed fill level. The fixed level fill method is done in well vented areas, preferably outside, because propane will be released during the procedure. In using this filling method, the tank is first connected to the filling station and the on/off valve is opened. The person filling the tank will then start the transfer pump and open the fixed level valve. When the propane reaches the designed fill level, liquid propane is forced up the dip tube and released as a white mist out of the fixed level valve. At this point the tank on/off valve and the fixed level fill valve are closed. The transfer pump is turned off and all fittings are disconnected. The fixed level valve should be checked to see that it is closed using a soapy water solution. In theory, it should not be possible to overfill the tank because once filled all the extra propane would be forced up the dip tube and out of the fixed level valve. But in practice, it is possible to pump the propane in faster than it can come out the fixed level valve, especially if the valve is not opened enough or the pumping pressure is high. Therefore the filling person should remain in attendance while filling the tank and avoid becoming distracted.

The second method of filling the propane tank is by weight. In this method the full weight of the tank is calculated ahead of time and the tank is filled until it reaches the correct weight. To determine the full weight, one first needs to get the water capacity (WC) and tare weight (TW), or empty tank weight. These numbers are usually stamped on the outside of the lifting collar around the tank on/off valve along with the dip tube length (DT). For my 20 lb tank the WC=47.1, the TW=18, and the DT=3.9. These water capacity and tare weight values are in pounds. The dip tube length is in inches. To calculate the full weight multiply water capacity by 0.42 and add the product to the tare weight. This value is 85% of the specific gravity of liquid propane at room temperature (which in other words is the ratio of the density of propane to the density of water). Therefore 0.42 times the water capacity is the weight of the propane to be added for an 85% fill. Thus, in my case, the full weight of the tank is 47.1 x 0.42 + 18 = 37.78 lb. With this method, math errors or inaccurate scales can cause problems.

As you looked around for the WC, TW and DT values, you may have noted a date stamped on your tank such as 9 88. This is the date of manufacture of your tank. Twelve years after this date, you will have to get your tank recertified before you can get it refilled any more. Recertification can be done by many suppliers of industrial propane bottles. They will check the tank inside and out for any signs of corrosion or other indications of impending failure. If it passes, a new certification date will be stamped on the tank. It will have to be recertified every five years from then on.

Whenever you use your propane tank, it should always be standing straight up. The vapor is admitted to the on/off valve at the top of the tank. If the tank is on its side, the liquid level may be high enough to allow liquid propane through the valve and into the system. This could result in a build up of pressure inside the hoses as the liquid vaporizes, possibly causing them to burst.

© 1996 James Kervin

Equipment   41

Oxygen cylinders

Oxygen is available in cylinders from your local welding supply company. They will normally sell you the oxygen and rent you the tank it is in for a nominal monthly fee. This is the preferred situation. Some companies might require that you buy the cylinder. This is not desirable, because then you are responsible for its upkeep which includes things like valve maintenance and hydrostatic testing. Hydrostatic testing is the recertification method required for oxygen tank certification. It is required ten years after manufacture of the tank and every five years thereafter. During hydrostatic testing, a cylinder is pressurized with water to about 3300 psig. The cylinder, which is constructed from a single forging of a minimum of one quarter inch thick high carbon armor plate steel, expands under this pressure. The expansion of the cylinder and the value of permanent expansion after the pressure is released are recorded and determine whether a cylinder is safe to put back to use. Occasionally it will be necessary to heat up the cylinder to anneal out any stress that may have been put into it during operation. Sometimes the people testing the cylinder will also clean it out using a caustic solution. Leasing is convenient in another way, in that you can just drop off your old tank and get a new one, rather than having to wait for them to fill your tank.

As a courtesy to your oxygen tank rental company, you should return your oxygen tanks to them with 50 to 100 psig of oxygen remaining in them. This helps prevent getting any foreign material into the tank. Also if you have more than one tank, mark empty ones with a chalk "MT" written on its side after it is taken out of service. This can avoid possible confusion later.

Table 8. Data on common oxygen cylinder sizes.

Oxygen Content* (cu ft)	Cap Height (in)	Outside Diameter (in)	Weight		Inside Volume (cu ft)
			Full (lb)	Empty (lb)	
20	19	5 3/16	13 1/2	12	0.115
80	35	7 1/8	70	65	0.463
150	51	7 3/8	92	80	0.858
251	56	9	153	133	1.453
337	60	9 1/4	172	146	1.950
* Final oxygen volume at 70°F & 14.7 psi assuming initial tank at 70°F & 2200 psi.					

The cylinders come in a number of sizes which are rated by oxygen capacity in cubic feet at standard atmospheric pressure and temperature. The most common sized tanks are listed in Table 8 along with pertinent information about them. The service pressure of your cylinder will be marked near the top in accordance with Department of Transportation (D.O.T.) regulations. (Do not accept a tank where the label is not legible.) As an example you may see the marking D.O.T.3A-2015. This indicates that the cylinder has been manufactured in accordance with D.O.T. regulation 3A and the cylinder filling pressure is

© 1996 James Kervin

42   Glass Beadmaking

2015 psi at 70°F. Current D.O.T. regulations on non-liquefied, non-flammable gases permits a 10% overfilling of cylinders. Your oxygen cylinder falls into this case. No other compressed gas tank should be substituted to hold oxygen. Some other gases are pumped using oil and this can allow an oil film to build up on the inside of the tank. If this equipment is used with oxygen, a fire or explosion may result.

Generally the oxygen that you get will be in a green painted cylinder. Unfortunately this is not always the case and cylinder color coding is no longer reliable. Instead look for a paper shoulder label on the top portion of the cylinder where it starts to narrow down. This label will give information on chemical content, any health hazards and gas reactivity (i.e. oxidizer, flammable or non-flammable).

On the top of your oxygen tank, as seen in Figure 9, is an on/off valve similar to the one on your propane tank. It is constructed of forged brass. In addition to the on/off valve, there is a regulator port off to one side and a pressure relief feature to the other. It has no fixed level valve because the oxygen in your tank is a gas and is filled to a fixed pressure. The valve is protected during shipping by a metal cover that screws onto threads cut into the collar at the top of your tank. Always keep this cover and use it whenever transporting your cylinder. Because the oxygen is a gas, all of it is immediately available to do work if the valve should be damaged. You may have heard horror stories of tanks taking off and flying through brick walls like a rocket when a valve got broken. Well these stories have some basis of fact, so you should always handle your tank with some degree of respect. You have to remember that each cubic foot of oxygen has been compressed down to about 10 cubic inches. This is 1/173rd of its original volume.

In looking at the regulator port, you first notice that the threads are on the outside of the port where they are more susceptible to damage. When you get the cylinder from your supplier these threads will be covered with a plastic cap to protect them. Save this cap and use it to prevent damage to the tank valve during transportation. You may get that tank back someday. If you look closely at the fittings on your regulator port, you will see that they are right-handed. This prevents you from accidentally mixing up oxygen fittings with propane fittings. All of your right handed fittings will be smooth and do not have the notch in them that the left-handed fittings do.

The pressure relief feature is also different from that which was on the propane tank. It is a frangible disk. The small cap, that you see over the disk, prevents access to the disk and also prevents you from getting hit by flying pieces of the disk if it were to rupture. The disk is a thin piece of metal that bursts if subjected to too high a pressure. It is sized to burst considerably above the cylinder service pressure but below the hydrostatic test pressure of the cylinder. The object here is again to provide a controlled way for a tank to fail if it should somehow become over pressurized. The disk thickness is sized to fail at about 3000 psig. Again you should not play with this fitting. Never tamper with the frangible disk or its safety protector.

© 1996 James Kervin

Equipment 43

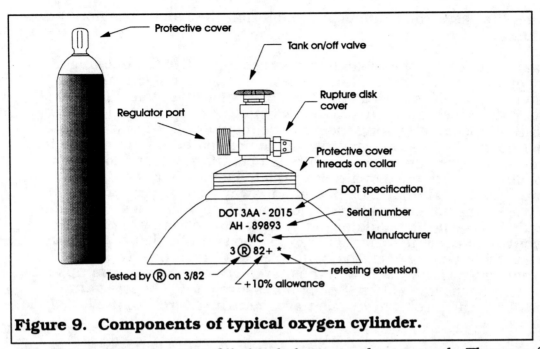

Figure 9. Components of typical oxygen cylinder.

Oxygen cylinders are also filled only by trained personnel. They are filled by connecting them to a gas system and allowing the gas to flow into the tank until it reaches the right pressure. You should not have to worry about this procedure, as much as with propane, because the facilities at which they are filled are more specialized, and the personnel that fill them tend to be better trained. You may notice that the pressure in the tank when you get it back may vary a little from the 10% over or 2200 psig nominal value. This variation is due to a number of factors such as the temperature at which it was filled or the speed with which it was filled.

Treat your oxygen cylinder with respect. Never allow it the chance to fall over or bang against other objects. Never drag your tank. If you don't have a hand cart with which to move it, move it by standing it almost upright and rolling it on the bottom rim. Always put the protective cap on your oxygen tank whenever you move it. Whenever you are using oxygen, you should open the on/off valve completely. This is because the valve is what's called a back reacting valve and only prevents leakage around the stem when the valve is completely open or completely closed. Sometimes the valve may leak some even if it is completely open because of previous mistreatment. For this same reason, it is also best to close the on/off valve completely whenever the tank is not in use. If a cylinder leaks around a valve or frangible disk, tag it to indicate the problem and move it out to a safe well-ventilated area immediately.

Propane regulators

The pressure in your oxygen and your propane tank is too high to be used by your torch without modification. If hooked directly to your torch, the gas would be coming out so fast that it would just blow itself out. Therefore both the fuel and the oxygen tanks use regulators to lower the pressure supplied to your torch down to a few psig. At this

© 1996 James Kervin

44 Glass Beadmaking

pressure, the gases come out slow enough that the flame does not blow itself out.

Regulators work by using a balance of forces to control the opening and closing of a valve. To explain this process, let's look inside a propane regulator. Figure 10 shows a cross sectional view of a typical propane regulator. The propane regulator screws into the propane tank with a male fitting. Before attaching the propane regulator, blow out the gas cylinder opening. This can prevent any foreign material from getting into the regulator that might interfere with its operation. When blowing out the opening, be sure to be in a well-ventilated area where no flames are present. Blow out the valve by pointing it away from anyone and then quickly opening and closing the cylinder on/off valve a crack. Now you are ready to attach the regulator to the tank. Once in place, propane from your tank can enter the regulator as shown in the left of the figure and leave the regulator from the right to go to your torch. The on/off valve that controls the gas flow is the movement of the lever arm up and down. This opens and closes the high pressure port. The lever arm rotates about the pivot that in this view shows as a circle to the left of the lever arm.

The regulator operates as follows. When the right end of the lever arm is pushed down by the adjusting spring, the left end of the arm rotates up. This opens the high pressure port. Propane then flows into the low pressure chamber faster than it is flowing through the exit to the torch. As excess propane fills up the low pressure chamber, it pushes against the diaphragm. The diaphragm pushes upward against the adjusting spring, pulling the right end of the lever arm up with it. This continues with the lever rotating around the pivot point until it closes the high pressure port. At this point, the force exerted against the diaphragm by the propane in the low pressure chamber equals the applied force by the adjusting spring. Thus this spring force directly controls the pressure in the low pressure chamber. As propane flows out of the chamber to the

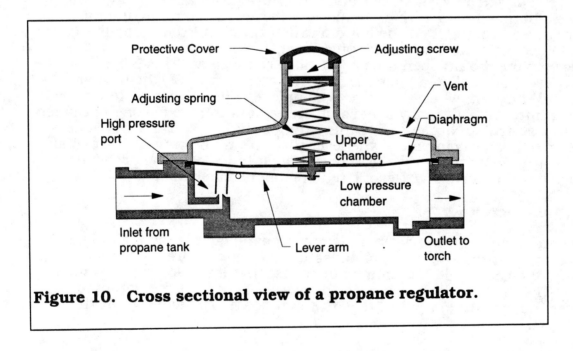

Figure 10. Cross sectional view of a propane regulator.

Equipment   45

torch, the adjusting spring once again pushes down against the lever arm opening the high pressure port and things start over.

From this explanation, you see that the pressure that is fed to the torch is controlled by the adjusting spring tension. Screw down clockwise on the adjusting screw and the tension of the spring increases. The pressure in the low pressure chamber thus has to be higher to push back against the spring and close the high pressure port. Likewise, if you reduce the tension on the spring, by unscrewing the adjusting screw counterclockwise, the pressure fed to the torch will be reduced. You will notice that the upper chamber, in which the adjusting spring is located, is vented to the outside atmosphere. This prevents any back pressure from being exerted on the diaphragm by the air in this chamber as the volume is decreased.

If you think about it, the propane also has to push against this atmospheric pressure when it pushes against the diaphragm. Thus the pressure setting of the spring is that over and above atmospheric pressure. This is again what is meant by gage pressure, that over and above atmospheric pressure. The normal propane regulator that you will use in beadmaking has a spring that allows adjusting of the output pressure between about 1 and 10 psig. You will want it set to about 4 psig when using a surface mixed torch. If you are working pyrex on a premixed torch, you need to set the propane pressure up a little higher, in the range of 5 to 8 psig. (The different torch types will be discussed shortly.) The question is how to do this if you don't have a pressure gauge on the downstream end. Many propane regulators don't have gauges because the vapor pressure is relatively constant as long as there is propane in the tank.

The propane regulator can be adjusted as follows:
1. With the propane tank on/off valve closed, remove the protective cover from the propane regulator. Unscrew the adjusting screw on the propane regulator. (On some propane regulators there may be a handle like on the tank on/off valve instead.) Clear away any combustibles from the end of your torch because the flame could get almost a foot long.
2. Open the gas valve on your torch all the way. No gas should be coming out yet. Open the propane tank. Some gas might start coming out of your torch now. If so, light it immediately. If not, gradually screw down on the adjusting screw until you can light it.
3. Slowly continue to screw down on the adjusting screw. As you do so the flame will get larger as the gas flows out faster. Continue screwing down until the flame just leaves the end of the torch or blows out.
4. Immediately close the torch gas valve and then the propane tank on/off valve. Your propane regulator is now adjusted.

Put the protective cover back on. (If your regulator has a handle, tighten the locking nut on the handle to prevent it from being turned unintentionally.) This setting is permanent and does not have to be repeated unless someone changes it on you or you switch torches.

© 1996 James Kervin

46 Glass Beadmaking

Oxygen regulators

The operation of your oxygen regulator is very similar to that of the propane regulator. Its construction is different because of the higher pressures involved. Your propane regulator lowered the pressure from about 100 psig to 4 psig. Your oxygen regulator has to be able to lower the pressure from 2200 psig to about 10 psig. These higher pressures require a more positive closure of the high pressure port. You can see the differences in construction by studying the cross sectional view of the oxygen regulator in Figure 11.

Before you open your oxygen tank on/off valve and admit oxygen into the regulator, you should unscrew the adjusting handle counterclockwise until all spring compression from the adjusting spring is removed. Next you should stand off to one side of the regulator before opening the oxygen regulator. This is because regulators have been known to blow out upon pressurization. As oxygen is allowed into the regulator by slowly opening the oxygen tank on/off valve, it is admitted to the high pressure chamber in the back of the regulator. You open the valve slowly to avoid sudden pressure surges which can weaken the valve body over time. Here the oxygen is trapped until the adjusting handle is screwed in to put compression on the adjusting spring, which in turn opens the high pressure port by moving the valve.

At this point you are probably wondering why we just didn't leave the adjusting handle screwed in and the adjusting spring in compression in the first place. The reason is that when there is no gas pressure in the high pressure chamber and there is compression on the adjusting spring, the valve ends up being a lot more open than in normal operation. Then when 2200 psig oxygen is suddenly introduced into the regulator, much of this gas quickly flows into the low pressure chamber and causes the high pressure valve to slam shut with a much greater force than normal. This slamming shut can damage the seat of the valve on the high pressure port. A damaged seat on the high pressure port can leak and allow higher than normal pressure to build up in the low pressure chamber. If this happens, you have to take your regulator into the shop to get it fixed. Therefore to prevent damage to your oxygen regulator, always unscrew the adjusting handle out after you close your tank and double check that it is out before opening your tank.

Let's get back to the normal operation of the regulator. High pressure gas is in the high pressure chamber, and the valve starts out shut from the force of the spring in this chamber. At this point the needle on the tank pressure gauge, the gauge on the right, will slowly swing to indicate the tank pressure. The needle swings slowly because the opening from the line to the gauge is made very small to admit the gas slowly. This protects the gauge from the damage that could occur with sudden applications of pressure. A full tank will register about 2200 psig. You can use this gauge to tell when your tank is out of oxygen.

The high pressure valve will stay closed until the adjusting handle is screwed in enough on the adjusting spring to apply a force equal to that of the valve spring and that of the high pressure gas pushing on the back of the valve. At this point, a small amount of gas will be admitted into

© 1996 James Kervin

Equipment 47

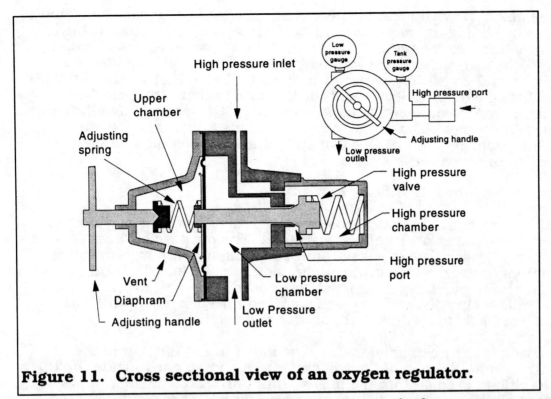

Figure 11. Cross sectional view of an oxygen regulator.

the low pressure chamber and it will register on the low pressure gauge. The gas in this chamber will also push up against the diaphragm. If the force from the gas pressure against this diaphragm is greater then the difference of the spring forces and the high pressure force mentioned above, then the valve will get pushed closed. As some of this gas is bled off from low pressure chamber out into the gas lines and is consumed by your torch, the pressure in the low pressure chamber will drop. As it drops below the difference value, the high pressure valve will open again. The gas pressure in the low pressure chamber required to close the valve is a function of the compression of the adjusting spring. The more this spring is compressed the higher the gas pressure in the low pressure chamber has to be to push the valve closed. Thus the more you screw the adjusting handle in clockwise, the higher will be the regulated low pressure.

For beadmaking using a surface mixed torch, you will want the low pressure regulated somewhere between 5 and 10 psig. Just as you increase the propane pressure when using a premixed torch, you also need to increase the oxygen pressure to about 25 psig. You may have to readjust the adjusting screw slightly once your torch is operating and constantly consuming oxygen to get it right. The pressure required by your torch varies slightly depending on the size of tip you might be using.

Before attaching your oxygen regulator to the tank, you may want to flush out the tank valve. Sometimes some debris gets in there during the filling of the tank. To flush this valve, secure the tank in its rack. Take off the protective cover. Turn the tank so that the regulator port is not pointed at anyone. Quickly open the on/off valve just a crack (about an eight turn). You will get a loud burst of oxygen. Close the valve

© 1996 James Kervin

immediately. Now you can connect your oxygen regulator to the cylinder. Do this by sliding the regulator nut back, inserting the round fitting of the regulator into the regulator port on the tank valve, and screwing in the nut clockwise. Screw down finger tight. Then while holding the regulator in the position you want it with one hand, tighten the nut with a well fitting wrench. Because of the ball and socket fitting on the regulator, you do not need to tighten too hard. Never use any lubricants on oxygen fittings. Also try to keep your hands free from oil when attaching your regulator. Oils can spontaneously combust with pure oxygen to produce serious fires.

Check valves and flashback arrestors

Another kind of fitting that needs to be included in your gas system is either check valves or flashback arrestors. The purpose of these fittings is to prevent back flow of gas possibly resulting in a fire in your hoses, regulators or tanks. One or the other should be included in both the oxygen and the fuel gas line. Most glass beadmakers use a check valve because it is cheaper and they use surfaced mixed torches which are much less likely to flashback than premixed torches.

Flashback is the phenomena where the flame burns back from the tip of your torch into the rest of the gas system. It can go back inside the tip to the torch and even on into the hoses. If not protected against, it may proceed all the way into the fuel or oxygen tank with explosive results. Again this is mainly a problem with premixed torches for reasons that will be explained later. Warning signs of a flashback in progress include: squealing or abnormal hissing sounds and a sudden smoky or sharp pointed flame. These indicate tip blockage. If you get a flashback, immediately extinguish your flame by first closing the torch oxygen valve and then the fuel valve. Allow the torch to cool for a few minutes. A flashback indicates major problems with your system, the most likely of which is a partially plugged tip. Check everything out. Purge each of the hoses separately. Check the regulator settings. When you have found and corrected the problem, only then can you safely relight your torch and resume working.

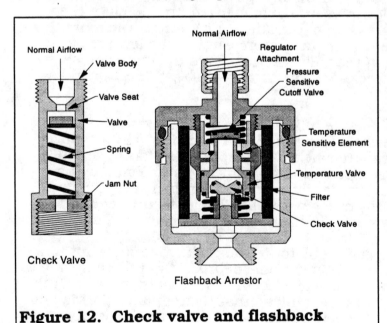

Figure 12. Check valve and flashback arrestor.

A check valve is a valve that only a only allows gas flow in one direction from the regulator to the torch. It may be mounted on either the torch or the regulator. The preferred location is on the inlet of the torch because that prevents any back flow into the hoses. But this is not easy to do on most torches, so they are usually mounted on the regulator. As illustrated in Figure 12, it operates through the action of a spring loaded valve. Gas flowing in the normal direction compresses the spring and flows around the valve. Gas trying to flow in the opposite direction assists the spring in pushing the valve against the valve seat thus closing off flow. This can happen if the tip of the torch gets plugged and tries to push oxygen into the fuel tank. Check valves are sensitive to dirt and damage to the seating element. To assure their proper operation, they should be checked regularly, at least every six months. You can check the proper functioning of your check valves by blowing into both ends and seeing that air will only flow in one direction. A check valve should not be reused if it is exposed to a flashback

A flashback arrestor is a little more complex device and actually combines a number of safety functions into one unit. The arrestor illustrated in Figure 12 includes the following: a check valve, a pressure cutoff valve, a stainless steel filter and a heat sensitive valve. It also has a small internal volume to absorb the energy of the flashback as it travels up the hose. It mounts to the regulator and eliminates any chance of explosion in your regulator or tank. In the event of a flashback, the small orifices in the stainless steel filter prevent propagation of the flame and the incoming pressure wave pushes the cutoff valve closed preventing any further flow of oxygen to the flame. The check performs the same function as explained above of preventing back flow of gas into the regulator. Lastly, if the arrestor is exposed to heat, the temperature sensitive element will melt allowing the temperature valve to close the pressure cutoff valve. Because of the

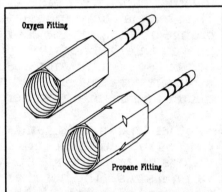

Figure 13. Oxygen and propane hose fittings.

multiple safety functions incorporated, it is suggested that you use one. A flashback arrestor is reusable after a flashback but not after a fire where the thermal sensitive element has melted. You'll know if this has happened because it will no longer pass gas.

Tubing and fittings

To connect your torch to your regulated gas supply requires tubing and fittings. The type of fitting used most by glass artists in connecting their hoses are barbed hose nipple fittings with hose nuts. These fittings are available with both right and left hand threads on the hose nuts for connecting to your oxygen and your propane supply respectively. The way to tell them apart as shown in Figure 13 is to look for the notch on the nut portion of the fitting discussed previously. The most common barb size is a 1/4". Hose barbs are also available with male pipe fittings on the other end. You will have one of these fittings on each of the inlets to your torch and on the flashback arrestors attached to your regulators. This type of fittings is used with low pressure fittingless tubing. The

Glass Beadmaking

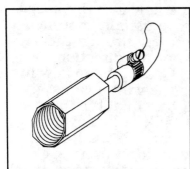

Figure 14. Use of hose clamp to hold hose on nipple.

tubing is slipped on to the fitting and clamped into place using hose clamps as shown in Figure 14.

A number of kinds of tubing are available for use with these fittings. Again the most common size of tubing has a 1/4" inner diameter (ID) and a wall thickness between 1/16th and 1/8th of an inch. The most widely used tubing is made from black neoprene rubber and is preferred because of its flexibility, light weight, ruggedness and durability. Another popular choice is pure gum rubber tubing that you may remember on your Bunsen burner from high school chemistry. This amber colored tubing is also flexible and light but is not as durable. It eventually darkens and becomes hard and brittle. Another good choice in tubing is Tygon® tubing. It is available as a double color-coded Tygon® tubing bonded together called Twintube®. The tubes are orange and green color coded. The green is conventionally used on the oxygen connections and the orange on the propane connections. This tubing although slightly heavier than rubber tubing is still quite flexible. It can soften some when heated, so be sure your hose clamps are tight. Being a bonded tubing means fewer tangles of tubing running around your studio which gives a neater and safer atmosphere.

Another type of fitting and tubing available is that used for commercial welding and cutting operations. They incorporate high pressure tube fittings of the ball and cup type, see Figure 15. They are available in various sizes. The hoses are of a heavy double wall construction reinforced with fiber. It is available as either single tubes or double tubes of various lengths. Because of its higher pressure rating and integral end connectors, it is the only type of connectors and tubing endorsed by the National LP Gas Association. One disadvantage for some glass workers is that it is less flexible, making it is a little more awkward to use. This is not usually a problem with beadmaking since you do not move your torch around.

When making up your system, blow out the hose to clean out any foreign material that may be in them. After making your hose connections, check them all for leaks using a solution of liquid dish detergent and water. Paint it on all your fittings while they are pressurized. Any leaks will cause the solution to bubble. Repeat this procedure occasionally to check for cracks or punctures in your tubing. Keep your tubing out of underfoot by hanging it from the underside of your workbench. Never walk on it if you can help it because this can cause eventual

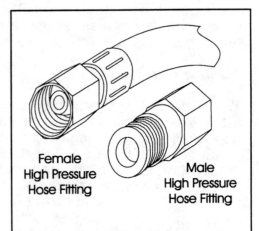

Figure 15. Illustration of industrial high pressure hose and fittings.

© 1996 James Kervin

Equipment   51

splitting of your hoses. If a hose is ever damaged or burned in a flashback, replace it. Flashbacks often burn the inner wall of a hose, weakening it. Also, don't even think about trying to repair a hose by wrapping it with tape. This can allow pinhole leaks over time, creating a dangerous situation.

Fuel-oxygen torches

The fuel-oxygen torch is the most important piece of equipment of the glass bead artist has. The whole purpose of his needing a gas system was to supply the torch with gas. The type and size of torch that you select will depend on the type and scale of work you intend to do.

Therefore it is important to think about what other areas you may also expand into (like flameworked sculptures, neon, etc.) before purchasing a torch.

Premixed torch

A type of torch commonly used by flameworkers is the premixed torch. Premixed means that the oxygen and the fuel are mixed inside the torch prior to being burned at the tip. Many premixed torches are also multipurpose, meaning they can use either oxygen or air to burn the fuel gas. This is accomplished by changing the tip. As mentioned earlier though, oxygen is preferred because of its higher temperature and more complete combustion. A good multipurpose premixed torch is a National 3A Blowpipe by Veriflo. It is widely used as a hand torch as well as a bench torch. One of the advantages of a premixed torch is that its "hard" high-velocity flame transfers heat to the surface of your work so rapidly that the inside of your piece remains relatively cool in comparison at first. This allows attaching constructions to the work without getting the whole thing so hot that it droops.

Premixed torches may have many different tips available. The wide choice of tips allow shaping the flameworkers most important tool, the flame. Different operations require flames of different shapes and size, thus different tips. (Some manufacturers use the term burners instead of tip.) With a large tip you can work glass rod up to an inch in diameter with a National 3A. Anything larger than this would require a larger torch. Smaller scale work can be accomplished by changing to a smaller tip.

When using a premixed torch, remember to adjust your propane pressure and oxygen supply pressure up to about 5-8 psig and 25 psig respectively. Otherwise your flame may get too close to the tip, allowing it to heat up and possibly ignite the fuel prematurely inside the torch. This condition is very dangerous because it can possibly lead to flashback.

Figure 16 shows a National 3A torch along with some of the tips available for use with it. The first tip shown is a gas/air tip. They come in a number of different sizes. The next is a single orifice tip. They are available with orifice sizes from a #1 with a .042" hole to #5 with a .100"

© 1996 James Kervin

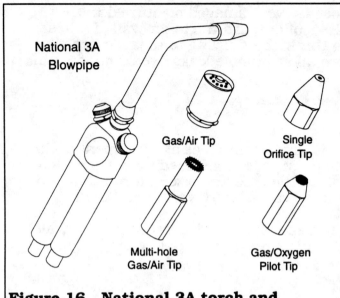

Figure 16. National 3A torch and associated torch tips.

hole. (Using tips larger than about a # 3 gives diminishing returns, you would be better off switching to a multihole tip.) A micro tip variation of this also exists with a smaller hole (.035") to give a needle-like flame. The next two are small multi-hole tips that spread the flame out over a larger area. Variants of these torches which spread the flame out a lot more are commonly used in tubing work for things like neon and are known as ribbon burners.

Because the fuel and oxygen are mixed inside a premixed torch, a plugged tip can allow pressure to build up inside it, leading to possible backflow up whichever hose is at the lowest pressure. Without a check valve at the torch inlet, this would normally allow oxygen to push its way up into your fuel tank. For the case of an almost empty oxygen tank, fuel gas could push its way up your oxygen hose. For this reason many premixed torches may have check valves integral to them. Since these integral check valves can become damaged over time, you may want a backup of a flashback arrestor on the regulator. A partial blockage of a premixed torch can result in a flashback for similar reasons.

Do not confuse a flashback with a backfire. A backfire is an instantaneous extinguishing and reignition of a torch flame. It is usually the result of holding your work too close to the tip of your torch and is confined to the torch head. Blocking the flow at the tip causes the gas velocity to slow enough that it no longer feeds enough gas to keep the flame lit. Then as the gas again builds up, the hot tip may relight the gas. It will typically stop immediately. If not, extinguish your torch and check out your system as discussed for a flashback. Look for loose connections, leaky hoses, incorrect gas settings of the regulator or anything else that could cause gas starvation at the tip. Under certain conditions a backfire can progress on to become a flashback. So if you have a backfire watch for flashback symptoms.

Surface mixed torch

The type of torch preferred by many wound glass bead artists over a premixed torch is a surface mixed torch. Examples of these are the minor and major bench burner made by Nortel Manufacturing, Ltd. or the new Delta 7 or Atlas 19 Jet burners. There is also a new burner available from Nortel with a tip surface area between that of a minor and a major burner. In this type of torch the oxygen is directed up to the burner tip through what I believe is stainless steel hypodermic tubing

Equipment

that are formed into a tapered nozzle. The propane flows around and between the tube cluster to the end of the nozzle. The gases mix at the surface of the nozzle. Surface mixed torches should be used with the gas pressure set at lower pressures than premixed torches — about 4 psig for propane and 5-10 psig for oxygen.

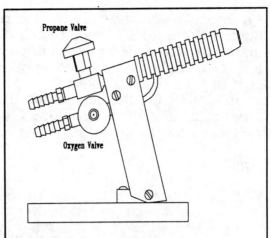

Figure 17. Surface-mixed minor bench burner.

- Ideally the aluminum cylinder around the stainless steel tubing should act as a heat sink and radiator to prevent them from getting too hot and melting. If this barrel is slid back, it will not work as well and you can possibly overheat the tubing and ruin your torch. Unfortunately on a minor bench burner this cover does not make very good contact with the tubing bundle and therefore does not help all that much. This can be a problem even with the cylinder slid forward if you are using fuels other than propane. I have heard of people trashing their minor burners by trying to use it with acetylene. The flame was just too hot and melted the burner face. This could also be a problem with Chem-o-lene. (The minor head on a major burner may be even more susceptible to this since it does not have the aluminum heat sink.) Because of the slower gas flow these burners can suffer from buildup of carbon on the face of the torch from impurities in the fuel gas being burned. This is more of a problem with the major bench burner than it is with a minor burner.

This type of torch is preferred over the premixed torch for a number of reasons. The flame is more spread out. A slower gas velocity out of the torch tip results in a more uniform and quieter flame. It does not transfer heat to your work as quickly as a premixed torch so the heat has more of a chance to penetrate into your work allowing it to achieve a more uniform temperature. Lastly this type of burner does not suffer from the irritating popping backfire that the premixed does if shut off incorrectly (i.e. if you turn the propane off first).

Hybrid torches

There are torches on the market that combine features of both premixed and surface mixed torches. One example of this type of torch is a Carlisle torch which has a central premixed torch core which is surrounded by a surface mixed one. Controls on the torch allow individual adjustment of either portion of the flame.

Stands

When using a torch as a bench burner to make beads or for other types of flameworking, a stand is a necessity. Some torches like the minor bench burner come with stands. Others like the National 3A do not. A stand frees both hands for working with the glass.

© 1996 James Kervin

54   Glass Beadmaking

A number of commercial stands are available to convert hand torches like the National 3A into a bench burner. A couple of features that you might consider when purchasing one are: easier removal, ability to adjust height or angle, and a heavy enough base that it does not have to be fixed to the table. A poor man's alternative to a commercial stand is a setup similar to that for the handheld torch using two small C clamps and a right angle bracket. One C clamp holds one leg of the bracket to the table and the other holds the torch to the bracket.

Lighters

A torch may be lit in any of a number of ways. You might think that most people would just light the torch with a match, but this method is considered neither safe nor reliable by the National Fire Protection Agency and the National Safety Council. The reason for this is not immediately obvious. You would think that everyone would be familiar enough with the use of matches, that they would be the preferred method. The problem with them, besides the fact that they get your hand too close to the flame, is that they can be blown out if the gas velocity on your torch is turned up too high. Then if the torch is not turned off, it may release enough gas into your workspace to cause a small flame up or explosion by the time the second match is lit. Therefore the use of matches to light your torch is discouraged.

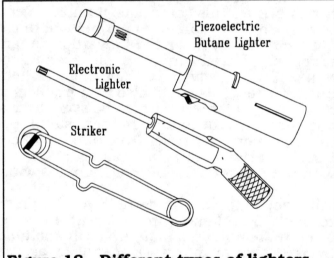

Figure 18. Different types of lighters used for torches.

The most common tool used to light a torch is a striker. Seen in Figure 18, a striker works by scraping a small flint across an irregular metal surface similar to a file. This is the same technique used to spark a cigarette lighter. Scraping the flint causes a spark to jump that can ignite the gas from the torch. In most strikers the spark is generated in a small cup which serves to trap a pocket of gas to make lighting it easier.

Another device used by some artists to light a torch is one of those butane lighters for barbecues. This uses pressure on a piezoelectric crystal to generate a high voltage spark that then lights a small butane flame from a refillable reservoir all at the pull of a trigger. It is a very reliable mechanism but can be a hazard. If you are the kind of person that uses something and does not immediately put it back in its proper place, this tool can be dangerous. Hoyt reports of an incident he was made aware of that happened when someone inadvertently placed a piece of hot glass down on a lighter that had not been put away. The glass melted through the plastic butane reservoir and ignited it causing a flash

© 1996 James Kervin

fire. Luckily no one was injured but this demonstrates why use of this type of lighter should be discouraged.

A good lighter for torches is the electronic lighter manufactured by Coleman Company. It uses an electrical oscillator circuit and transformer like on your car to generate a pulsating high voltage arc from a C cell battery. The arc is not strong enough to hurt someone and can barely be felt. At the same time, it is sufficiently strong enough to reliably light a low velocity stream of propane.

Lampworking hand tools

There are also a number of hand tools that you should become familiar with before starting to work. Some of them you may already have around your shop or alternative choices of equipment which may work almost as good. The first three of these tools are used to cut glass to length. The next five are used to shape the glass and to hold decorations being added to a bead. The last tool is used to form the core of a wound bead.

Glass cutters

Depending on the kind of glass with which you are going to work, the appropriate glass cutter may be a standard cutter like that used in stained glass. Some artists choose to use scrap glass from fusing to make their beads and this cutter is just fine for that application. Since most of the dichroic glass being used in beadmaking is manufactured in sheet form, the stained glass cutter will be used by artists working with dichroic glass.

Other artists prefer to use glass which is specifically manufactured for flameworking (Moretti or Satake glass) that comes in three foot long rods. A standard glass cutter does not work well to cut this material into manageable lengths. There is a tool manufactured specifically for this task, called a glass cutoff knife, which is pictured in Figure 19. It consists of a rectangular tungsten carbide blade mounted in an anodized aluminum handle. The blade is removable and can be reversed to expose four new cutting surfaces. Tungsten carbide is an extremely hard material used primarily for things like machine tools. In fact, used lathe tools can be a cheap alternative to a cutoff knife if you know any machinists. Tungsten carbide besides being very hard is also a brittle material. If you drop your knife, you can break off a section of your blade. (I learned that the hard way.)

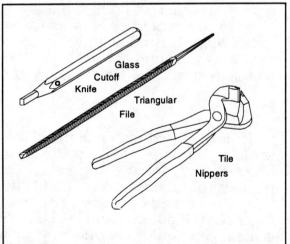

Figure 19. Some of the tools used for cutting glass rods.

56   Glass Beadmaking

To use your cutoff knife, hold the handle with the four fingers of one hand and push a rod against the blade with your thumb. Then make a score around the rod by twisting the rod all the way around with your other hand. Next take the rod in both hands putting your thumbs about one half inch on either side of the score. Bend and break the rod using your thumbs as a fulcrum and pulling toward you with the tips of your fingers.

Nippers

Nippers are hand cutting tools made for cutting ceramic tile. They are used similar to how grozing pliers are used in stained glass work. As seen in Figure 19, they have short tungsten carbide blades mounted at the end of their jaws. When you squeeze the handle, the blades which are mounted perpendicular to the way blades are on scissors, come almost together. They are used to nip off small pieces of tile. In our situation they can be used to nip off a section of rod.

A new type of mosaic cane nippers, the Leponitt Mosaic Glass Cutter, has recently come on the market, which has two replaceable tungsten carbide blades. The carbide disk blades have a sharpened, 85° included angle cutting edge. With a diameter of ¾" the disk has a total cutting surface of about 2½" compared to the usual ½" on most nippers. When the part of the disk that you are currently using becomes dull, you just grab the included Allen wrench, loosen the screw holding the disk and rotate it to bring a fresh cutting surface into play. The cost of a new set of disks is only about ¾ that of a new tool. This tool cuts your cane more uniformly and with more control than a tile nipper. They also don't tend to shoot your cane slices across the room like tile nippers do. Being a specialized tool though, it tends to be a lot more expensive than tile nippers.

Triangular file

A triangular file can also be used to score your glass rods for breaking. To do this, hold the rod down on the table with one hand and take the triangular file in the other. Push the triangular file perpendicularly across the top of the rod away from you. This should put a score in the rod. Rotate the rod slightly and continue scoring until it runs about 1/4 to 1/2 way around the rod. Wet the score. Then break the rod with your hands as described for the glass knife.

Paddles

Paddles are used to shape the glass while it is hot and pliable. Hot glass workers often use cherry paddles (soaked in water to prevent the wood from burning) for shaping glass. That is too messy for our work. The paddles that flameworkers and beadmakers use are made from graphite. Graphite is used because it will not stick to hot glass as metal will when it gets hot. Paddles can also be used as marvering plates to form the glass if you don't have one on your workbench. For handwork, small paddles on the order of 1 1/2" x 1 3/4" are preferred by most beadmakers but paddles are also available in 1" x 4", 2" x 3", 3" x 4", etc. There is now a little graphite block (mini-marver) available that mounts

© 1996 James Kervin

Equipment 57

to the top of your torch. This makes it always conveniently available for use without having to hold it in your hand

Most paddles have rectangular solid faces but there are some new ones on the market shaped like a small rubber spatula with an increasingly sharp edge on one side and a rounded edge on the other side as seen in the left of Figure 20. These paddles, sometimes called Stump Shapers after Loren Stump, allow you to poke groves and creases into hot glass, shaping it to your will.

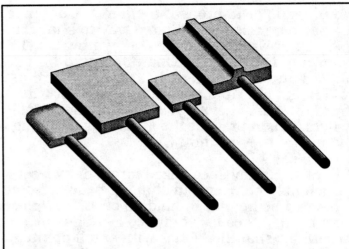

Figure 20. Some of the types of paddles available.

There are also paddles as seen in the right side of the figure which have sort of an upside down T shape. This type of paddle is used to shape cylindrical beads with rounded ends. The sides of the cylinders are shaped by rolling in one of the two rounded creases. Which one depends upon the size of the bead. Then to form a nice rounded end you turn the mandrel perpendicular to the crease and roll the end of the bead along the crease. Most beadmakers just shape cylindrical beads on a flat paddle and get the rounded ends by jockeying around the paddle to form it.

Some paddles are available with multiple sized hemispherical and tear drop shapes carved into them to help shape beads if you like. They may even have grooves for your mandrel. These blocks can also be used to make hemispherical cabochons and marbles. Hemispherical cabochons can be made by just getting the glass on the end of a rod hot and pushing it into the cutout in the mold. The proper way to use these molds to form beads and marbles is to use one size hole to help get the right amount of glass built up on a mandrel or punty and then use the next smaller hole to shape the object by gently rolling it on the lip of the cavity. If you try to use the volume of the cavity for shaping, you inevitably form undesired folds in your work.

Tweezers

Tweezers, like those seen in Figure 21, are used to pick up and hold hot constructions that you want to add to

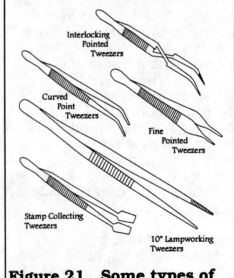

Figure 21. Some types of tweezers available.

© 1996 James Kervin

your beads or to preheat them in the outer reaches of your flame. They can also be used in a limited way to shape and form your beads or to pick off unwanted features off of a bead. The special long tweezers shown in the figure are manufactured for use in flameworking and come in 6, 8 and 10 inch lengths. Tweezers are usually made of thin steel and will not stand up to a direct flame. For this reason, remove your bead from the flame before you use any metal tool to form and shape it. This will also help prevent the glass from sticking to the tweezers which can happen if they get hot.

There are many specialized forms of tweezers available for other reasons which may be useful in shaping beads. Some tweezers are self-locking. This can be helpful in holding on to tiny pieces that you are trying to add to a bead. Ones for stamp collecting have small flat ends that can be useful for shaping. Ones with small pointed ends also come in handy for pulling out feature details. You will also want to collect a wide variety of tweezers for your work.

Pliers and pinchers

Pliers can be used like tweezers to shape your glass but are a little more resistant to the heat because of their larger mass. This means that they also chill the glass faster and you may want to preheat them slightly before touching them to your bead to prevent thermal shocking it. This is less of a problem when the glass is really hot. They can be used to add twists and ridges, or to pull out and move around sections of your bead. The ideal pliers for this type of work is a good needle-nosed pliers.

Special jawed pliers can be made by brazing different kinds of shaped plates onto cheap swap-meet pliers (or purchased premade). Examples of such pliers are illustrated in Figure 22. It is called a mashing or squashing pliers. It is used to squeeze molten beads to flatten them out. A smaller version with square jaws, called a "mini-masher", is used for squishing small details in sculptural beads is also available. Flat jawed mashers are also available such that the jaws do not completely close together. They close at the inside of the jaws where they are brazed on but they are open at the outside end of the flat. These types of mashers are used to make star millefiori and Rosetta beads. A variation on the flat jawed mashers are one with curved jaw faces. These are used to give a little curvature to tableau beads (discussed later).

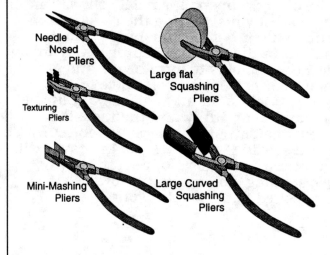

Figure 22. Different types of glass pliers.

You can also make pliers with jaws having textures or shapes. I call these types of pliers, "pinchers" for lack of a better name. They texture the glass as well as shape it. Commercial ones are available to make leaf-like ridges, squigglely lines and square lines, but with a little imagination I am sure that many other ideas may come to mind. They come with the pinching surface of the pliers either perpendicular to the end of the jaws like a normal mashing pliers, or aligned along the jaws which ever is easier for you to use.

If you decide to make your own specialized pliers, try making your jaws out of brass as it does not seem to leave as much scum on the glass as some other materials. If you want to make pliers that can texture the glass as you squash it try welding on sections of a wood rasp (file). This puts in a number of parallel lines like veins on a leaf.

Reamers and shapers

Reamers are primarily used to flare out the ends of blown beads. They come in a number of different types some of which are shown in Figure 23. The most common being a straight graphite rod with a point on one end and an insulated handle on the other. Graphite rods, which are available in a number of diameters from flameworking suppliers, can also be used to shape a work. Graphite reamers are also available with a hexagonal cross section. This reduces the contact area with the bead and thus the heat loss as you twist it in the hole.

Another common type of reamer for large holes is made out of brass and shaped like a triangle at the end of a rod. One of this type is also seen in the figure. This type is very useful for shaping and distorting the surface of a bead. When using reamers made from brass or steel, lubricating the tip with beeswax prior to use helps prevent it from sticking to the glass and vice versa. Other tools that can be used like reamers to shape glass include razor blades and exacto knifes.

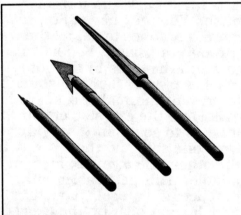

Figure 23. Reamers for shaping beads.

Tungsten pick

A tungsten pick is used in a number of ways. It can be used to rake glass, to pick off undesired elements, shape features and drill holes through the glass. Tungsten is used because it does not stick to the glass as easily as does a lot of other metals, even when hot. A good straight pick can be constructed using some of tungsten wire used for tig welding and is easily obtained from a welding supply house. This wire can be held in a wood dowel handle or a pin vise. A pin vise is a small handle used to hold things like small reaming tools, scribes, etc. It has a central hollow in which fits a collet. Over the collet a screw-on cap is applied that causes the collet to tighten on whatever is inserted into it as the cap is tightened.

© 1996 James Kervin

Tungsten is used because glass for two reasons. First, it is very resistant to the heat. Second, it does not stick to it as much as other metals (unless both the pick and the glass are hot). If one is cooler than the other then it will not stick. This feature can be put to good use to allow a pick to act as a temporary mandrel in building up beads out of tubing. Here you can temporarily bond the tubing to the pick by heating one end of the tubing and the pick. The bead can be released later heating the pick real hot and twisting the bead off.

Tungsten picks are available with small hooks on the end as seen to the left in Figure 24. These are used to shape features and indentations into the surface of the glass. I will talk about their use when I talk about making a face bead. They are also available with right angles on the end. This kind is used for raking and is not really necessary because you can usually rake with a stringer but you may want to purchase one anyway. Both of these are a little hard to make since tungsten is so brittle, so you may want to purchase them.

To drill a hole in a piece of glass with the tungsten pick, you get the pick red hot and poke it through the glass twisting it back and forth as you push. You may have to repeat this more than once to get all the way through the glass. You will also have to warm the glass in the outer reaches of your flame to soften it and to prevent thermal shock. To prevent distorting the exit side of your bead, it helps to go about ½ way through from one side and then ½ way from the other side trying to meet in the middle. This gets easier with practice. If you get trapped in the middle, just heat up the exposed portion of the pick and twist it out. For making larger holes, it helps to make a pilot hole first with a smaller diameter pick and them ream it out with a larger one.

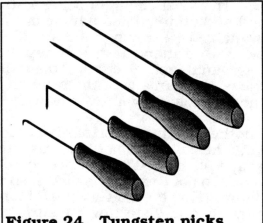

Figure 24. Tungsten picks available.

Scissors

Another tool that you will use occasionally is a pair of scissors. Besides for the obvious use of cutting things like metal foils, scissors can also be used for cutting molten glass. When looking for a set of scissors to use on glass beads, look for scissors with thin blades. This will minimize the heat conduction from the glass when cutting it and allows you to cut further before the glass cools enough to get hard. A good scissors for use with glass is one of those like used in Bonsai. Scissors can be used to square off ends of parts or to make cuts into something where you want to pull out sections of it out for something like a feather for a wing.

Hot fingers

Sometimes when you are making beads, you want a tool to cradle the bead in the fire without burning your finger tips. The perfect tool for this

Equipment

is a set of hot fingers. They consist of four steel fingers mounted in a handle that grip the bead by adjusting a slide forward as illustrated in Figure 25. This causes the fingers to come together. You can purchase one of these tools or make your own. The ones pictured use round cross section brass tubing to form the handle and square cross section tubing to form the slide. A ring is soldered on the end of the adjusting slide to prevent it from sliding into the handle. The fingers themselves are made from steel wires (which could be from old bead winding mandrels) that are soldered into the handle. You can bend the tips of the fingers to suit the job at hand. The circular tips shown are good for handling spherical beads. Hammesfahr and Stong show an simpler fabrication technique for hot fingers.

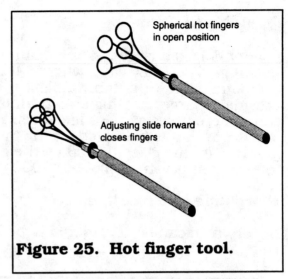

Figure 25. Hot finger tool.

Winding mandrels

The easiest of the beadmaking techniques available to a typical glass artist, as will be described later, is that of making wound glass beads. In this technique, beads are wound around a mandrel. The most common mandrel employed by wound glass beadmakers is stainless steel filler rod used in TIG welding. It is available from welding supply houses and is commonly available in 3 foot lengths of 1/16th, 3/32nds and 1/8th inch diameter. Copper coated steel rods are also another good alternative, but be sure you do not get the flux-coated rods. For beads with holes larger than this, stainless steel tubing is suggested. Stainless steel is the recommended material for a number of reasons. It holds up well to the heat without distorting. It does not oxidize appreciably and its surface remains smooth under repeated use. Lastly it is a poor conductor of heat. This allows you to hold the rods relatively close to the bead without burning yourself.

Some artists like to attach handles to the winding rods by sticking them into counter drilled wood dowels or by using a pin vise. This is especially important when making big heavy "monster" beads. Another convenient option is to use one of those mechanical pencils made for drafting that have a little, normally-closed pin-vise like mechanism that opens when you press the button on the end of the pencil. The extra thickness gained from any of these options helps give you a little more control during winding by making the rods easier to handle. They may also help prevent putting stress on your ligaments and joints reducing the chances of repetitive motion injuries. The other thing that you may want to think about doing is adding weights to the end of your mandrels or mandrel handles to counterbalance the weight of the bead on the other end of the mandrel. This will also help to make the mandrel easier to handle.

Glory holes

A glory hole is a large heating chamber used by glassblowers to heat and reheat glass as they work with it. It is used by bead makers to make components, most notably millefiori, for inclusion in their beads. It provides a larger heating area than is possible using a torch. It does not contain crucibles of glass like a glass furnace and is usually in the shape of a drum that is insulated on the inside. In order to be able to manipulate the glass heated by the glory hole, it must maintain an internal temperature of about 2000° F.

Glory hole construction

A glory hole can be considered to be composed of three main components: metal framework, refractory lining and heating system. The design of each of these components involve tradeoffs to meet the designer's requirements. Factors to consider include: heating capability, ease of use, durability, safety and of course cost. There are a few glory holes currently on the market that are fine for the kind of work that we will be talking about in this book. They include the Murphy Fire Bucket made by Fusion Glass, Inc. and another by Denver Machinery. You could also, if so inclined, build your own. For plans see either of the following three references listed in the back: "Advanced Glass Fusing" by Boyce Lundstrom, "Glory Hole is Heart of Glassblowing" by Karl Platt or "A Glory Hole Design" by John Nickerson. Figure 26 shows a cross sectional view of a typical glory hole. You will want to keep things small for most beadmaking applications.

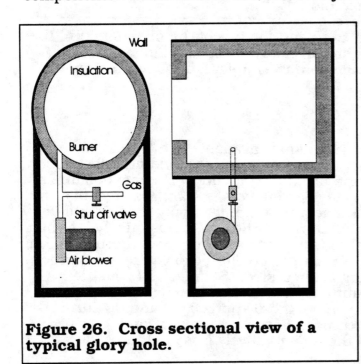

Figure 26. Cross sectional view of a typical glory hole.

The first design component, the metal framework, provides the strength and durability of the system. It consists of a metal cylinder and stand, usually constructed from steel to withstand the high temperatures and erosion incurred in daily use. The most common sources for the cylinder is large pipe or small steel drums. The cylinder wall provides for protection of the refractory lining, which tends to be fairly fragile, from mechanical damage during use. To it is mounted the rest of the stand framework which positions the glory hole at the proper height for work and to which the burner system is mounted.

Equipment   63

The choice of the second component of the glory hole, the refractory insulation, involves tradeoffs in durability, cost and energy efficiency of the system. Most glory holes are insulated strictly using alumina fiber blanket material rigidized with a refractory cement. This is because fiber blanket is cheaper and easier to work with than many other types of refractory materials. More rugged and efficient glory hole designs include multiple layers of different fibers and possibly fire brick or castable refractory liners. The inner liner should have the highest temperature rating since it is directly exposed to the flame. Successive layers will have lower and lower density to provide higher insulation capability. If your glory hole has a castable liner, you should make sure that it has been properly prefired prior to your first use. Otherwise you will want to take it easy and fire the glory hole at a low temperature the first time you use it to make sure all the chemical reactions that occur during a curing cycle have been done completely and gradually. This is sort of like breaking in a new car where you don't push it right away. Even after curing, a castable lined glory hole should be heated up slowly during each use to prevent thermal shock cracking. Practicing these precautions will pay you back with increased durability to the flames.

The combustion system feeds both air and fuel, usually propane or natural gas, to the burner in the side of the cylinder. Most likely you will have a propane fueled glory hole that will use a propane tank and regulator identical to that which have already been described in the discussions of propane-oxygen torch systems. The burner is located off center from the center of the cylinder and feeds the flame into the chamber tangentially to the surface of the wall. This causes the flame to make a swirling vortex inside. The burner may simply consist of a piece of pipe or it may have a nozzle to increase the speed of the incoming combustion gases. It will be buried inside the insulation to protect it from erosion by the flame. Air flow is supplied by a mechanical blower. Gas feed will be regulated by a gas regulator and a throttle valve.

Glory hole operation

The operations that we will be doing with the glory hole will require either preheated materials or annealing of constructions after they are formed in the glory hole. For this reason, it should be located in close enough proximity and without obstructions to your kiln. There should also be plenty of room available to turn around, back up and do the operations that will be required. This is especially important as you are lighting it with a handheld propane torch and it lights off with a loud roar.

The use of a glory hole involves an open flame that produces a lot of heat. For this reason it should be located away from combustible materials and fuels (oils, paints, etc.) Have your propane supply tank located as far away from the glory hole as practically possible; you still want to have easy access to the tank for on/off control. Always keep a fire extinguisher close at hand. The flame contains some unburned fuel by products so use it only in a well ventilated area. Make sure that all your propane connections are leak tight.

If this is your first time using an a glory hole, you are in for a thrill. It sounds really powerful and can scare you. But if you are careful,

© 1996 James Kervin

64   Glass Beadmaking

understand your equipment and follow the correct operating procedures, you should not have any real problems. The basic operating instructions are as follows:

1. Check to see that the fuel throttle valve to the burner is closed.
2. Turn on the propane at the propane tank. Check for any hint of propane smell in the air or the sound of any leaks. (You did leak check all your fittings when you set up the system.)
3. Turn on the air blower. Hear how noisy it is. Could you have heard any propane leaks if you turned it on first?
4. Some glory hole blowers may have a valve to throttle the blower air. If yours does, throttle it down to prevent it from blowing out the flame while you are lighting the glory hole.
5. Light a handheld propane torch like those discussed earlier to light the burner. You use this instead of something like a match since it is less likely to blow out.
6. Hold the torch with the tip as far inside the mouth of the glory hole as necessary to ensure that the flame reaches the burner as you point the flame point at it. Make sure that you are not so close that the flame is blown out by the air flow inside the glory hole.
7. Slowly open the gas throttle valve. The burner should light almost immediately. If not, close the gas throttle valve and try to determine what the problem is. Do you have propane? Can you smell it? Is the torch still lit?
8. Adjust the propane so that you just have a small blue-yellow flame at the outside of the burner.
9. Allow the glory hole to warm up. (In just a couple minutes it will be glowing red.) Then turn up the throttle on the blower.
10. Adjust glory hole temperature and atmosphere by throttling your propane feed.

Turning off the glory hole is much easier. Turn off the propane first at the throttle valve and then at the tank. Never turn off the air first because the flame could travel into your gas system. Allow your blower to continue running for a few minutes to cool everything down.

Kilns and annealers

A kiln or annealer is an insulated container in which glass can be heated. Unlike the glory hole or a torch, which we have already discussed, a kiln allows precision temperature control from room temperature to over 2000°F. As a beadmaker you will primarily use your kiln for annealing stress out of your beads as will be discussed later. Of course you might also decide to pursue fabrication of beads by one of the more common kilnworking practices such as fusing or Pate de Verre. You will also find a kiln useful in making millefiori, in making drawn beads and in applying lusters or enamels to your beads. There are also a number of general operations besides fusing that can be done in a kiln. Each has its own characteristic temperature. Table 9 provides a list of temperature ranges and what types of kiln processes are done in each of these temperature ranges.

© 1996 James Kervin

Equipment   65

Table 9. Temperature ranges for various kilnworking processes.

Temperature Range (°F)	Process
RT- 100	
100- 200	
200- 300	Removal of physically bound water from molds and kiln furniture (212°F)
300- 400	Removal of chemically bound water from molds and kiln (375-450°F)
400- 500	
500- 600	
600- 700	Lusters stop smoking (600-625°F)
700- 800	
800- 900	
900-1000	Organics finish burning off Firing bright metal lusters on lead glass (960°F)
1000-1100	Firing Reusche enamels (1080°F) Firing Thompson low-fire enamels (1050-1150°F) Firing bright metal lusters on soda lime glass (1040-1100°F)
1100-1200	Firing Fuse Master enamels (1125°F) Firing low temperature lusters (1100°F)
1200-1300	Firing bright metal lusters on Pyrex or quartz (1200-1250°F) Firing most lusters (1250-1325°F)
1300-1400	Firing high-fire Thompson enamels (1350-1450°F) Firing most clear overglazes Devitrification range for susceptible glasses
1400-1500	Paradise paint matures (1450°F)
1500-1600	
1600-1700	
1700-1800	Raking of hot glass fusing
1800-1900	
1900-2000	Melting glass in a crucible for pouring

How kilns work

Kilns like glory holes are composed of three main components: a structural framework, an insulating liner and a heat source. There is nothing really complex about a kiln so don't be afraid of it.

The framework of a kiln usually consists of an exterior metal skin and a stand to get it up off the floor. The exterior skin serves a number of important services, the most important of which is to serve as a framework to which you mount your insulation. It also protects the insulation from mechanical damage during normal operation. The framework of the skin also serves as a convenient place to mount control boxes and lids or doors. The kiln will usually be mounted off the floor on a stand for two reasons. The first is so you will not have to bend down so low to put things into and take them out of the kiln. The second is to allow air to circulate around your kiln and help keep the exterior cool.

© 1996 James Kervin

66   Glass Beadmaking

Like a glory hole, the insulation of a kiln may be composed of a number of layers. The bottoms of most kilns are made using fire brick to provide a strong heat resistant surface upon which to stand kiln hardware. The inner walls of most pottery kilns will also be made from fire brick because of the higher temperatures needed to process pottery. Most glass kilns these days are being lined with alumina fiber blanket that has been rigidized. This is sufficient because the processing temperatures with glass are typically 500°F lower than that used for pottery and the alumina fiber can withstand these temperatures without breaking down. The alumina fiber blanket provides a big advantage in that it has a much lower heat capacity (meaning that it soaks up less heat) allowing faster temperature cycling through a kiln cycle. (There is some concern that the alumina fiber blanket material is carcinogenic and becomes more so with repeated application of heat. For this reason, many safety conscious people advocate a fire brick lined kiln.)

Firebrick, on the other hand, will take longer to heat up because its higher heat capacity requires more energy to heat it up and, for the same reason, it will take longer to cool off. This phenomenon is called rebound and can be used to provide slow cooling down after a firing without the use of power. Behind the inner exposed layer of either firebrick or fiber blanket is usually a layer of loose ceramic wool for more insulation. Even the sides of a kiln may be made from insulating fiber board to provide extra insulation. With all this insulation, the inner surface of the kiln may be at 2000°F while the outside may be cool enough to touch.

Almost all of the kilns being used in glass studios are electric fired because of their many advantages over gas fired kilns. These include: providing more uniform heating, being easier to control both for temperature and atmosphere, being quieter and requiring less maintenance. The main difference to be found between different glass kilns is in where the elements seem to be placed. Some only have elements on the ceiling of the kiln which provides a more uniform heat distribution over the surface of the glass. This also allows faster heating rates on large glass projects without risk of cracking from thermal stress. A disadvantage of this configuration is that it does not allow heating a second shelf of glass beneath the top one. For this reason top firing kilns are usually fairly shallow but larger in length and width. The other fairly common element configuration is to have the elements mounted on the side. Here the rate of temperature rise has to be slowed slightly for large glass projects to allow the heat from the elements to penetrate to the center of the shelf and thus prevent stress buildup from expansion of the edges faster than the center of the work. This configuration also allows for heating of stacked shelves, although, you have to make sure that the spacing between them is sufficient to allow proper air circulation and heat convection. For this reason, kilns of this configuration will tend to be deeper than top fired ones. These two configurations can also be combined as shown in Figure 27 to make a versatile kiln for either situation. For beadmaking either configuration will do fine because the pieces that you will be making are small and will not develop large thermal differences.

For an annealer which you will be reaching in and out of quite frequently, you want to make sure that you never touch a live element.

Equipment   67

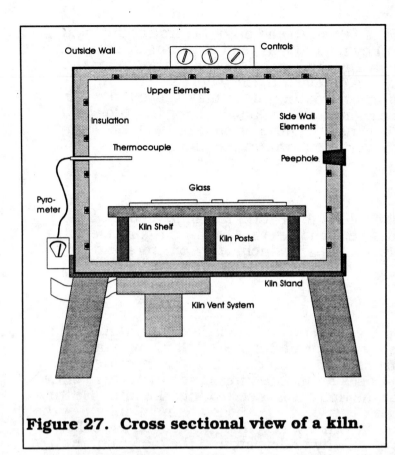

Figure 27. Cross sectional view of a kiln.

One way to do this is to have a "dead man's" switch (contact switch) mounted to the door in such a way that whenever the door is open power is turned off to the kiln. But many artists work with the door open for a long time which may allow the annealer to cool too much. You could try to hide the elements in grooves in the sides of the annealer but that is not fool proof and no one likes playing the fool in this situation. A safer alternative is to encase the elements in quarts tubing. The heat can still get out of the tubing since most of the heat is transferred by radiant energy. This arrangement is not as good for a fusing kiln because it can cause the elements to over heat and burn out a little sooner.

The heating elements in your kiln work just like those in your stove or oven. As electricity moves through the wire, its flow is slowed or resisted by the atoms in the wire. The energy expended in pushing against this resistance to flow is released as heat. Flow through the elements and thus heat to the kiln is controlled by infinity switches on the front of your kiln. These switches will typically be numbered from 1 to about 10 where the higher the number, the higher the fraction of time the kiln is on. Their control range is from about 5% to 100% of the time. These switches operate by using interior bimetallic strips similar to those in a thermostat. As power flows through them, they heat up and bend, opening the electric circuit (shutting off power). They then cool down, unbend and reclose the electric circuit. Rotating the infinity switch controls the amount of time that the kiln is on by controlling how much the strip has to bend to pull away from the contact to shut off the power. The electrical power required for your kiln may be either 120 or 240 volts.

Your kiln may have its door on either the top or the front. Opinion is divided as to which configuration is better. Top-loading kilns are touted as being easier to load and use because they provide complete access to the inside surface of the kiln. Others say burns to the face and arms are more likely when using a top-loader as you peek into the kiln to see how the firing is progressing. During peeking, top-loaders are more

© 1996 James Kervin

68   Glass Beadmaking

susceptible to having particles fall off the lid onto the project during a firing. This can be really annoying and may lead to pitting or cracking of your glass during cool down. The other possible configuration for the door, on the front, provides less of a view of the whole kiln during peeking, but provides a better view of the side to make sure that your beads are not slumping or sagging. Having a side-firing front-loader is not the best configuration because the missing elements on the door makes for large temperature variations within the kiln.

Measuring kiln temperature

Since the whole purpose of a kiln is to heat things up in a controlled manner, let's discuss the different choices that we have to precisely measure the temperature in a kiln. They include pyrometers and cones.

Pyrometers

A convenient device to monitor the temperature inside your kiln is called a pyrometer (literally translated to mean fire meter). It allows you to monitor your kiln temperature so that you do not end up heating it too high or at too fast a rate. It uses a thermocouple made from wires of two dissimilar metals welded at the tip that is inserted into the kiln. Heating the welded junction between the two wires causes the metal in one of the wires to pull electrons from the other wire. This physical effect, called the Seebeck effect, causes electricity to flow around the loop from the thermocouple through the pyrometer. It is actually a quite common effect between metals, but certain metals produce a much higher voltage potential than others. Some specially developed alloys, like chromel, alumel and constantan, make thermocouples so sensitive they can measure the temperature increase from holding them in your hands. The pyrometer actually measures the amount of current that is flowing through it, but since that is directly proportional to the temperature of the thermocouple, the readout is calibrated in temperature. The wires that connect the thermocouple to the gauge have a calibrated resistant and should not be shortened or exchanged except with acceptable replacement parts.

The scale of the pyrometer itself will generally be calibrated both in degrees Fahrenheit and Centigrade. They will have a range from 0° to about 2500°F. The pyrometer and thermocouple are sensitive instruments and should be treated respectfully. It should not be subjected to dust, moisture or being bumped around. Never connect anything else across the pyrometer terminals except the connecting wire to the thermocouple. You can break the pyrometer if you do. To test to see if your system is hooked up correctly, hold a match under the thermocouple junction and see if the temperature reading on the pyrometer rises. If the gauge needle is reading below zero, then you have the wires to the pyrometer reversed. Switch them and it will then record correctly. There is a little resistant to needle movement that can be overcome by tapping slightly on the face of the pyrometer. This will give a truer reading.

© 1996 James Kervin

Equipment   69

If you look at the thermocouple, you will see that it is sheathed in a ceramic body. This provides insulation from accidental contact with the elements. The thermocouple is generally inserted into the kiln though a hole drilled into one of the fire brick plugs for a peephole. It should be inserted well into the kiln away from the sides and elements, preferably out over your work. Try to always position it in the same place so that the conditions that you will get inside the kiln are consistent for the same pyrometer reading. After a thermocouple has been used a lot, it will start to oxidize and can eventually be completely consumed by the oxidation process. The oxide layer can insulate the thermocouple junction and should be cleaned by light abrasion using 0000 steel wool. Try not to flex the junction or you may crack it. If you get no reading with your match test of the thermocouple and you are sure everything is hooked up, it is possible that the junction or the metal has been completely oxidized up.

The meter of the pyrometer needs to be kept cool to read correctly. If the outside of your kiln gets hot, then you should not mount the gauge there. If mounted to the kiln, it should be in such a position that it does not get heated when you open the kiln door to peek in. Wherever you keep the meter, mount it firmly so that it can not be accidentally knocked to the floor.

Cones

Another method commonly used to measure kiln temperature, the use of cones, does not really measure temperature. Instead it measures what is commonly referred to as heat work. Cones are slender pyramid shaped objects of unfired clays that have been carefully formulated to react to heat in a predictable manner. They are placed inside your kiln where they can be viewed through the peephole. As they heat up, they soften and bend under their own weight. By controlling their formulation, the amount of heat work which causes the bending can be controlled. The temperature at which the cone deforms is a function of the heating rate. These are published by the manufacturer of the cone and should be controlled for about the last 200°F of the firing. As an example, Orton's large and self-supporting cones are calibrated for a heating rate of 270° F/hr. A properly fired cone will have its tip bend over in a smooth curve until its tip becomes even with its base.

Cones range in number from 022 to 42. The larger the number, the more heat work that is required to deform the cone. You might wonder at the leading 0 on 022. Originally cone numbers started at 1 which was used for a processing temperature of about 2100° F. Demand soon developed for lower temperature cones to serve as indicators during firing of decorations, lusters and enamels as well as for use in glass fusing. Rather than renumbering all the cones from 1 again it was decided to number backwards from 1 by adding an 0 in front of the number to indicate it is a heat treatment less than 1. So 022 is less than 015 and thus requires less heat work.

Cones come in three different sizes. The first is large regular cones which are 2 1/2" high and require mounting in cone plaques or clay

© 1996 James Kervin

70 Glass Beadmaking

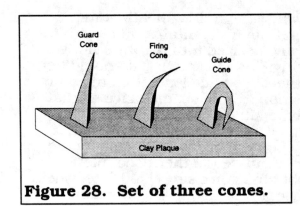

Figure 28. Set of three cones.

pots. They are inserted such that exactly 2" of the cone sticks out of the plaque and it is at an angle of 8°. Small regular cones are 1 1/8" high and are mounted so that 15/16" is exposed. A guide should be used to ensure that either of these regular cones are mounted at the correct angle. They should also be positioned such that they will not fall against each other during the firing. The last kind of cone is a self supporting cone. These cones already have their own preset base such that they are mounted at the right height and angle.

The recommended way to use cones is in sets of three. A center cone is chosen to indicate when the proper heat work for your process is complete. This is referred to as the firing cone. A first cone that is one number lower than the firing cone. This "guide" cone's bending will indicate that you are approaching the proper heat work condition and need to pay more attention to the kiln. The third cone is to guard against overfiring your project. If you see it start to bend, then you are getting too hot and need to reduce the temperature in the kiln as soon as possible. If you want, you can place the same set of cones in a number of locations around the kiln to investigate how uniform the heat conditions are inside it. This configuration of cones is illustrated in Figure 28.

The performance of a cone may vary somewhat from the established value if conditions vary from that for which they were calibrated. Besides the effect of heating rate which we have already discussed, cone performance is also affected by soaking at a temperature and the kiln atmosphere. Soaking for one hour at temperature requires using a cone one cone number higher to indicate proper heat work. A three hour soak requires a cone two cone numbers higher and a nine hour soak three cone numbers higher. This is because you are putting in extra heat work from the hold at temperature. If for some reason you have a very reducing environment in the kiln, say because you are burning out organics, you should use an iron free cone. They do not require oxygen to mature properly as do standard cones.

Kiln Sitter®

A Kiln Sitter® is a mechanical device developed and manufactured by W. P. Dawson Co. that is designed to shut off the power to the kiln after the designated heat work has been achieved. To accomplish this, the kiln sitter uses a small cone or pyrometric bar to record the heat work. The Kiln Sitter® senses the condition of the cone by a mechanical linkage that puts it in three point bending. The cone is rested on two pins and the mechanical sensing rod is placed on top of the cone. As the cone is worked, it gets softer and the weight of the sensing rod causes the cone to bend. When the cone bends a preset distance, a claw attached to the

Equipment 71

other end of the rod is disengaged from a switch by pivoting about a linkage point. This releases a spring loaded switch which then slams open, shutting off the kiln power.

The Kiln Sitter® is not a complex device and is used as follows: 1) before setting up, turn off the power at the infinity switches. 2) ensure that the sensing rod swings freely and does not bind in the ceramic tube. 3) apply a thin coating of kiln wash to the cone pins and sensing rod on the inside of the kiln. 4) raise the sensing rod and insert a cone into place on the pins. 5) raise the spring loaded switch and hook the claw over the face of the switch. 6) close the kiln and turn on the power at the infinity switches.

There are pros and cons as to whether to use a cone or a pyrometric bar with a Kiln Sitter®. The pyrometric bars, because of their uniform cross section down the length of the bar, will bend more controllably from firing to firing. Their bending is not as much a function of where the sensing rod is suspended on the bar. Cones on the other hand have a variable cross section and will bend a little sooner and result in a lower heat work firing, the closer the rod is placed to the small end of the cone. Some people like this feature because they feel that it gives them as much as 1/2 a cone variable control over the firing. Others do not like this because it gives them one more way to mess up.

When properly fired, the cone in the Kiln Sitter® will be bent approximately in a 90° angle. If yours is not, then your sensing rod may be bent. This may result in either an underfiring if the rod is bend upward or an overfiring if you rod is bend downward. Check on the function of your kiln sitter by using either your pyrometer or a set of witness cones. If you detect differences, you can try to adjust for them by changing the cone position in the Kiln Sitter®. Be aware too that the sensing rod can become oxidized and corroded to the point where it looses enough weight that this can also affect the firing you receive.

Setting up your kiln

First and foremost read your instruction manual to develop an understanding on how to use and set up your particular kiln. How you set up your kiln can greatly affect the safety of its operation. It should be kept at least one foot away from any flammable materials and ideally should have one foot of air space all around it to carry away excess heat. It should be located on a fire proof surface preferably concrete. If not, install some other insulating fireproof material underneath it. It should not be located near gasoline, oils or other flammable materials. It should not be set up in a damp area. The space in which you set it up should have plenty of ventilation because there are times when items that you are firing in the kiln may release toxic vapors. It should also be out of the way so that you or others are not continually tripping over it and it should have plenty of room around it so that you can access it safely.

Get the kiln all set up before connecting it to power. Make sure that you hook the kiln into a circuit with the right voltage. Also you should try to hook it directly into a circuit receptacle without using an extension cord

© 1996 James Kervin

72   Glass Beadmaking

if at all possible. Make sure that the power cord is not in contact with your kiln so that it will not melt during use. If you have to use an extension cord, make sure that it is properly constructed for the voltage and current used by your kiln. As an example, a 120 volt 15 amp kiln requires an extension cord of at least #12 copper wire. If you have to install an extra circuit for your kiln, make sure that it is done by an electrician. Your receptacle should not be more than about 50 ft from the junction box and should have a minimum of other outlets on the same line to prevent overloading the circuit. Other items in the same circuit may cause variations in your firing. Likewise power delivery to your house may vary during the day and change the amount of power available to your kiln.

Kiln care

If your kiln has never been used or has not been used in a long while, then you should do a tempering run before using it. A tempering run is a slow heat up and dwell at a low temperature to drive off all moisture in the insulation. To do this first empty and clean out your kiln. A vacuuming with a soft brush nozzle works best. Check to see that there is a good layer of kiln wash on the floor of the kiln. Kiln wash is a refractory separator material like that used on the winding mandrels. (Its use is described shortly.) If the kiln wash layer is not in good shape, then apply a new coating. Now close the kiln lid but vent it by propping it open about an inch with a piece of ceramic kiln furniture. Turn the kiln on low, allow it to heat up slowly to about 300°F and hold it there for an hour to get rid of the physically attached water. Then proceed on up to 400°F and hold for another hour to get rid of the chemically attached water. Then turn off the kiln, close it and allow it to cool slowly back to room temperature. Besides helping to make your kiln last longer, this process also reduces the amount of moisture in your firing. Moisture can cause bubbling if it is trapped beneath your glass and reacts with the surface of hot glass to corrode it.

You should occasionally check your kiln over to see that everything is in good shape. The exterior should be intact to hold everything together. Check over the inside of the kiln. (Always turn off the kiln power by unplugging it whenever you are doing any maintenance on it.) Cracks in fire bricks are part of normal wear and tear. They allow expansion and contraction during the firing cycle and do not need to be repaired. Chips and crumbled areas are another thing altogether. They reduce the thickness of the thermal insulation and should be repaired. They can be patched using repair cement available from your ceramics supply store. Spatula it into place, let dry overnight and then sand it lightly to smooth it. If the damage is extensive, then you may have to remove part or all of the brick. For a partial brick replacement, cut a piece from a new brick to fit and fill in around it with repair cement. For an entire brick, replace it with a new brick that you have trimmed to size to match the old brick. Remember there will be a slight gap between the bricks to allow for thermal expansion so don't make it too tight of a fit.

Next check out the elements. Are they bulging out of the grooves? Sometimes all that has happened is that the staples have come out. If so, just push them back into position using a screw driver. Other times

© 1996 James Kervin

Equipment   73

the coils may have actually grown in length from thermal cycling. If so they will need to be resized slightly and anchored back into their grooves. To resize the bulged out sections, take a needle nosed pliers slightly shortening the distance between each coil loop by squeezing them together. Do this carefully because elements tend to become brittle with age. As the bulged out area is shrunk, insert them back into position. When done working the elements back to size, anchor them in place with an element staple. Put the staple over the bottom portion of the loop in a groove. Push it part way in with the needle nose pliers at a slight angle so that the staple will hold better. Then use the tip of a small screw driver to push it to the bottom of the groove. If your elements are coming out at the corners, then you need to lengthen them to fit. This uses essentially the same procedure. Use a snap ring pliers (one that opens when you squeeze the handle) or a screw driver to open up the distance between a number of loops. Then staple it in place.

If you have had your kiln for a long time and it seems that the firings are starting to take longer and longer, then the elements may be starting to wear out. With time they will not be able to carry as much energy as they used to be able to and will need to be replaced. This process is accelerated if you have been doing reducing firings for some reason. I suggest that you consult your kiln manual as to how to replace them or get a qualified repair person to do it for you. Elements can also become damaged if they make contact with glass during a firing and the glass can short across the elements. So if you have thermal shock kiln explosions, I suggest that you check out the kiln afterward to remove any glass that may have gotten onto the elements.

Occasionally you will have to replace an infinity switch. This is because the contacts in the switch that turn the power on and off deteriorate over time. As they open, the electrical flow does not stop immediately and a spark jumps across the gap at the contacts. This is the muffled pop that you hear as your kiln cycles. This arcing concentrates the electrical flow over such a very small area that metal in the switch actually gets melted. Arcing is made worse by a high humidity or dusty environment. Over time the contact area gets so pitted and corroded that they build up a heavy resistive layer and no longer work correctly. To remove the switch, first remove the knob by gently prying it off the shaft at the face of the switch using a screw driver under the base of the knob. Unplug the kiln and then open the protective switch box in which the switch is mounted. Remove wires from the old switch, one at a time, and either mark where they came from or install them directly onto the new switch to keep their order correct. Remove the locking nut on the outside of the shaft housing and slip the old switch out. Slip in the new switch, lock it in place with the locking nut, close up the protective housing, replace the knob and you are back in business. These are the simplest and most frequent repairs that may be needed on a kiln. For anything more extensive than this see your manual or get a repairman.

Kiln safety

There are a number of aspects to safely using a kiln that we have not discussed. First and foremost, a kiln uses a large amount of electricity that can be dangerous if not used correctly. Therefore always operate

© 1996 James Kervin

74 Glass Beadmaking

your kiln according to the manufacturer's directions. Never reach into a kiln unless the power to it is shut off. Make sure that the wires that come out of the kiln are in good shape. On a 110 volt kiln that plugs into a normal wall socket, the plug should have a ground pin (i.e. the third round pin beneath the other two flat ones). Never use one of the three pin to two pin adapters that are available in the hardware stores to plug your kiln into a socket with only two prongs. That third wire is hooked up to the exterior of your kiln to carry away any current that may somehow leak to the exterior if you were to have a short in the kiln wiring somewhere. Without that ground properly hooked up, a short can potentially be a very shocking experience. In fact it would probably be a good idea to check that this ground is hooked up correctly by using an ohm meter to measure the resistance between the round pin on the plug and the exterior of the kiln. It should be a low number.

The next safety concern about working around a kiln is how to dress properly. A kiln puts out a lot of heat and when opened during a firing, it can very easily burn you. So you definitely need to wear protective clothing on your hands and arms when you reach into it. On your hands, you should wear some of the non-asbestos high-temperature gloves now on the market. Check them over to make sure that they have not developed any holes in them. To protect your arms and upper body, you should wear some heavy clothing of natural fiber. Natural fibers are a must because man-made ones will melt and can become fused to your skin resulting in some nasty burns.

Lastly the other thing that you need to protect from the heat of the kiln is your eyes. Welder's shades of at least a #3 are required to prevent damage to your eyes from exposure to the infrared radiation coming out of an open kiln.

Suggested further reading

Althouse, Andrew D., Turnquist, Carl H., Bowditch, William A. and Bowditch, Kevin E. Modern Welding, Goodheart-Willcox Company, Inc., 1992

Fraser, Harry. Electric Kilns, Watson-Guptill Publications, 1974

Hammesfahr, James E. and Stong, Clair L. Creative Glassblowing, W. H. Freeman and Company, 1968

Nickerson, John. "A Glory Hole Design", in Hot Glass Information Exchange 1979 John M. Bingham editor

Olsen, Frederick L. The Kiln Book 2nd edition Materials, Specifications and Construction, Chilton Book Company 1982

Platt, Karl. "Glory Hole is Heart of Glassblowing" Glass Art Vol. 3 No. 3 (March/April), 1988

Ritchie, Ralph W. and Ritchie, Fern J. Electric Kiln Handbook, A Studios West Craft Monograph, 1981

© 1996 James Kervin

Glass

Now that you know a little about beadmaking equipment, let's talk about the material that you will be working with, glass. Glass is a unique material formed from melting a number of oxides together. When heated, this brittle material will get softer, gradually deform or slump and eventually melt to form a viscous liquid. Unlike other materials, this does not occur as a sharp transition at a specific temperature but instead occurs gradually over a temperature range. When molten glass is cooled, this process occurs in reverse and whatever shape that was introduced while soft is retained in the material. To understand glass a little better, we need to spend some time discussing about its chemistry and how this affects its properties.

Glass chemistry

As stated earlier, glass is made up of a mixture of oxides. The main oxide used in these mixtures is silicon dioxide (SiO_2). If the only oxide you had in your glass was SiO_2 then you would have fused silica or quartz. Silica glasses are not composed of distinct molecules but instead consist of an interconnected random three dimensional matrix. The basic structural component of this matrix is the silica tetrahedron. This is a four sided pyramid with oxygen atoms at each vertex of the pyramid shielding a silicon atom at the center. Each oxygen atom is part of two tetrahedrons that are orientated randomly with respect to each other and are thus is referred to as a bridging oxygen atoms. Silica glass is held together by a strong network of covalent bonds (electron sharing between atoms) which results in a relatively sharply defined, high melting point (3115°F). This occurs at a much higher temperature than what you are used to working with in your studio. Many of the refractory materials that are used in our kilns would not stand up to repeated exposures to such high temperatures.

To lower the melting temperature of the glass, a number of other oxides are added to randomly break up some of the covalent bonds between the bridging oxygens by attaching them to a metal atom instead. This will end one section of the chain making the whole chain less rigid and more mobile. These other metal oxides also strain the glass matrix as it cools because of size differences of the metal atoms compared to the silicon atoms. Some of the additives do not form strong covalent bonds with oxygen but instead form weaker non-directional ionic bonds. Upon heating up a glass, these weaker bonds and less rigid structure allow the glass to break up at much lower temperatures (about 1800°F).

© 1996 James Kervin

76   Glass Beadmaking

Variations in chain length widen the temperature range over which this happens.

The types of other oxides added and their proportions thus determine when the glass starts to soften and when it will effectively melt. The weaker the ionic bonds, the lower the temperature at which softening will occur. Also the more of the modifying oxides that are added, the shorter will be the resulting silica chains in the glass and the more fluid the glass will be once it starts to soften. Glasses that soften at lower temperatures said to be softer while those that soften at higher temperatures are said to be harder.

Types of glass

Let's look at some of the most common glasses and discuss how their composition affects some of the properties relevant to making beads. These properties are summarized in Table 10. To do this, let's start with the basic building block.

Table 10. Average properties of some basic glass types.

Glass Property	Lead glass	Soda-lime glass	Borosilicate glass	Quartz glass
Softening point (°F)	1145	1337	1400	2876
Annealing point (°F)	840	1022	1000	1983
Strain point (°F)	775	940	775	1753
Thermal expansion coefficient (10^{-7} in/in/°F)	50	50	27	3.1
Density (lb/ft^3)	218	156	144	137
Refractive index	1.6	1.51	1.49	1.459

Quartz

Quartz, or vitreous silica as it is sometimes referred to, is made by heating pure silicon dioxide to about 3137°F. The resulting liquid is so viscous that any gas bubbles trapped between the grains of sand as it melts come out very slowly if at all. When cooled, the rigid three dimensional matrix of this material causes it to have a very low coefficient of thermal expansion (COE). This also accounts for its relatively high softening, annealing and strain points. It has much too viscous and too high a melting point to use in beadmaking.

Soda lime glass

In order to decrease the viscosity of vitreous silica and thus make it more workable, fluxes or network modifiers in the form of metal oxides are added to the formulation. In soda lime glasses, the metal oxides that are added are calcium oxide in the form of lime carbonates and sodium oxide in the form of soda ash. Both of these materials release carbon dioxide gas as they react with the molten silica. Typical compositions are

Glass   77

between 70 to 80 % silica by weight, 8 to 12 weight % lime and 12 to 17 weight % soda. During manufacture of the glass, the soda (Na_2CO_3) releases carbon dioxide to form Na_2O. The lime does likewise transforming from $CaCO_3$ to CaO.

As discussed earlier these materials serve as network modifiers. Too much lime makes the glass susceptible to devitrification, too little results in a glass that is susceptible to chemical attack. Other additives are added to make the mixture more workable. One of these is alumina which also improves the chemical durability. The large size of the metal atoms in the modifying oxides cause lower viscosity making the glass easier to shape into beads. It also results in a higher COE from asymmetric vibrations of the molecules. Thus requiring more annealing of the beads to remove stresses. Most commonly available fusing glass and Moretti glass (that used by most wound glass beadmakers) are of this type.

Borosilicate glass (Pyrex)

Boron oxide forms a plane triangular matrix unit that helps break up the silica matrix and also migrates to the surface of the glass where its structure reduces the surface energy of the glass. This makes the glasses to which it is added as a modifier, very stable chemically. The smaller size of the boron atom compared to the calcium and the sodium atoms introduces more freedom of motion and less stress into the glass matrix resulting in a lower coefficient of thermal expansion.

Borosilicate glass is a fairly high temperature glass and it really needs a lot of heat from your torch to work because of its stable structure. It also remains much more viscous and has to be really pushed around to shape it in comparison to soda-lime glass. Its lower COE makes it much less susceptible to thermal shock. Because of its high working temperature, many of the metal oxides used to color soda-lime glass will burn out of borosilicate glass. Therefore its color palette is much more limited than soda-lime glass.

Lead Glass

Lead oxide is usually used as a network modifier of the silica matrix but when added in high enough concentrations can act as a network former. Lead oxide is a good flux that bestows the glass mixture a large working range over which the glass changes very little in viscosity. For this reason it was used for centuries to produce fine tableware and art work.

In flameworking, lead glass finds its main use in neon tubing although Satake glass from Japan is lead based and is used for beadmaking. It has 70 colors available and is easy to work.

Colorants

Colors in glass are formed by three major processes: dissolved metallic oxides, colloidal suspensions of particles, and inclusions of crystalline materials. Metallic oxides can be dissolved uniformly into molten glass

© 1996 James Kervin

78   Glass Beadmaking

just like sugar in water. They actually become part of the solution and will not settle out again. When the molten glass is cooled and allowed to solidify, the oxides remain dissolved in the solid glass phase. Each metallic oxide absorbs characteristic wavelengths of light and pass the rest through. The result is color.

A second way that glass is colored is to disperse tiny particles uniformly throughout the melt. Although this may seem the same as the previous method, it is not. This is more like the mix of fine silt in river water. There the particles are suspended because of the motion of the water molecules, but they never really become part of the solution. If you were to take that water and run it through a centrifuge, you would be able to separate the particles out. If you held glass at high temperature for a long time, these colorant particles would settle out. In this situation, the size of the suspended particles dictate the wavelengths of light that they can reflect. The remainder of the light is absorbed.

The third way that glass is colored is through the addition of materials, that when the glass cools, form tiny crystalline inclusions in the glass. Because they have a different structure than the rest of the glass, they refract the light differently than the bulk of the glass. This leads to an opal-like effect.

To color clear glass, first lay out some of the colorant on your marver. (High temperature Pyrex glass will not necessarily work well with all of the colorants as we discussed earlier, especially enamels.) It has been found beneficial to heat the oxide before mixing it with the glass. Form a gather on the end of two rods and roll them in the colorant. Bring them together in the flame and twist the rods in opposite directions to mix in the colorant. Again roll the gather in the colorant and mix in the flame. Repeat this process until you get the depth of color that you are looking for. Then stretch the gather out into cane or rod of the desired thickness.

If you have clear tubing available, fuse one end onto some clear rod. Then fill the tube with the colorant and fuse a rod on the other end of the tube taking care not to fuse the second end shut. (It would shatter from the expanding air upon reheat if you did.) Now heat the tube in the largest possible flame starting at the fused end. As the tube starts to soften, force the ends together and rotate them in opposite directions to mix up the colorant. Again when satisfied with the final mix and the depth of color, pull out the blob into cane of the desired thickness.

Be careful when mixing your own colors because metal oxide fumes are not necessarily good to breathe. Some oxides like lead, cadmium and uranium are highly toxic. Mixing should always be done in an area with good local ventilation pulling the fumes away from you. In addition the space itself should also be well ventilated to prevent any buildup of stray fumes.

Table 11 lists some colors of glass you might want to try making, colorant materials you can add to get that color and approximate amounts of that colorant needed.

© 1996 James Kervin

Glass   79

Table 11. Glass colorants and the colors that they produce.

Color	Shade	Colorant	%
white		fluoride opals (fluorspar)	
		phosphate opals	
		tin oxide	
	cream	silver oxide	2-4%
yellow		vanadium oxide	
	greenish	silver nitrate	0.2%
	transparent	silver oxide	
		selenium	
orange		cadmium & selenium	
red	ruby	gold	
		copper oxide (red)	
	flat	copper oxide (black)	
		cadmium & selenium	
	pink	tin oxide & chromium oxide (2/1)	
purple		manganese dioxide	0.5-1%
		nickel	
blue		cobalt oxide	0.05%
		cobalt carbonate	0.2-1%
	greenish	copper carbonate	0.4-1%
	pastel	cobalt carbonate & tin oxide (1/3)	
green	yellowish	iron oxide	0.4-1.5%
		iron chromate	0.5-1.7%
		potassium dichromate	0.2-0.8%
	dark	chromium oxide & cobalt carbonate (1/1)	1-2%
	pastel	chrome oxide & tin oxide (1/1)	
		chromium oxide	0.2%
		copper oxide (black)	0.2-0.4%
	transparent	copper oxide (red)	0.2-0.4%
black		manganese dioxide	6+%
amber		sulfur	1.5%
		iron oxide	2-5%
brown		silver nitrate	
		nickel carbonate	0.2%
		copper oxide (red)	
gray		nickel carbonate	0.2%
	smoky	nickel oxide	0.2-0.6%

© 1996 James Kervin

80   Glass Beadmaking

Blending colored rods

Most of you will almost exclusively work with precolored glass rods such as Moretti. Their color palette can sometimes be limiting because you may not have all the shades that you may want for highlights. To alleviate this limitation, what you need to do here is mix two different colored rods together to get one of a new third color. This will allow developing color variations for shading and shadowing as well as more realistic vegetation and flesh tones — a place where the Moretti palette is definitely lacking. To blend colors, start with two rods of your base tint (usually the lighter color) and one of a darker "pigment" color. Paint some of the pigment color onto the outside of one of the base tint rods for a length of about an inch. This is done by getting the tip of the pigment rod red hot and then painting it on by pushing down and towards you on the base tint rod. At the end of each paint stroke, lift the pigment rod off the base tint rod and burn off any stringers in the flame.

Once you have applied enough pigment to the base tint rod, you are now ready to mix it up to get a nice uniform color. Grab your other base tint rod and attach it onto the pigment colored end of the first rod. Heat up the whole pigment colored region until it is hot and globby. Twist one rod in one direction and the other in the opposite direction. To assist you can swirl one rod around the other. Stretching the glob out and pushing it back together also helps. You will not be able to see what you have at this point but you should be able to tell if it is well mixed or not by looking for striations in the red hot glob which would indicate incomplete mixing. When done mixing, pull out the glob into a fairly thick cane.

As you start blending colors, you will find that you won't always get the color that you would expect from consulting a color wheel. Blue and red for example won't necessarily make purple. The different metal oxide colorants may interact in unpredictable ways. Some colors, like reds, may break down after prolonged mixing into an ugly brown. Likewise turquoise once it starts to sparkle will burnout. Some colors are not necessarily what they seem either. As an example, Moretti black is actually a very dark purple. Transparent colors mixed with opaque colors will usually result in streaky transparent colors. To start getting a feel for what you can achieve with blending, try blending white or ivory with a little red to get better flesh tones or green with a little "black" to get more natural greens.

When blending colors, as in mixing your own colored glass, you have to be concerned with toxic heavy metal fumes coming out of the very hot glass. Make sure that you use proper ventilation.

Coatings

The appearance and color of glass is also changed by coatings that are added to it. Like a mirror coating, they change the reflective and refractive properties of the glass. Some of these coatings will stand up to the heat of the torch allowing them to be incorporated into beads - others will not. So let's look at some of these coatings.

© 1996 James Kervin

Iridized coatings

Iridized coatings are surface coatings of stannous chloride that are sprayed on to the surface of the glass when it is still fairly hot. They give the glass a little extra sparkle. These coatings are lost when they are worked in a torch but will stand up to the heat of a kiln. Such coatings can of course be applied after shaping of the bead is complete.

Dichroic coatings

A relatively recent coloration technique that has been applied to glass is metallic vapor deposition. The process to be described shortly deposits thin metallic coatings on the upper surface of the glass. These layers are very thin, on the order of the wavelength of light. Because of this they have some relatively striking optical properties. When viewed by looking through the glass at a light source, the glass will look one color as you look straight through it, but if you move your head so that you are looking at the glass from a different angle that color will change. These colors are referred to as the transmitted colors of the coating since the light is being transmitted through the glass. If instead you view the glass by light reflected off the glass, you will see another color. This is called the reflective color. The changing color effect of dichroic glass is a result of how the coating refracts the light.

Dichroic glass is available in a number of transmitted colors. The most common of which tends to be blue, cyan, magenta or yellow. Red, orange and green are also available but are more expensive because they require thicker coatings and thus more time. Those artists who use this material feel it is worth the price, about $1 to $5 a square inch. They feel it adds a new dimension to their beads.

The method to apply dichroic coating was developed to provide optical filters and partially reflective surfaces for scientific applications such as lasers. It consists of cleaning the glass and putting it into an ultra-high vacuum chamber. Here the glass is heated up and cleaned again by bombarding it with high speed electrons that have been accelerated by a high voltage potential. The glass has to be ultra clean or the coatings will not stick to it. The electron beam is then directed onto targets containing the material that is to be plated on the surface of the glass, which are usually metal oxides like titanium oxide. The process, called evaporative coating, heats up the surface of the targets to incredibly high temperatures, as high as 3000°C. At these temperatures the surface of the target vaporizes. These vapors then travel across the vacuum chamber to the clean glass surface. If the chamber were not at high vacuum, the vapors would not be able to cross this gap. All during this process, the glass is being rotated in order to achieve a more uniform coating. The deposition rate of the material is controlled by the temperature to which the target is heated. The thickness of the coating is then precisely controlled by the process time. The number and thickness of the different layers deposited on the glass determines the resulting optical properties. By masking the glass with shields, coatings with different patterns can be made.

82   Glass Beadmaking

Almost any glass can be evaporative coated and you see dichroic coatings on both rods and sheet glass, although sheet dichroic is much more common. Because of limitations in vacuum chamber size, most sheets are not more than 16" on a side.

Compatibility of dichroic glass is a function of the base glass to which the coating was applied. Much of what is available has been made for fusing work and can be used in beadmaking but it has a COE of 90. Dichroic Moretti glass is also now available from some suppliers. Be sure to ask your supplier if the coating is appropriate for high temperature applications because some are not. I have been told that GM coatings seem to hold up better than most. Also be careful when handling the coated sheets since they are only a surface coating that can be scratched.

Temperature regimes of glass

As you work with a glass, you will notice how its physical properties vary with temperature. The variation in properties can be described in terms of different temperature regimes for that glass.

The brittle solid regime

The regime with which you are probably most used to working with glass is that around room temperature. In this temperature regime, glass is a solid material that breaks in a brittle manner when stressed. A small scratch or crack will propagate quickly through the material with great ease.

Glass in this regime expands and contracts at a near constant rate with changes in temperature. The amount of expansion is, as was explained earlier, quantified by the glass's Coefficient of Expansion (COE). This number which is expressed in 10^{-7} inches per inch per degree centigrade, is the average expansion over a defined temperature range. The usual range tested in the laboratory is from 0 to 300°C (32-600°F). The upper end of the temperature range for the brittle solid regime is somewhat higher than this. For soda-lime glasses it is on the order of 700°F.

As the temperature of the glass is changed in the brittle zone, the parts of the glass that get warmer faster will try to grow in size relative the cooler glass around it. This causes the silica tetrahedrons to try and slip and stretch past each other until they lock up say on a larger colorant atom. These slippages build up at locations like this, straining the natural order of the atoms in the glass and resulting in stress. In the brittle regime, the only way that stress in the glass can be relieved is by fracture.

The non-brittle solid regime

As the glass is taken higher in temperature, the atoms become more mobile as their vibrations and tetrahedron rotations increase. They start to be able to jump around any obstructions that may have pinned them

© 1996 James Kervin

previously in the brittle solid regime. This does not happen all at once, but gradually as the vibrations of the glass atoms increase with increasing temperature. This motion allows any stress that may have built up in the glass to start to relieve itself.

This temperature regime for soda-lime glasses extends roughly from about 700 to 1000°F. Within this regime, the glass continues to expand and contract with temperature change, but the COE is different than it was in the brittle solid regime. (In fact, the COE is not really a constant and varies throughout both temperature regimes.) The increased mobility of the atoms allows any built up stress to relieve itself. It is still possible to change the temperature of the glass faster than the stress can be reduced by the movement of the atoms (in other words you can still thermal shock in this regime). It is this temperature regime in which glass is annealed. Many artists have been taught to think that annealing (stress relief) takes place at a particular temperature, but that is not correct. What that temperature actually represents is a compromise. The compromise is a temperature at which the atoms are mobile enough to allow relief of the stress in a reasonable time, minutes, without being so high that the actual glass itself starts to flow in the same sort of time period.

The flexible regime

As you continue to raise the temperature of a soda-lime glass to above 1000°F, it starts to become more and more pliable. Left at this temperature, it will start to droop or flex under the influence of gravity or muscle power. The atoms are now so mobile that it is no longer possible to thermal shock the glass. Its properties start to resemble something more like taffy. Its surface also starts to get sticky. It will stick to other glass or to other materials such as separator coatings or kiln wash. These attributes become more pronounced with increasing temperature until about 1400°F when soda-glass starts to enter the last temperature regime.

The fluid regime

In this temperature regime, manipulation of the glass becomes possible. The glass exhibits fluid like properties. This is the regime that you are operating within as you wind, shape and decorate beads on your torch. This regime is also where full and flat fusing takes place in a kiln. By careful control of the temperature of your piece you can determine how the glass can be worked. You can make it so that it flows like a thick fluid or have it so that it can be sculpted like clay.

Glass compatibility

As mentioned earlier, the kinds and amounts of oxide modifiers used in making a particular glass, strain the silica matrix differently and affect the rate at which the glass shrinks when cooled. This rate, as mentioned earlier, is commonly known as the coefficient of expansion (COE) and is usually expressed as a whole number. As an example, the Bullseye compatible glasses all have a COE of 90. What this means is that in the

© 1996 James Kervin

84 Glass Beadmaking

solid regime a 1 inch long piece of one of these glasses will shrink 0.0000090 inches (90 x 10^{-7}) for each 1°C reduction in temperature. Thus a 10 inch piece of glass will shrink about 0.051 inches in cooling from its annealing temperature (about 1100°F) to room temperature. Similarly a 10 inch piece of Moretti glass with a COE of 104 would shrink 0.060 inches.

Therefore, if you were trying to fuse together 10 inch strips of these two types of glass, the difference between the shrinkage of one strip and the other is 0.009 inches. This is about the thickness of 5 sheets of paper. That may not seen like much on our ordinary macroscopic level, but when you compare it to the size scale of reference, atoms, it is enormous. As a result the piece would literally pull itself apart.

Table 12. Coefficient of Expansion (COE) of some common art glasses.

Manufacturer	COE (in/in/°C)
Northstar	32
Pyrex	33
GNA	81
Shott Clear	83 & 87
Bullseye	90
Wasser	90
Uroburos	90
Kugler	82-94
Zimmerman	74-94
Spectrum	96
Novi	104 (No longer available)
Morreti	104
Satake	120

As anyone who has done hot glasswork before knows, you have to make sure that whatever glasses you use in making your beads are compatible. Some manufacturers cater to hot/warm glass artists and have initiated good quality controls to ensure a consistent self-compatible glass line. Also for bead work (small pieces of glass), small variations (1-3 points) in COE will probably not cause any major problems. But as most good fusing manuals will recommend, you probably should check the compatibility of your glass yourself for large beads. Table 12 lists published values of COE for many of the common art glasses.

In actuality this concept of a constant COE value for a given glass is a highly simplified version of what really happens. First of all, as mentioned, COE is not a constant. It varies with

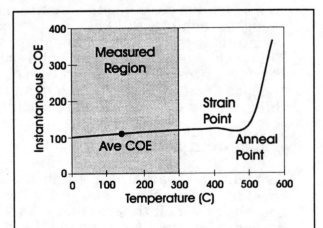

Figure 29. Variation of COE with temperature.

© 1996 James Kervin

Glass   85

temperature as illustrated in the graph in Figure 29. What is really reported in Table 12 is the average COE value for the shaded test region from room temperature to 300°C. As long as the glasses are of similar composition, they will behave similarly over the rest of the temperature region of interest. If not, they may vary widely in that region and so even if they had the same average value in the shaded region, they may not be compatible because of the differences at high temperature.

Be aware too that not all the glass from a manufacturer will have the same COE and be intercompatible. As an example, unless labeled as compatible, not all Bullseye is compatible. Also some people have tried to tell me that all GNA is compatible and I have learned the hard way that this is not true. So unless a glass is labeled as compatible, don't assume it is. Test it yourself as will be discussed later.

Suggested further reading

McLellan, George W. and Shand, Errol B. Glass Engineering Handbook 3rd edition, McGraw-Hill Book Company

Scholes, Samuel R., and Greene, Charles H. Modern Glass Practice, 7th edition, Ceramic Book and Literature Service, 1993

Weyl, W. A. Coloured Glasses, Brady & Serban, 1954

© 1996 James Kervin

86   Glass Beadmaking

© 1996 James Kervin

Flameworking techniques

Let's now turn our attention to the topic of how to operate your equipment and learn some basic flameworking skills that will be needed in beadmaking. To begin with, let's discuss how to operate your torch.

Handheld torch operation

Operation of a handheld torch is fairly simple. These are generally used with propane but some can also be used with disposable canisters of propylene or MAPP Gas® depending upon their construction. Read the manufacturer's instructions. Let's first assemble the torch head onto the tank. Start by ensuring that the torch on/off valve is turned off. If you look closely at the handle of the on/off valve, it will usually be labeled with the direction to twist the knob to turn it off. That direction is usually clockwise. Next insert the shaft of the torch head into the throat of the fuel tank and screw the torch head on. The torch head will screw on in a clockwise direction. In installing the torch on the tank, hand tighten it only, as over tightening can distort the threads. Whenever attaching or removing the torch, do it in a place where no open flames are present. This is just in case fuel is released at the connection between the torch and the tank. Also allow the torch to cool before removing it from the tank, but please do remove it – do not store them attached together.

To light the torch, set it down upright or in its stand on the work table. Light a match and hold it slightly below the edge of the opening on the torch tip with the match head slanted slightly down. Turn the fuel gas on medium low by turning the on/off valve counterclockwise. Slowly lift the burning match into the flowing gas and the flame should catch. If the rush of fuel gas blows out the match, turn off the gas and start over. For some reason I find the hardware store torch harder to light. (Possibly because gas flow is faster near the edge of the tip.) Adjust the gas flow using the on/off valve until you can no longer see yellow in the flame. To turn the torch off, twist the on/off handle clockwise. Be aware that the torch will continue to burn for a couple of seconds after the knob is in the off position.

On the hardware store torch, you do not have any real adjustment capability. It is either all the way on or all the way off. This is because of a difference in how the valve works. When you open the valve, you uncover a hole. When you close it, you cover the hole. There is no way to have it partly open. On the TurboTorch® and the Hot Head®, you

© 1996 James Kervin

88 Glass Beadmaking

have what's called a needle valve, where as you open the valve you are withdrawing a needle out of the hole. This effectively changes the size of the hole and thus the gas flow through it.

In these small handheld torches, you will want to work out in the flame just past the blue portion where you lose all signs of color. This is the hottest portion of the flame and is generally about 1 1/2" to 2 1/2" from the tip of the torch. Most people tend to find themselves drifting back closer to the tip of the torch because they can see this portion of the flame better or they just want the bead closer to them. Try to keep pushing yourself back out into this hot portion because, besides being easier to work the glass out in this location, this is also a less reducing portion of the flame. As such, it will be less likely to cause the colorants in the glass to be reduced. This is where the flame steals oxygen from the metallic oxide colorant reducing it to a metal atom that look dull and gray.

Another thing of which you should be aware is to always have the fuel tank upright or tilted to the upright. This is so you do not push liquid fuel out the torch tip. Remember that most of the fuel gases exist as a liquid inside the tank until they evaporate or boil. You can tell the liquid level because the tank will be cooler and will sweat at this level on a hot day. The reason you do not want liquid propane coming out of the torch is that it will result in more fuel coming out than you want and the torch will flare up. This is why the stands that I discussed for the handheld torch, position the tank slanted upward on an angle.

Fuel-oxygen torch operation

The glass beadmaker's most important tool is his torch. Other artists have a number of special tools, each of which has a special function. A woodworker has different sized saws and drills that he can use to shape his work. Likewise, the beadmaker has different adjustments that he can make on his torch that change his flame, depending on what he is trying to do. This is accomplished by changing the gas flows or by working in a different section of the flame. Learning to make these adjustments will help lead to mastery over your work.

Turning on the gas

If you have never used a mixed gas torch before, don't worry. It's not hard and you will soon get the hang of it. Begin by getting a feel for how the valves operate. Start with the valves on your torch while your fuel gas, usually propane, is turned off.

Look at the valves on your torch. There are two of them, one for the propane and one for the oxygen. The propane is usually connected up to the red valve (which is conventionally on the right) and the oxygen is connected to the green valve (on the left). These valves are needle valves that screw a tapered needle in and out of a soft tapered seat when they are operated. They should never be turned off real hard because that can cause the needle to deform or scratch the soft valve seat. Either of

© 1996 James Kervin

Flameworking Techniques   89

these conditions can lead to developing a leaky valve that will need to be replaced.

With the gas turned off at the cylinders, try opening and closing your torch valves. They are opened by turning the handle counterclockwise and they are closed by turning them clockwise. Try to develop a feel for this. If your valves are difficult to turn and you are sure that you are turning them in the right direction, then you may have to adjust them. (Remember that we do not want to use any lubricants with oxygen fittings because they can cause a fire.) This is done by slightly loosening the locking nut under the valve handles. Tightening this same nut will make the valve a little harder to turn. This adjustment should always be made with the valve open so that you are not jamming the needle deeper into the valve seat. This is also the adjustment to make if you notice any gas coming out through the valve handle.

Now close the torch valves. Look at the adjusting handle on your oxygen regulator. Check to see that it is screwed out and is not exerting force on the adjusting spring. Open the on/off valve on the oxygen cylinder. You should not hear any rushing gas or hissing. If you do, close the tank and check for leaks. At this point, the only place that could be leaking is the connection between your tank and regulator. If you have any leaking, unscrew the regulator from the tank. Clean the fittings with a clean dry cloth. Examine the fittings for scratches. If the tank seat is damaged, take it back to the supplier. If everything looks okay, fit the regulator back into the tank valve connection and screw down a little tighter this time on the regulator nut.

If you can open the oxygen tank valve and not hear any sustained leaks, you should see the tank gauge slowly register the pressure in the tank. Remember that you have to completely open the oxygen valve to prevent leakage around the valve stem. Nothing should show on your low pressure gauge at this time. Now slowly screw down on your regulator adjusting handle. After you start to feel resistance on the adjusting handle, you should start to see pressure register on your low pressure gauge. Set it in the 5-10 psig range for a surface mixed torch. (When working with a surface mixed torch, you generally keep the oxygen to gas ratio at about 2 to 1.)

If you hear a leak at this point, first check to see that your torch valve is turned off. If it is, check to see that the oxygen hose is connected properly to all fittings and that there are no holes in it. Check also to see that all your hose clamps are tight. Try closing the oxygen tank valve and seeing if you can detect any perceptible drop in the pressure reading on the high pressure gauge.

Let's now check out how your torch valves operate. Don't worry about releasing a little oxygen in this operation as it is perfectly safe to do so and you will only lose a few cents worth. Think of your valve like a water faucet. The further you open the valve, the more water flows out and the faster it rushes out. Now try slowly opening and closing your torch oxygen valve. Listen to the sound of the oxygen flow as you open and close it. Observe how you don't have to close the valve very hard to stop the gas flow. Get a feel for this. Your propane valve operates exactly the

© 1996 James Kervin

90   Glass Beadmaking

same way, but you do not want to play with it like this because you would be releasing propane out into your workplace, creating a possible explosive hazard.

Once you feel comfortable with the operation of your torch valves, you are ready to proceed on to the next step, turning on the propane. Check to see that the torch propane valve is closed. Reach down and open the propane tank on/off valve between one half and a full turn, no more. This allows plenty of flow but makes closing the tank quicker in an emergency. Take a second to listen and smell for any leaks. If you detect any, check quickly to see if the torch valve is open. If not, immediately close the tank on/off valve and check all propane connections. Once you have corrected any gross leaks, again open the tank valve. Check all your fittings and tubing for small leaks by painting a solution of liquid dish detergent in water on them. If you see any bubbles, then you have a leak at that joint that must be fixed before lighting the torch. If you don't detect any leaks, you are ready to go. This procedure should be repeated any time you disconnect and reconnect your propane fittings for two reasons; first, to prevent explosive propane hazards, second to prevent biological hazards of propane. Propane vapors can give you a terrible headache or even worse in large exposures. Repeat this procedure to check your oxygen fittings for leaks; this prevents wasting oxygen.

With this procedure completed, we are now ready to proceed on with discussing how to light your torch.

Lighting the torch

Flint strikers are commonly used by most artists to light their torches. The strikers are inexpensive and reliable once you are accustomed to them. To light the torch with the striker, hold the striker a couple inches in front of the tip of the torch with the hollow of cup facing the tip. Open the gas valve on the torch slightly, about a quarter turn counterclockwise or less. Any further may cause the flame to deflect off the cup once lit and may lead to burns. Immediately strike a spark to light the gas in the cup by squeezing the arms of the striker together. This scrapes the flint across the file in the cup. You may want to practice this ahead of time because it is not quite as easy as it sounds. If you are not familiar with using a striker, you may not exert enough force on the arm to hold the flint against the file. Without that contact you can not strike a spark. You should be able to do this every time you try because as you are trying to light the torch the propane is continuing to be released. If you take too long to get a good spark, enough propane will build up around the end of the torch to cause a flameup that can be frightening as well as dangerous.

The electronic lighter is operated similarly. Open torch fuel valve such that the flow of gas is low. Then depress the button on the lighter and the high voltage arc should light the flame. If it doesn't work, immediately turn off the propane and check to see that the lighter is arcing. A weak battery may be the culprit They have to be changed after about 50 hours of use. You may also have had the gas on too high. These lighters are more expensive, initially and over their lifetime than

© 1996 James Kervin

Flameworking Techniques

the flint strikers. Their ease of operation may make them worth it to you though if you are having trouble getting the hang of using the flint striker and are being constantly exposed to those frightening flameups.

If you decide to use one of the butane lighters, light the pilot flame on the lighter first by pulling the trigger. Then open the gas supply to the torch and immediately light it with the pilot flame. Remember to put this lighter off to the side, outside of your work area and well away from hot glass before starting to work.

If this is the first time that you have had the torch lit, you may want to go through the procedure for adjusting the propane regulator that was explained previously. Otherwise let's proceed onward and learn more about how to use this tool.

Adjusting the flame

Slowly open the propane valve until you have a yellow flame about 4 to 6 inches long as shown in the top of Figure 30. The flame may also be a little smoky or sooty because without any oxygen added to the flame the propane is not being completely burned. This is called a blowy flame and is sometimes used in flameworking to flame anneal borosilicate glass. This flame can build up black soot on your beads. Because it is very low in oxygen, it is a very reducing flame. This can cause some of the metal oxides that color your glass to be reduced (lose oxygen) and change color.

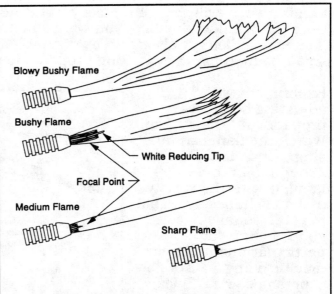

Figure 30. Different flame adjustments possible with your torch.

Open the oxygen valve on the torch slowly. Soon your will get a flame that looks like the second picture in Figure 30. This is a bushy flame. It is also used for flame annealing and preheating large constructions. It applies heat to a fairly large area. In this flame you start to see a faint blue cone extending out into the flame from the torch tip. You will also have bright white tips at the end of the blue flame The blue cone will become more pronounced as you add more oxygen. The tip of the blue cone is called the focal point and is the hottest part of the flame. The bushy flame is still a reducing flame as indicated by the prominent white tips at the focal point. Notice how as you add oxygen to the flame that the white tip become less pronounced. The size of this feature is a good indicator of how reducing your flame is.

© 1996 James Kervin

Add more oxygen to the flame and watch the blue cone become more pronounced and draw in toward the tip of the torch as well as the white portion draw in and diminish. When the flame looks about like the third picture in the figure, it is what is referred to as a medium flame. The blue tips have been reduced to about one quarter of an inch in length and are relatively equal in length. This flame is now oxygen rich and is thus called an oxidizing flame. It can reoxidize some of the metal colorants in the glass if you have accidentally reduced them. This is still a fairly large flame and can be used for overall heating of a large bead. This is the type of flame most commonly used in beadmaking and the portion of the flame that you will be working in is about two thirds of the way out in the flame.

Adding still more oxygen will result in a more pointed flame called a sharp flame as is seen in the bottom illustration in Figure 30. As you add more oxygen to get this pointed flame, you will also notice that your minor burner will get a little hissy from the oxygen flow. This flame is used for detail work where you want to limit the area over which the flame is applied. It also is an oxidizing flame. You can quickly get a small pointed flame by cutting propane flow of a medium flame.

Experiment with adjusting both the propane and the oxygen. Watch the flame change shape and size. Do this enough to become familiar with the variety of flame shapes available to you. Usually one shape is best for a particular operation you may be doing. Through experience you will learn to be able to quickly adjust your torch to get the flame that you desire. Note also that different portions of the flame are hotter than others. The focal point is the hottest part and you should be working out past it. The area closer to the torch is also more reducing and working here may change the color of your glass as well as possibly boiling it. As you move toward the edges of the flame, it is cooler and good for slow heating. Figure 31 shows some of the functions of different portions of the flame.

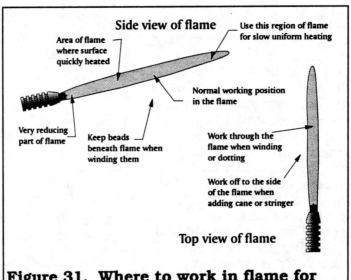

Figure 31. Where to work in flame for different processes.

One common mistake that beginners make is that they concentrate so intensely on manipulation of the beads and glass rods, that they completely forget about the possibilities open to them through flame adjustment or operating in different positions in the flame. Try to be aware of your flame and adjust it as needed to make your work easier. In most of your beadmaking work, a medium flame with blue cones on the order of about 1/4 inch long are indicative of the proper size flame.

Flameworking Techniques 93

Also listen to the noise generated by your torch. A noisy flame probably has too much oxygen.

Shutting off your equipment

Shutting off your torch is a lot simpler than turning it on. The only thing that you need to remember is to turn off the oxygen first and then the propane. If you reverse this order you can get a loud popping on premixed torches. Again do not over tighten the valve knobs on your torch or you can damage the valve seats. Then turn off the gas and oxygen at the tanks and unscrew the adjustment handle on the oxygen regulator. Lastly bleed any pressure from the hoses by opening the torch valves one at a time. Remember to close them before starting up next time.

General torch care tips

After you have been using your torch for a while (about one half hour or so), you may notice a build up of some glowing material on the end of the torch. This build up is carbon and should be cleaned off to prevent the possibility of transferring it to your beads. It is cleaned off by scraping your tweezers or any other tool that happen to be handy across the face of your torch. You do not have to turn off your torch when you do this. This may produce a snapping sound but don't let it bother you. You will also be developing a build up of carbon in your torch. A small cleaning tool is usually included with your torch to ream this out. You should do this regularly. Do not attempt to do this while the torch is running. This may seem obvious, but I have been told of one incidence where this was done and the reamer melted off inside the torch and ruined it. (Although how the person was able to do this without getting burned is beyond my comprehension.) You may also want to invest in a little better set of reamers that can be purchased at a welding supply house.

If while you are making beads, you should happen to get glass on the tip of your torch, immediately turn off your torch. Cool it and clean the glass off the torch. If you don't do this, the hot glass can flow into the tip of your torch and block the holes.

Glass manipulation basics

Now that you know the basics on how to safely operate your torch and a little about different types of glass, you are ready to start working glass in a flame. In this first section you will develop an understanding of how glass behaves in a flame and some basic flameworking techniques that you will need in order to become proficient. After that you should practice these skills by making some components that can be used in decorating your beads. At that point we will move into different beadmaking techniques.

Holding the glass

In most flameworking situations and in beadmaking, you will hold the glass rod feed stock in your dominant hand. Your right hand, if you are

© 1996 James Kervin

right handed, or your left, if you are left handed. How you hold it in that hand depends on what operation you are doing at the moment. In some operations you will hold the glass rod like a pencil, in others you will hold it like a tennis racket. In all cases though, you will hold it lightly not firmly.

A maneuver that you will have to get used to when you start to work with molten glass on the end of your rod is rotating the rod. The rod has to be rotated constantly during heating for two reasons. The first is to evenly heat the rod around the circumference and allows glass to flow uniformly. If you only heat from one side of the rod, the other side will not flow or stretch. This can cause the glass to pull and exert force on objects to which you are trying to add

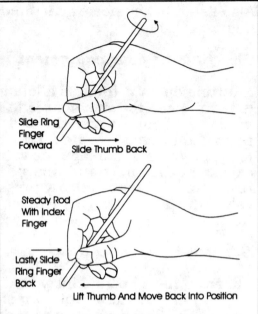

Figure 32. Pencil grip for glass.

glass. The other reason that you need to rotate the glass rod as you heat it is to prevent the heated glass from sagging under the influence of gravity. As the glass forms a molten drop on the end of your rod, it will want to bend down and drip off. By rotating the rod, down continually changes direction and the drop stays centered on the end of the rod.

Now that you know why you want to rotate the rod, you need to learn how to rotate it. In the pencil position, you rotate the rod by sliding the rod between your thumb and ring finger while using the index finger to steady the rod as shown in Figure 32. Here the rod is rolled by sliding the thumb back toward the palm of the hand and the ring finger is slid away from the palm. During this motion, each finger will move between a quarter and a half of an inch. At this point the thumb is lifted and moved back out to the starting position while the rod is temporarily held in position between the index finger and the ring finger. The thumb is then placed back against the rod and holds it against the index finger. Lastly, the ring finger slides back to its original position and we are ready to start the whole motion over again. In actual practice this motion becomes one continuous one. The process is hard to describe but with a little practice you will understand it and the motion will become an automatic one. It is easier to do

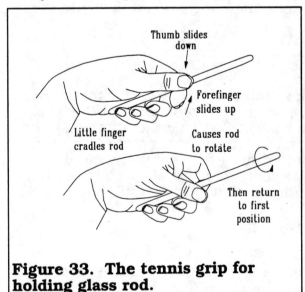

Figure 33. The tennis grip for holding glass rod.

© 1996 James Kervin

Flameworking Techniques 95

once it becomes automatic and you stop thinking about it.

In the tennis racket grip, the motion is a little bit different and a lot easier. Here the rotation is accomplished by rolling the rod between your thumb and your index finger as illustrated in Figure 33. The thumb, which is pointing toward the end of the rod, slides downward while the index finger and maybe also the ring finger, which are pointing downward perpendicular to the rod, slid upward. The rod rotates between them while at the same being cradled between the remaining fingers and the palm of your hand. This cradling allows both the thumb and the index finger to be lifted and moved back to the starting position simultaneously without losing control of the rod.

Heating the glass

Now that you know how to hold the rod, let's discuss how to safely get it into the flame without thermal shocking it. This has to be done before you can work with it. Thermal shocking is where the glass builds up more stress then it can withstand as it is being heated up and shatters. As explained earlier, this is a problem mainly in the low temperature regime where glass still reacts as a brittle solid. So the objective is to heat the glass rod slowly through this regime and into the non-brittle solid regime where all stress flows easily through the material. Thermal shock is more common with large diameter glass rods or ones with freshly cut ends. Strips cut from sheet glass with their many cut edges, as our dichroic beadmakers are well aware, can also be problematic.

There are three ways to do this. The first is to take the glass rod in your dominant hand in a tennis grip and wave it quickly in and out of the flame. You will want to start out near the end of your flame. Do this until you can start to see the sodium flare over the top of your didymium glasses. Some glasses will also change color as they heat up which serves as an additional indication of correct preheat. As the glass heats up, slow down your waving and bring the glass into the working point, about two thirds of the way out in your flame. The tip of your glass should start to glow. At this point you should be able to stop waving the glass and hold it in the flame. As the end of the rod becomes molten, you would start rotating it.

Another way to introduce the glass into the flame is to start by holding the glass rod way out at the end of the flame. As it starts to glow a little bit, you can slowly slide it through the flame toward you until you get it into the proper working position. The last and easiest way to preheat your glass is to have a section of your hot plate or annealer available to do this. Some annealers come with little racks to help balance the portion of the rod that protrudes out of it. Just set the rod down here and let it get hot. Be careful of short rods which may get too hot to handle.

With some glasses or operations, you may have to heat up more than just the tip of the rod. You may have to heat up as much as an inch of the end of the rod to prevent thermal shocking. You can do this by plunging the rod repeatedly into the flame as needed and pulling it back

© 1996 James Kervin

96   Glass Beadmaking

out. This is especially a problem with filigrana and aventurine because they seem to have a lot of residual stress in them.

Gathering

In order to decorate beads with dots, spirals, or many other applications, it is required to be able to gather a molten glob of glass at the end of the rod. The gather is made up of glass from the rod itself that is collected and held at the end of a rod as it melts. This is achieved, as illustrated in Figure 34, by introducing the rod into the flame as was just explained and keeping the end in the flame. By rotating the rod, you can keep the molten drop that starts to form at the end from dropping off. As you keep the end of the rod in the flame longer and longer, more of the rod will melt and become part of the drop at the end of the rod. In most cases in beadmaking, you will not gather more than about a 3/8" diameter drop before using it. With practice of your rotating skills, gathering this much and more will be simple.

There are also times that you might want to develop a gather somewhere else along the rod rather then at the end. To do this hold the rod in one hand and introduce it into the flame at the point at which you want to gather. You do this by slowly waving this point through the flame just as if it were the end of your rod. As you get it to the point where you can continue to hold it in the flame, you want to grab the other end of the rod with your other hand. Start rotating the rod with both hands to keep it from drooping as it gets soft. As the center softens, you will have to be careful to rotate both sides at the same speed or the gather will be twisted and distorted. As it melts, you can

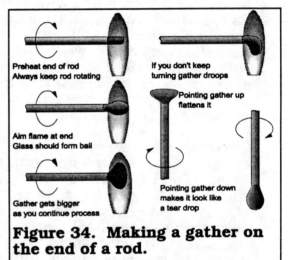

Figure 34. Making a gather on the end of a rod.

speed up the gathering process by gently pushing the two ends of the rod together as you rotate them. When the gather is of the desired size, lift it out of the flame and continue rotating it while you allow it to cool. This is necessary because it can still droop at this point. Also you may want to be careful to keep the two ends of the rod aligned if desired as the gather cools.

If you notice tiny bubbling or scuzzing on your gather, this is an indication that you are overheating the glass. To prevent this, you need to work out further in the flame from the tip of the torch. Remember the ideal location is about two thirds of the way out in the flame.

Fusing rods

One way to practice gathering is by fusing two shorter rods together to make a longer one. Practicing this skill will help improve both your rotating and your gathering skills, as well as, your whole feeling for how the glass responds in a flame. To do this cut two short pieces, each

© 1996 James Kervin

Flameworking Techniques

about six inches long, from one of your rods. Take one piece in each hand and get an end of each into the flame as explained earlier. Then gather a small drop on each just barely bigger then the end of the rod.

If while doing this, one piece gets ahead of the other, just remove it from the flame for a few seconds or hold it out further in the flame. It can even be allowed to stop glowing and be put immediately back into the flame without thermal shock damage. There is a point though, that if left too long out of the flame, that it might cool so much that slow reentry would be necessary. You will develop a feeling for this as you get more experienced.

Anyway, after you have your two small gathers on the ends of the rods, you are now ready to join them. Do this by bringing the two gathers together in the flame and holding them there just long enough for them to join together into one gather in the center of what is now one rod. While doing this you will have to continue to rotate both rods otherwise your gather will droop. Once touched together, the rods will have to be rotated at the same speed or the gather will get twisted and distorted. Increase the size of the gather until it gets to be just slightly larger than the rod diameter.

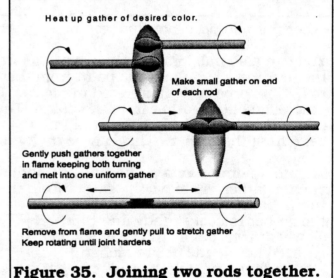

Figure 35. Joining two rods together.

Once the gather at the junction is the right size, remove it from the flame. Lifting it up is the easiest way to do this. Continue rotating both rods until the glow starts to go away while also trying to keep them aligned. Then gently pull on the ends of both rods just enough to shrink the gather down to the original diameter of the rod. Keep it aligned and rotating just long enough to chill solid.

If your rod is not straight or of uniform thickness, just stick the gather area back into the flame, reform the gather and try again.

Drawing a point

There are times in beadmaking when you might want a small glass point, a narrowed down section of rod, to apply glass in a controlled manner or to use as a tool in manipulating a bead. There are two ways to draw such a point: either from a gather at the end of a rod or from one in the middle of the rod.

To draw a point from a gather at the end of a rod, start by forming such a gather. Then grab another rod with the other hand. Pull the gather out of the flame and touch it to the cold rod. Give it a second or two to chill

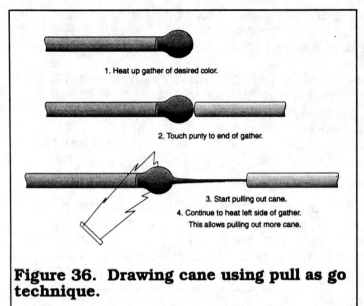

Figure 36. Drawing cane using pull as go technique.

and then slowly pull it away from the cold rod. The slower that you pull it away, the thicker will be the point that you draw. Larger gathers and longer points might require you to rotate the rod slightly while pulling. When the point is of the desired length, hold it stretched out for a couple seconds to allow it to get hard before you put it down. Once cool you should be able to break the point free from the cold rod because it will not have formed a good joint. If the other rod had been hot this would not be the case.

You can also pull longer points (or cane) from a rod by continuing to heat the first rod as you pull the point from the end of gather with the second rod. This process is illustrated in Figure 36. To start heat the rod on the other side of the gather from the point. The gather itself is outside of the flame. Continue to feed more rod into the flame as you continue to pull cane from the gather. This can be tricky until you perfect it.

To pull a point from a gather in the middle of a rod, start by forming such a gather. Remove the gather from the flame while continuing to rotate both ends of the rod. Allow the gather to cool slightly and then slowly draw it out as in the previous case. When to the desired length, stop pulling and hold it outstretched a couple seconds to allow it to cool. Then break it in the middle and you have two points to use. Remember that the longer you wait before pulling and the slower that you pull, the thicker your cane will be.

Flame cutting

Flame cutting is very similar to drawing a point from a central gather. Start with a rod, get it into the flame and just to the point where the central area is starting to gather. Lift it out of the flame and pull just slightly. This will form a stretched region in the rod. Allow it to cool slightly and put this thinned out region back into the flame slightly

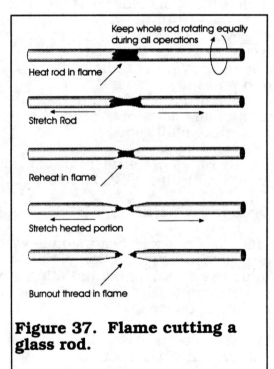

Figure 37. Flame cutting a glass rod.

Flameworking Techniques 99

more on one side than the other. This area, since it is thinner, will heat faster than the thicker region around it. If this region was made thin enough in the first draw by having minimized the gather, you should now be able to pull the pieces apart in the flame without much stringing. If it is stringing out, wind the string from the thinned end that was more out of the flame than the other, around the other with a small circling motion. Do this until the string is burned through by the flame and then separate the pieces. You may want to take a second to melt the string into the gather on the piece you wound it about before putting it down.

Punty use

There may be times when you have been working on a glass bead or decoration for a glass rod and you want to work on the area where it is attached to the rod. To do this you need to temporarily attach another rod to the bead at a different location to act as a handle.

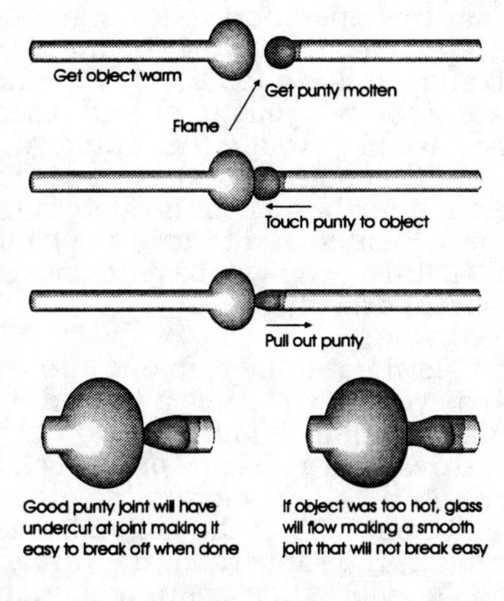

To attach another rod, you make a small gather at the end of the new rod and touch it to the bead at the desired location. This is often referred to as puntying but I am not sure if that is a real word. How permanent this attachment becomes depends upon how hot the bead was at the attachment point. If the bead was almost molten, the glass will flow from the rod to the bead and make a good permanent attachment. Many times though you do not want a permanent attachment. In these cases you will keep the bead a little cooler so no material flows from the rod to the bead. If you look closely at a temporary punty joint, you will be able to see the temporary joint between the two.

Get object warm

Get punty molten

Flame

Touch punty to object

Pull out punty

Good punty joint will have undercut at joint making it easy to break off when done

If object was too hot, glass will flow making a smooth joint that will not break easy

Figure 38. Attaching a punty.

The glass on the punty will have drawn in at the attachment point leaving a sharp meniscus all the way around as shown in Figure 38.

If you want to make a permanent attachment, get both the rod and the attachment point hot (slightly glowing) and press them together so that they form a slight bulge. Then gently pull on the joint until it contracts down to form a smooth joint as shown in the bottom right of the figure. If it still has some sharp undercut to it like the bottom left picture, you will need to sharpen up your flame point and reheat this area. Sharp joints are crack initiators and will almost never last.

Sometime the object that you are handling is so big that you want a pretty substantial sized glass punty but Morreti glass, if that is what you are working with, only comes in about one quarter inch diameter. What you can do is use a large diameter pyrex rod as your punty. Compatibility is not a problem because you are going to remove it before

© 1996 James Kervin

100   Glass Beadmaking

it cools. Just be sure to remove all traces of the punty when you are done and throw away the last little bit of what you are making that was attached to the pyrex.

Compatibility testing

With the basic skills that you have just learned, you already have the skills necessary to be able to test the compatibility of your glass. To do this heat about the three quarters of an inch of the two glass rods which you want to test for compatibility. Start to get a gather on the end of one of the rods and attach it about one half of an inch from the end of the other rod. Then fuse the two rods together by aiming the flame onto the joint between the two rods. Turn the rods to heat both sides of the joint. Heat one of the rods at the joint surface where it connects with the overlap area to soften it and move it down on center of the joint region between the two rods. (You can refer to the first couple of steps for making latticino in Figure 39 if you are unclear on what you are doing.) Repeat this operation with the rod on the other end. Keep heating the overlap area of the two rods until the joint area contracts into a molten glob shaped like a football. While heating the joint, you will have to keep rotating the two rods to prevent them from drooping. You will also have to be careful to rotate them uniformly so that you do not develop any twist in the molten glass. You may also find it helpful to incline the rods back and forth to keep the glob in the right position. Once you have properly heated and formed the glob, pull it out from the flame and let it cool slightly. You will have to continue to rotate the rods to prevent the glob from drooping.

Then slowly pull the glob out into a long thin thread without twisting the glob as you do so. After it is stretched to full length hold it tight for a few seconds until it solidifies. If you have done this right you will have a long thin thread with a stripe of one color on one side of the thread and a stripe of the other color on the other side of the thread. Break off the thread from both of the original rods. If the glasses are compatible (shrink at the same rate), the thread will remain straight. If the thread bends by more than about one quarter of an inch over a twenty inch length, they are on the border line of being incompatible and probably should not be used together. The glass on the inside of a bow has the lower COE. For glass to be used as a surface decoration you may want to have less than one eighth of an inch deflection because they are more susceptible to breaking off.

If you want a quantitative value for the COE difference of the two glasses, you need to carefully measure the length of the thread, its diameter (this will require a micrometer to do accurately) and the bow. Substitute these values into the following equation to get a good approximation of COE difference:

$$COE = \frac{16*10^7*\text{thread diameter}*\text{bow}}{\text{thread length squared}*\text{temperature difference}}$$

The term 10^7 is equivalent to 10,000,000. All dimensions should be in the same units, such as inches. Thread length squared means the thread length multiplied by itself. For a temperature difference, you might assume that you would use a value expressing the difference from

Flameworking Techniques 101

when the glass solidifies back down to room temperature. This would be about right if the COE values did not have the large non-linear changes above the strain point that we saw back in the last chapter. By trial and error, I found a value of 1700°C to be a good approximate temperature difference to use.

If you are not the type of person that feels comfortable with equations, you can use the following table to help determine COE differences. For bows larger than those in the table, multiply the table COE value in the last column for that thread diameter by the ratio of your measured bow to the largest bow listed (your bow/0.625).

Table 13. COE difference values from thread testing.

Thread Diameter (in)	Bow (in)				
	0.125	0.250	0.375	0.500	0.625
0.010	0.2	0.4	0.6	0.8	1.0
0.020	0.4	0.8	1.2	1.6	2.0
0.030	0.6	1.2	1.8	2.5	3.1
0.040	0.8	1.6	2.5	3.3	4.1
0.050	1.0	2.0	3.1	4.1	5.1
0.060	1.2	2.5	3.7	4.9	6.1
0.070	1.4	2.9	4.3	5.7	7.1
0.080	1.6	3.3	4.9	6.5	8.2
0.090	1.8	3.7	5.5	7.4	9.2
0.100	2.0	4.1	6.2	8.2	10.2

Some things that may cause problems with determining COE differences by this technique are cracking and non-ideal thread geometry. For threads with very large COE differences, even small diameter threads may develop very small cracks or crazing that will release some of the stress in the thread that causes bowing. This will result in an underestimate of the COE mismatch. In deriving this equation, I had to make a number of assumptions about the thread geometry. Violations of these assumptions effect the accuracy of the calculated value. The first assumption that I made was that the thread diameter was constant along its length. If this is not true, try to break the thread into a shorter one with more constant diameter. A second assumption was that the cross section of the thread was round. If not, approximate an average diameter for the cross section. Lastly I assumed that the cross section was split equally between the two glasses. Large differences in viscosity of the two glasses may make one side pull thinner than the other which will result in an underestimate of the COE mismatch.

Flame annealing

When making large beads, a lot of stress can end up in the glass from having one part of the bead being almost molten and the other end being solid. Also there may be times that you spend a lot of time on one portion of a bead, while the rest of the bead is cooling some. In these cases, the stress may get so large that the bead can crack during its initial cooling before it can be kiln annealed. To help prevent this from

102   Glass Beadmaking

happening, you can flame anneal the bead in a medium flame before burying it in the vermiculite. Hold the bead out near the end of the flame and get it uniformly hot just at or beneath the temperature where it starts to glow (the dull red state). If you start building up soot on or getting color change in your bead, the flame is too reducing and you need to add just a little more oxygen to it.

After you have heated the bead uniformly, pull it out of the flame and allow it to cool slightly such that it is not glowing. Then bury the bead in your heated vermiculite to let it cool. If you put the bead into the vermiculite too hot, the vermiculite will dent it or stick to it. The pot of vermiculite should be heated to about 300 to 400°F. Then when done for the day, turn off the hot plate under the vermiculite and allow it to cool for about one half hour, depending on the size of the bead before you remove it. Be sure that you feel the top of the vermiculite to see how warm it is before you pull the bead out. Try to refrain from peaking ahead of time at your masterpieces before they are cool to prevent thermal shock. Kiln anneal them afterwards.

General glass manipulation comments

One thing always to be aware of when working on a bead or other glass construction is to always keep the whole thing warm. Every once in a while go back and rewarm the whole project to about the dull red state if possible. It is very easy to get so absorbed in one area of the construction that you let another area cool off. Nothing is worse than seeing your bead crack before your eyes as you rewarm a section that got just a little too cool. You can sometimes fix the cracks by reheating this region to lightly glowing red but this will mean losing any surface detail in the process. If you suspect that a portion of the bead has cooled off, reenter the flame gradually as if the bead were a cold rod of glass.

Along those same lines I discussed earlier how by careful temperature control of the glass that you can vary considerably its viscosity and thus how it may be worked. To do this you really have to get a feel for how to read its heat and where to heat it in the flame. Overheat it and it will run away from you. Control its heat well and you will be able to sculpt it like clay. Heating very fast will get the outside hot while leaving the inside relatively cool. To thoroughly heat you have to heat slowly removing it from the flame occasionally to let the heat sink into the bead.

Component construction

As a way to practice some of the skills that you have just learned, you can make some constructions that can be used to decorate the beads that you will make later. So let's discuss a number of different kinds of decorative constructions.

Latticino or twisted canes

One of the easiest constructions that you can make to decorate your beads are basic latticinos. Latticino literally translates from Italian as "little milk-white glass strands." This describes the traditional latticino

© 1996 James Kervin

Flameworking Techniques

which is made by twisting white and clear rods together to create small candy cane like white stripes suspended in clear glass. Now-a-days beadmakers use almost any color combinations imaginable to make similar twisted cane constructions. In this book, I have generalized the term latticino to apply to these structures too. This generalization is not universally accepted by all glass artists but no better term has been developed.

The overall latticino manufacturing process is illustrated in Figure 39 and is very similar to the process that was use in thread testing for compatibility. You start by preheating about an inch of two rods and attaching them together with an overlap by touching the gather of one rod to the other rod about an inch in from the end of the rod. Then bend it over to touch the gather on the other rod (a & b). Join the two rods in their overlap region by heating along the joint. Next heat the rod handles and move them onto center (c). Melt the joined area down into a uniform glob that looks like a football. Then lift the glob out of the flame continuing to rotate it to prevent droop. Let the glob cool slightly. Start to introduce a counterclockwise twist by rotating one rod in one direction and the other in the opposite direction (d). Slowly pull the glob apart. Twist faster and faster as you stretch farther and farther. When done, hold the latticino stretched out for a few seconds to allow it to finish hardening up.

Remember that you can control the thickness of the latticino as you pull it out, just as you did in pulling points for cane, by controlling the speed with which you pull it out of the glob. The slower that you pull it, the thicker it will be. Slightly thicker sections and ends can be pulled out some more by lightly reheating that section in the edge of the flame and repulling. This can be tricky though because the small diameter rod heats very quickly. It may also help to hold the end on an angle in the flame as you reheat it.

There is another way to make a basic latticino. This method is called the pull as you go technique. For this technique you get the two rods hot as you did before and join them together with an overlap of about three quarters of an inch as you did before but this time do not melt them into a ball. Instead get one end hot, then pull and twist out latticino again in a counterclockwise direction. Keep the flame off the region that you are pulling out, instead be preheating the area just ahead of that region. This method can be made a little easier by holding the rod at angle to the flame because it allows preheating of a larger area. An advantage of this method of making latticino over the last method is that it can have more texture to it. By

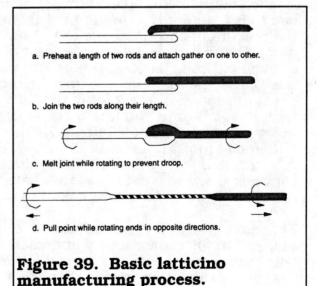

Figure 39. Basic latticino manufacturing process.

© 1996 James Kervin

Glass Beadmaking

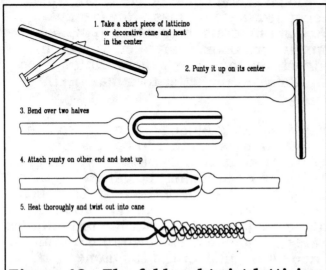

Figure 40. The fold and twist latticino manufacturing technique.

keeping the glass a little cooler, a texture resembling that of a rope can be developed that gives the latticino just a little more uniqueness when lightly fused to the surface of a bead.

This last technique can also be done using a single short piece of rod as illustrated in Figure 40. Here you heat the short piece of rod in the middle and punty at this point onto another rod. Next by heating the middle of the short rod you can bend it in half to have the ends together and lightly join them along its length. Then heat the ends and pull them out while twisting at the same time.

As you make latticino, you might have the problem that it will change from looking like a stripe of one color on the second to that of a stripe of the second color on the first. This problem usually comes from not moving the rods back on center or not shrinking the joint down uniformly into the football shape before pulling it out. One way to eliminate this problem, if you just can not get it to work the normal way no matter how hard you try, is to join a short section of the second color to the center of a longer rod of the first. Then when you pull it out you will always have more of the background color than the stripe color and your Latticino may look more consistent.

Latticino can also be made of more than just two colors. As an example, let's examine making one of three colors. To do this, start out by joining two rods together but do not heat them up to form a glob. Flame cut off the remaining portion of one rod. Now add another color by heating a new rod and attach it along the joint of the two other rods. Move the attachment rods back on center and work the three rods together into one glob by heating and melting the rods. Try to prevent trapping of air down the center of the joint of the three rods by working from one end to form the glob until you finally reach the other. The reason that you do not want to trap any air bubbles is that they will pop as you reheat the latticino to apply it as decoration to your bead. Once you have the glob fully formed, you pull it out at the same time putting in the counterclockwise twist as before. Latticino can similarly be constructed from four colors. After four colors the effect starts to be lost.

There are many different variations to the latticino theme. Basic latticino made from filigrana are very impressive looking. This makes a latticino with very fine well defined lines that spiral around each other in a clear casing. Another variation is to make a rainbow colored latticino with a white core. The white core emphasizes the color of transparent colors.

As an example, a red, yellow and blue white core latticino would be made by applying sections of color on a central white rod as shown in Figure 41. You would start by preheating the white rod and applying two stripes of transparent red equally spaced around the central white core. Use the pencil grip on the red rod as you apply it twisting slightly to evenly heat the rod as you apply it. The thickness of the transparent layers can be controlled by how you stretch and push the red rod as you apply it to the white rod beneath the flame. Next attach two stripes of yellow adjacent to the red stripes. Push down with the yellow rod into the joint area between the white and red to completely fill the joint and not trap any bubbles. Lastly apply two stripes of blue again pushing down slightly to completely fill the void between the red and yellow stripes. Attach a rod handle to the other end of the white core and heat up the striped area into a homogeneous blob. Then twist and pull out like any other latticino.

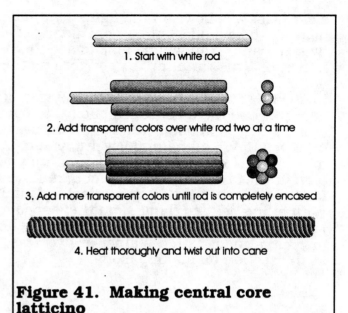

Figure 41. Making central core latticino

Another variation on the latticino theme is make one with an internally twisting ribbon. To make latticino like this, start by flattening out a large gather. Then pull it out into a short ribbon about a little over an inch long. Get the end of the ribbon hot and square it off with a scissors. This will become the ribbon that will spiral through the latticino. At this point, you can decorate the ribbon if you want. You could add stripes down the center or the sides, or any of a number of different options. The example, shown in Figure 42, has stripes added down the centers and the sides. Now case the whole ribbon in clear glass by adding successive stripes of clear glass pushing down to fill the voids. It helps to rock the clear rod back and forth in the flame as you apply it to heat it evenly. Remember to keep the whole ribbon warm as you do this. Eventually you will get the ribbon encased in a big cylinder of

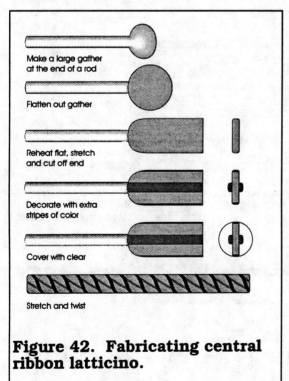

Figure 42. Fabricating central ribbon latticino.

© 1996 James Kervin

106 Glass Beadmaking

clear glass as shown in the figure. Attach a handle on the other end and heat up the cylinder into a homogeneous glob as usual and pull out into twisted cane. You will be able to see the ribbon twisting through this latticino. This variation is good for creating underwater plant life scenes.

I have presented but a few of the myriad of latticino variations to get you started. Use them as a springboard to come up with your own designs. Some latticino are so beautiful themselves that it is a shame to use them on a bead. When making jewelry, you can use that perfect latticino to make multi-colored dangles by just fire polishing one end and making a loop in the other. To make a loop, just heat up a small section of the latticino and bend it down on itself. Flame cut off the extra latticino. With a fine pointed flame, join the looped end to the main body of the latticino. Then shape the loop by lightly heating it in the flame and manipulating it with a reamer or tweezers. This will be better described in the section on making loops.

Ribbons

Another construction that is formed in a manner similar to latticino is ribbon. Here you lay up a number of rods one on another as you did for latticino but you keep the lay-up flat in a paddle-like arrangement as shown in part (a) of Figure 43. As you add each section of rod you join them on each end of the paddle. Try to keep it hot and straight. You do not attach an additional handle at this time because it is easier to flatten the ribbon on the marver without a handle. You then join the rods well along the joints and marver the ribbon flat (b). You should get the creases out to prevent it from stretching unevenly as you pull it out.

Now attach a handle to the well marvered end. When you do this, pull down some of the outside colors as illustrated in the figure before attaching the new handle on center (c). This pulling down helps the ribbon stretch evenly when you pull it out. Now burn off the original handle and flatten that end of the paddle (d). When the whole paddle is flat, reattach the handle to that side, again pulling down some of the outer color as shown in part (e) of the figure.

Then heat the paddle all up evenly by waving it in small circles in the flame, flipping it back and forth as it starts to droop. When it is uniformly

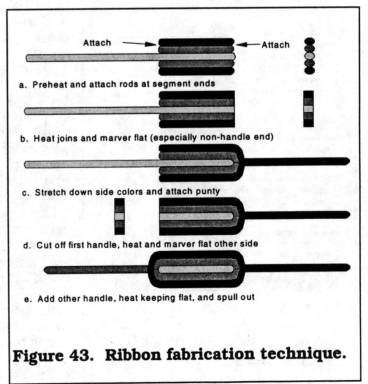

Figure 43. Ribbon fabrication technique.

Flameworking Techniques 107

heated bring it out of the flame and cool slightly, all the while continuing to flip it back and forth to prevent any droop. When cooled to the right temperature start to pull it out. Like with cane, the size of the ribbon can be controlled by the speed with which you pull it out. Also, if the ends start to cool and don't pull out quite enough, you can wave them through the flame to reheat them up enough to continue the pull.

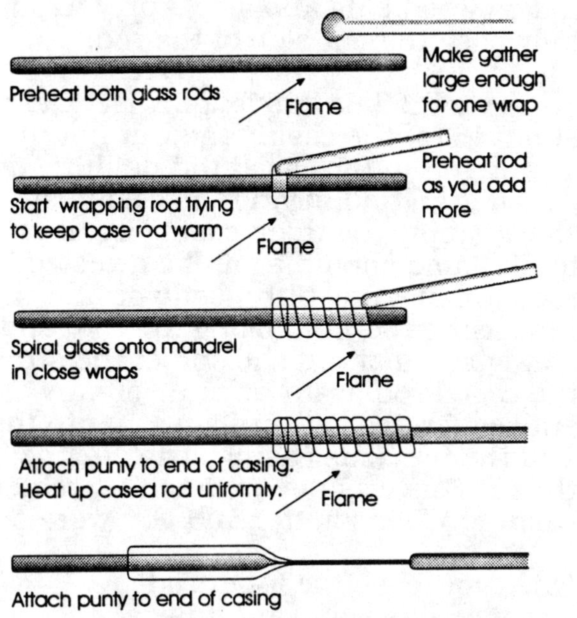

Cased rods

Often when you make decorations like flowers, you want a subtle blending of colors. One way to achieve this is by casing one color with another. Start out by preheating two rods as if you were going to make a latticino. You only want to lightly heat the rod of the color that you want on the inside so that it will not thermal shock when it is cased while holding it in the tennis racket grip. You do not want to get it soft. You get the color that you want on the outside hot and start to make a gather.

Figure 44. Fabricating cased cane with circumferential wraps.

Now start to wrap the cooler rod with material from the hotter rod. Do this by touching the hotter rod, which you are holding in the pencil grip to the cooler and rotating the cooler rod away from you as shown in Figure 44. (This is very similar to the basic wound bead technique to be described later. You may want to read that section before attempting this construction.) When casing, it is very important to keep the hot rod in the flame and the cooler rod below the flame. Make sure that you do not trap air between wraps as this can cause popping of the cane as it is applied. To make thinner outer coatings, try pushing down with the hot rod for wider application or pulling a point from the gather as you wind it on the cooler rod.

The other method of casing is to apply the casing color by using lengthwise applications. Here, like before, you start by warming up the rod to be cased and heating up just the tip of the casing rod. If you want a thin casing coat, you heat up about ½ inch on the end of the casing rod red hot while holding it in the pencil grip. Then apply the casing by pushing down onto the outside of the rod to be cased with the casing rod pointed slightly toward you. Quickly draw it down the length of the rod to be cased and then pull it away from the cased rod through the flame to burn off any stringers that develop as you pull away. For long cased areas, the flame can be situated such that it is pointing along the outside of the cased rod and onto the casing rod to continue heating the casing

© 1996 James Kervin

108   Glass Beadmaking

rod as it is being applied. Apply as many thin stripes as is needed to fully case the out side of the rod.

To apply thick layers lengthwise, warm the rod to be cased as before and about ½" of the casing rod but not quite as hot as before. Now apply the casing rod to the cased rod pushing down lightly (while holding it in a pencil grip) and having the casing slightly pointed away from you. Now slowly apply the thick casing by drawing the casing rod toward you. The torch flame should again be directed onto the junction where the two rods are meeting but mostly on the casing rod. To keep the back side of the casing rod from being too cool and pulling as you apply it, it helps to slowly rotate it. At the end of the stroke, pull the casing rod away from the cased rod again burning off any stringers in the flame. On subsequent coats, gently push into the interface between the cased rod and the previous casing stripe to ensure not trapping any air between them. This was not as much a problem with the thin coats because the casing rod was hotter and you were pushing harder.

Once you have the inner rod wrapped like you want, fuse a rod onto the end of the cased section. Then thoroughly heat the cased section to fill in between the wraps. You will have to rotate the rods as you heat to prevent droop. When a uniform hot glob is formed from the cased section, remove it from the flame and pull it out to whatever size you desire. While pulling it out you may find it easier to prevent drooping by rotating it back and forth instead of all the way around.

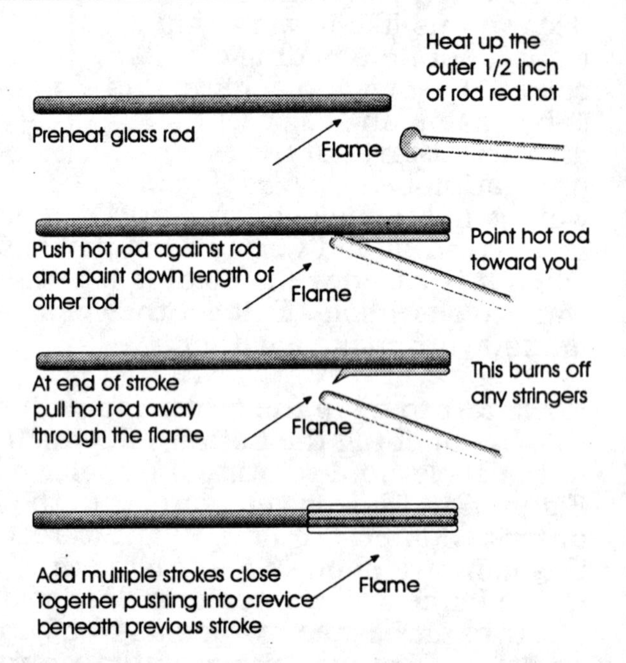

One form of cased rod that really looks good is to case opalescent white with a deep transparent color like rubino oro or bleu cobalto. These white core canes allow some beautiful transitional effects between the transparent colors by themselves contrasted to regions of transparent glass over the white.

Figure 45. Applying thin casings lengthwise.

Loops

With the flameworking skills that you have learned to date and the skill that you are now going to learn, you will be able to make one basic type of bead, a pendant bead. A pendant bead is a bead that, instead of having a hole through it, has a loop at the top like that suggested for use with the perfect latticino. These beads are usually tear drop shaped and are hung from the loop.

© 1996 James Kervin

The steps for making a basic single color pendant are illustrated in Figure 46. To start, take a glass rod and make about a 1/2 to 3/4 inch diameter gather on the end. Remember to keep the rod rotating to keep the gather on center. You might also find it easier to handle by tilting the rod up at about a 45° angle to the horizontal as you gather. The size of gather that you can handle will depend both on your skill level and the diameter of the rod. Large gathers are easier to handle on larger diameter rods. Let the gather chill slightly and then lightly attach a punty rod of the same color to the other end of the gather.

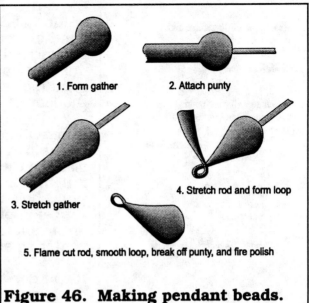

Figure 46. Making pendant beads.

Now reheat the joint between the original rod and the gather until it gets soft. Remove it from the flame and allow it to cool just slightly. Oh, by the way, you have been remembering to keep everything rotating haven't you. Next slightly draw out the gather to form a nice smooth tear drop shape. Now we are ready to make the loop. Heat the section of the original rod at the top of the tear drop and pull it out to a point. Quickly loop the point around on itself to form the loop from which the pendant will hang. Burn off any excess rod from the loop and shape it in the edge of the flame with a reamer or tweezers. Lightly reheat the whole bead except for the punty joint. Then break it off the punty, grab the loop end with your tweezers and fire polish the punty joint area.

The first couple times that you attempt loop making, you might want to use Pyrex rod so you do not have to concentrate as much on keeping your glass hot enough so that it does not crack. This also makes it easier because you can start from a larger diameter rod. If you want to add surface decorations as will be discussed later for wound beads, you would do that right after you first make the gather. Another variation suggested by the "Beadle" (see reference) is to insert a tiny bit of color into an otherwise clear pendant. This is done by putting a small bit of color on the end of a second rod drawn from clear color and pushing it into the interior of the initial gather. To push it in you have to reheat the gather to the point where you can just barely keep it on the end of the rod. Then again burn off the drawn rod at the surface of the gather and reheat the gather to regain a uniform shape before continuing.

Button holes and loops

A variation of loop addition which can be used to make button shanks was presented by Lewis Wilson in the reference at the end of this chapter. After attaching a medium diameter cane to the back of the button as shown in Figure 47, you can flame cut off most of the rest of

110 Glass Beadmaking

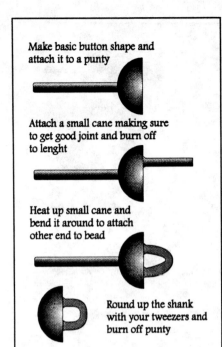

Figure 47. Attaching a loop-like button shank.

the cane. Then you heat up the short section of cane and use you tweezers to bend it over and attach it to an adjacent prewarmed section of the button back by pushing down and then gently pulling up to get a nice smooth joint. Finish by reheating the loop and shaping it with a reamer.

Another easily constructed raised button shank can be made by adding a small dab of glass to the back of the button and pinching it lightly to form a fairly thick shank. Then put a hole in the shank by using your tungsten pick to drill a hole from both sides of the shank that tilt down and join in the center as shown in Figure 48.

If you don't want a raised button shank, an easy variant of the previous technique can be used to construct a recessed one. Here instead of adding glass and pinching a raised shank, you push into and pinch to form a recessed one as shown in the figure. You then use your tungsten pick as before to drill the hole into the shank from both sides.

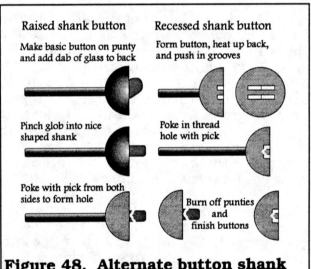

Figure 48. Alternate button shank construction techniques.

Suggested further reading

"Beadle, The Venerable", The Bead Column-Pendant Beads", Glass Line Vol. 7 No. 3 (October/November 1993)

Burton, John. Glass - Hand Blown Sculptured Colored Philosophy and Method, Bonanza Books, 1967

Dunham, Bandhu Scott, Contemporary Lampworking - A Practical Guide to Shaping Glass in the Flame, 1993 Pre-publication Edition

Hoyt, Homer L. Glassblowing - An Introduction to Solid and Blown Glass Sculpting, Crafts & Arts Publishing Co. Inc., 1989

Schuler, Frederic. Flameworking - Glassmaking for the Craftsman, Chilton Book Co., 1968

Wilson, Lewis. "Venetian Paperweight Buttons" Bead and Button No. 3 (June) 1994

© 1996 James Kervin

Millefiori and Mosaic Cane

The term millefiori (translated literally from Italian as "a thousand flowers") was established by the German scholar Heinrich Freiherr von Minutoli in 1827 to refer to the canes being produced at the time which in cross section contained stylistic floral images. Many artists now refer to any decorative glass cane which has patterns in the cane cross section as being made by millefiori techniques or as being millefiori and that is the way that I will use the term here. When the image gets much more complicated and is constructed of discrete elements, the cane is then usually referred to as mosaic cane. Millefiori and mosaic cane are usually used as thin slices which are applied as external decorations on beads. These thin slices are referred to as murrine (the singular is murrina). It is the pattern or image in the cross section that is usually the desired design element.

Figure 49. Some examples of Moretti murrine slices.

Ready-made compatible murrine are commercially available for use in your work from the Moretti glass factory in a wide variety of patterns. Figure 49 shows some of the patterns that they have available. Moretti murrine can be purchased by the ounce or the pound. You can get all of one design or mixtures of patterns graded according to size or coloration (clear or opaque). If you want, you can also purchase the millefiori cane instead of murrine. Or instead you may choose to make your own millefiori and thus your own murrine slices. Construction of millefiori and mosaic cane is the subject of this chapter.

Murrine can also used in building up mosaic images like are made in Murano Italy for pendants where murrine are fused together in a kiln. For this application, you want the murrine to be sliced a bit thicker, on the order of ¼" thick or more. If not, the glass will not flow to fill in the gaps between the murrine to form a uniform fused pendant. In making some of these mosaic pieces, I have also noticed what I believe to be some incompatibility between some of the murrine (especially between clear and opaque ones) that needs further validation.

© 1996 James Kervin

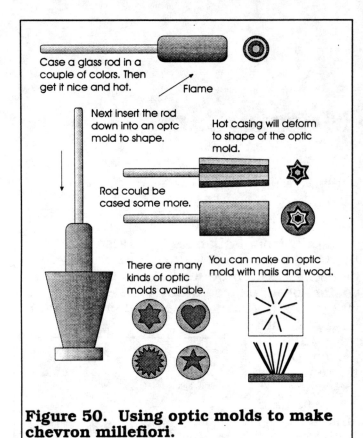

Figure 50. Using optic molds to make chevron millefiori.

Optic molds

The first method that I shall discuss to make millefiori cane is through repetitively casing layers that are occasionally manipulated for shape using molds. This is the typical technique that is used by furnace workers to form simple cross sectional patterns and is the technique by with most of the Moretti millefiori is made. To try this technique yourself, you might want to start out cheap and make a crude optic mold by nailing about six 4d finishing nails in a star pattern as shown in the bottom right Figure 50. Note that the tops of the nails are slanted outward to prevent capturing the glass.

Start the glassworking process by casing a rod of one color with another color using one of the processes that was discussed in the last chapter. Next heat the cased section of the rod until it is very soft. Then plunge it into the homemade optic mold as indicated in the figure to distort the casing and get the cross sectional pattern. Allow the rod to cool some and case it in another color.

When hand casing a distorted bundle, first add the new color down in the depressions made by the optic mold. Apply the casing really hot and push down hard to avoid trapping air. Again heat thoroughly and distort using the optic mold. Repeat this process as many times as you desire to get as large a piece as you want. Then heat the cased rod and draw it out into the desired thickness rod or cane for your work. Allow it to cool and chop it into about one eighth inch thick murrine slices or longer if you want to try fusing them. Professional optic molds can be purchased from one of the sources listed in the back of this book, if you so desire, and are available in a number of shapes. To use them, you have to preheat your mold on a hot plate and get your glass really hot (almost to the point where you lose control of it) and then plunge it into the optic mold. Personally, I have not found optic molds to be very useful for beadmaking, especially since handworking techniques are so easy to do.

Ribbed cane

Instead of using optic molds to introduce thickness variations in the color layers of your millefiori, you can accomplish the same thing by

© 1996 James Kervin

Millefiori and Mosaic Cane

handworking the bundle with a knife or reamer to put in creases. Just get the cased section hot and make axial slices down its length. An easily-made versatile tool to do this is a small reamer made from a small triangle of stainless steel or brass sheet metal held in an exacto blade handle. One side can be sharp and the other folded over to introduce wider grooves.

This is the technique used for construction of a very simple form of millefiori, ribbed cane. Ribbed cane is a form of cane that gives a natural looking color variation when used to make floral applications. Ribbed cane usually has a very simple pattern in its cross section and is not necessarily used as slices. Instead, the value of ribbed cane is for making floral applications. Here it is used for the variation in the thickness of the casing color on the exterior of the cane. This variation will show up as natural looking striations of color when the cane is applied to beads to make floral decorations as will be described later.

To make ribbed cane, start by making a good sized cylinder of a light colored glass on the end of a glass rod. Smooth it up. Then heat up one side of the cylinder and press inward with something like a shaper (one of those spatula shaped graphite paddles) or a knife. Then heat up the opposite side of the cylinder and make another groove. Make about eight equally spaced grooves all around the cylinder. Now fill the groves with a dark colored glass like black. After the grooves are all filled, lightly coat the entire outside surface of the cylinder with the dark color. Then uniformly heat up the cylinder and pull it out into a fairly thick cane. When applied to a bead, the thicker sections or ribs of the darker color will be apparent as darker streaks running through the application.

Bundled cane techniques

Bundled cane is a kilnworking technique that can be used to make more complex millefiori that may contain images like people or animals. This technique, commonly used by furnace workers, is a bit complicated and involves bundling rods and/or cane together cold and then fusing the glass in a kiln to form the desired image before being stretched out in a flame. Many glass historians and technicians have suggested that complex cane images created by this technique should more correctly be referred to as mosaic glass. This process is illustrated in Figure 51. In the first section, a number of points of various

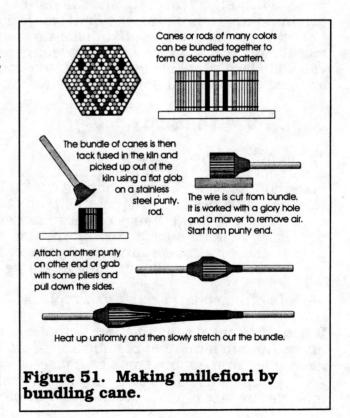

Figure 51. Making millefiori by bundling cane.

114   Glass Beadmaking

sizes have been bundled together using copper wire to create the desired pattern or picture. They were next put into a kiln and tack fused together so that they would stick together. Then by using a gather at the end of a punty, the tacked bundle is removed from the kiln. A molten glass collar is constructed around the punty end of the bundle. Quickly cut the wire from the bundle and keep it hot. Slowly heat up the bundle starting on the opposite end from the punty and work all the air out of the bundle as you work from one end to the other using your marver. Next attach another punty and gather to the other end large enough to cover the face of your bundle. Then you can either get the bundle all nice and hot and pull it out all at once or heat and pull as you go.

Once you have made a bundle and stretched it into cane, you can rebundle this cane with other canes and stretch it again to make more complex canes. You can also make components and bundle them together with filler cane to make detailed images. If you make half an image, you can combine it with the reversed image by flipping a piece of the same pull end for end to get a complete symmetrical image. These are some of the techniques that were used in antiquity to construct the famous Roman glass mosaics.

An alternate bundle working method you could try for making mosaic cane consists of taking the wired bundle cold and slowly heat one end until you get it fused together. Then attach that end to a punty. Now begin to fuse together the other end. Continue slow heating until you feel comfortable with how the bundle is tacked together and cut off the wire. Now proceed as previously described. The problem with this technique is that you are almost sure to have a couple rods or cane break as you heat them up and fall out of the pattern. In either of these two bundling techniques, the final resolution of the image is dependent upon the size of the rods that made up your bundle. If you look at a mosaic image made by a bundling technique under a magnifying glass, you will always be able to see the dot or pixel structure of the cane and any lines present will not really be straight.

Lampworked mosaic cane

As your experience in lampworking increases, you will find it possible to construct millefiori or mosaic cane images in the torch by adding material to a base rod and shaping it with hand tools. Besides being a relatively advanced technique, this process may also require some assistance. To make things easier to understand as I describe the process of making mosaic cane in the flame of a torch, I will continue to refer to the large image cane before stretching as a bundle, even though you are no longer really bundling anything.

Mosaic cane construction principles

When thinking of building up a complex image, it helps to break the image up into a number of subcomponent parts which are later assembled into a more complex image. As you will soon see, doing each section separately allows you to shrink each component separately to an appropriate size prior to assembly by stretching it. Before actually

© 1996 James Kervin

Millefiori and Mosaic Cane   115

describing the construction of any complex mosaic canes, let's start out by discussing some of the basic principles to consider during construction of mosaic cane pieces.

First, it helps to construct the basic cane bundle off of a borosilicate glass punty because its higher viscosity makes it stronger and more stable as you heat up the bundle. It is also more resistant to thermal shock in case you forget to warm it occasionally. If the bundle still breaks off of the punty during construction, don't panic. Just pick it up off the bench or the floor with some long tweezers that you keep handy just for that purpose and reattach it to the punty before you go on. Use a large diameter pyrex rod of about ½" for your punty because it is easier to handle as the bundle gets fairly big and heavy. Thin it down by about a half this diameter on the end that will attach to the bundle.

You could also used a pyrex backbone down the length of the bundle as is suggested by Lewis Wilson in his video on millefiori cane construction. This appears to work best if you make this backbone as the top of a pyrex T. The bottom of the T then works as a good handle so that you can keep flipping the piece back and forth to keep it evenly heated. After you are done, you just heat up the area around the T such that the Morreti glass is fairly soft while the pyrex is just flexible. Then peal the pyrex off the bundle. If you have some problem getting the last little bit off, reheat it and try cutting it off with your scissors. Then plop the whole thing into the annealer. If you want to see a demonstration of this, buy the video or take a class. The only problem with the T-bar technique is that it violates the second principle of mosaic cane construction that is discussed next.

The second principle is to start working on the image from a simple shape at the center of the image. This allows you to start from a single colored rod — at least for a the beginning of a subcomponent. A more complex image will probably by started off of a central subcomponent. By starting from a point near the center of the image, it makes it easier to judge and control the size of the image as you build it up. You will have a better feeling of where you are going with the image.

The third general principle is not to let your bundle get too long or you will have a hard time balancing it on the end of your punty, as well as keeping it warm enough to prevent thermal shock. One and a quarter to two inches seems to be about optimum size for torch assembly. This can be adjusted some depending upon the size of your torch flame.

The fourth principle is to understand that colored layers appear to lose some of their intensity as they get stretched out and made thinner in cross section. So go on and use bolder colors than those you might at first think. These layers are also easiest to apply lengthwise to the bundle as you build it up rather then circumferentially.

In order to properly know what the image looks like as you build it up, you need to observe the fifth principle — keep the non-punty end of your bundle clean. This allows you to view your image and see where you need to add more glass. For the same reason, smooth out each colored layer after you finish adding it. This allows you to really be sure of what

© 1996 James Kervin

the image looks like. It also prevents bleeding of colors through the crevices in the surface of a colored layer. Do this by marvering or shaping the bundle with a paddle. When shaping the bundle, only get the side of the bundle that you are working on hot and not the whole bundle. This gives you a rigid side against which to push and prevents the whole assemblage from bending as you push against it.

The last general principle that you should consider is that as you stretch out a bundle into a cane it tends to want to form a cylindrical cross section. Thus to avoid distortion of your image as you pull it out, it helps to make the bundle roughly cylindrical or oval to begin with before you stretch it. If nothing else, avoid wide variations in cross sectional thickness.

Beginning mosaic images — block letters

So with these principles in mind lets discuss how to go about making a fairly simple sort of mosaic cane — block letters. Many glass bead artists want to add identification to their work as they get better and more widely known. They feel that it makes their work more valuable and recognizable. One way to do this is through signature cane made with block letters.

There are three basic types of shapes that you will have to work with in making block letters: straight sides, partial curves and closed curves. The following letters have straight sides: A, B, D, E, F, H, I, J, K, L, M, N, P, R, T, U, V, W, X, Y and Z. The following letters have partial curves: B, C, D, G, J, P, R, S, and U. Lastly, the following letters have closed curves: O, and Q. As you can see, some of the letters have both straight sides and partial loops. Let's look at the construction of each of these types in turn.

Figure 52 show the construction technique for making one of the straight sided letters. For this illustration I chose one with straight sides only, an M. As in making all mosaic cane, it helps to start out at approximately the center of the image. In this case the wedge in the center of the M. Do that by making a gather of what will be you background color and making a wedge about an inch and a half long using a paddle and

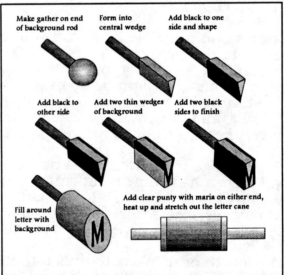

Figure 52. Making straight sided letter cane.

a marver. Then paint one long side of the wedge with black and smooth it out with your paddle. Make sure to keep the end clear. After that, paint the second long side of the wedge with black. If you were to stop at this point you would have a V. Now add a narrow wedge of background color to either side of the V. (If you were making a W instead of an M you would add wider wedges.) Add the final two black sides and the letter is

Millefiori and Mosaic Cane

completed. If you were to try and pull the bundle at this point, it would try to round up the edges, so add enough extra background color around the letter to ensure that it will pull uniformly. Now add a punty to the other side of the letter. Since letters are fairly small, you can get by using just a maria (a flattened gather on the end of a rod) made on a clear rod. You want clear so that you can see what you are doing. If you want to maximize the amount of usable letter cane, then you should burn off the original rod and add a clear maria on that side also. The get the bundle hot, remove it from the flame and pull it out.

The partial curved letters and the closed curved letters are really done pretty much the same except that you have curved surfaces to contend with. For this example, let's look at one of the harder ones, an S. Here you pick one of the central loops as a place to start. You make a shape to correspond to this out of background color. You next coat this about three quarters of the way around with black. If you were to stop at this point you would have a C or with a little shaping a U or a J. You should start to see how a lot of the letters are very similar. Next you add a thick stripe of background down below this. Then you carry the outside of the S around this background loop and the S is complete. Of course you want to fill in around it prior to pulling so that you keep the proper shape and add clear rods with marias on them so that you get a maximum amount of usable letter cane out of this pull.

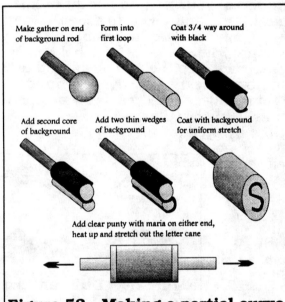

Figure 53. Making a partial curve letter cane.

Figuring out how to do the rest of the letters will be left as an exercise for you. Most of them will be pretty obvious. The B is a little bit difficult. I find it best to start with the flat side first, lay on one background stripe, cover it with black then lay on the other background stripe, cover it with more black and a little shaping work to finish.

Advanced mosaic images — faces

In any mosaic image you always start out by planning the individual subcomponents that you will need to construct ahead of time to make up your image. In this case, these components will consist of the eyes, the nose and the mouth. I will discuss each of these in turn and then describe how you combine them to make a mosaic facial image.

So let's start with a discussion of construction of eye cane. Look at an eye. From inside outward it consists of several parts: the pupil, the iris, the white, the eyelids, the lashes and some surrounding flesh. Each of these subcomponents can be made as simply or as complex as you want. The pupil can be a simple black dot, it could have a dash of white to simulate a reflection of light or in the limit it could even have a small image of something that it is looking at. The iris can be a single color like blue or you could try to show all the ribbing if its ligament substructure. The white can be just that or it could be the eye of the typical glass artist who has been up all night working with a complex bloodshot look. The lids can be thin or really baggy. Eye lashes can be represented by a single line or by any of a number of variations where you try to show the structure of the individual lashes. From this, you can see what I mean when I say that an image can be kept simple or made very complex.

With this in mind, the eye that I will discuss constructing here will be relatively simple. As I describe its construction, I will hearken back to some of the general principles presented earlier. Start out with a simple black pupil. (If you want something more complex, you will have to make a sub-subcomponent with the image you desire.) Warm up the desired one and a half inches on the end of the rod in your non-dominant hand. Pick up the iris color with your dominant hand and use it to case the pupil with the iris color. For a simple iris this involves just applying several lengthwise casing coats of the appropriate color. Use a bold color like a dark blue not a pale one. Remember to keep the end clean and to smooth out that layer before moving on to the next layer. As you build up the iris, be aware that most of the time, unless the eyes are wide open in surprise, that you will not see them as being circular. They are usually clipped at the top and the bottom by eyelids.

Next the white of the eye is added to either side of the iris to establish the basic eye shape. Remember that this basic eye shape, as illustrated simply in Figure 54, may very with either nationality of the person that you are trying to portray or the emotion with which you are trying to show them. Once you have this basic eye shape established by the addition of the white, it makes it all the more distinct if you apply a very thin coating of black all the way around the exterior of the eye shape.

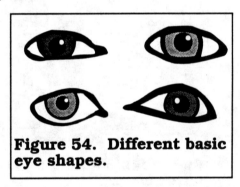

Figure 54. Different basic eye shapes.

Before doing this, you may want to transfer the bundle onto a pyrex punty if you have not already done so. If you do transfer it to a pyrex punty at this time, make sure that whatever end faces out away from the punty carries a clear image of the construction to guide your work. This usually means holding the bundle with a tweezers and burning of the rod handle and reattaching that same end to the punty. If you want to get as much as possible good mosaic cane pulled from the bundle, you may want to add a little glob of any color glass (although clear glass is preferred) to that end in which to embed the punty. Then you firmly implant the punty into this glob by getting the glass hot, sticking the warm punty into the glob and rocking it back and forth as well as side to side about 45°. This attaches glass from the glob up the side of punty forming a good strong joint. Lastly pull out slightly on the punty to get a tapered transition.

Millefiori and Mosaic Cane

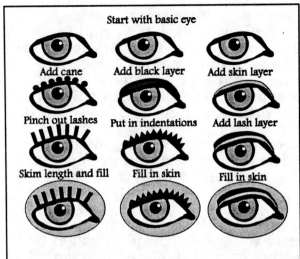

Figure 55. Some basic eyelash treatments.

With the mosaic eye construction now firmly attached to the punty, we are ready to continue on with an eyelid and eyelash treatment for the upper portion of the eye. The eyelid will usually be at most just a thin layer of flesh, but you might try varying its thickness for effect. The three different eyelash treatments that I will discuss are shown in Figure 55. The first allows making very large exaggerated lashes. Here you add some narrow stripes of black to the top of the thin layer of black around the eye shape was added last and squish them into tall thin ridges. A mini-masher is the ideal tool to use for this task. At this point the tops of the lashes are probably uneven. You can even them out by heating the tops slightly and then skimming off the top evenly with your black rod. Now fill in between the lashes with some super hot flesh colored glass and you are finished. The second lash treatment is to apply a thicker layer of black to the top of the eye and then use a graphite shaper to push little grooves into this layer which you then backfill with flesh color. The third lash treatment is to give a thin European eyelash. To achieve this first apply a thin crescent shaped upper eyelid that is thinned to almost nothing on either end. Then apply a thin layer of black over this lid.

At this point, the eye is really pretty much complete, but if you were to stretch it out, it would distort badly because of the large changes in cross section. So you want to add some extra flesh color around the image to at least make it an oval shape. Once this is done, build up a cap of clear glass on either end of the bundle that goes all the way out to the edge of the bundle. This will allow an even pull of the whole cross section of the bundle and will maximize the amount of usable cane that you get out of the bundle when you stretch it. If you don't add these caps you can end up pulling out the center of the bundle and having the outside pull inward unevenly at different sections of the cane. Clear glass is the best choice for these end caps for two reasons. First it is the cheapest color and second it allows you to see the image underneath the end cap. This allows you see what you are doing as you stretch out the bundle. You can imagine what the final face cane might look like if the eye cane inadvertently got twisted as you stretched it out.

Now as soon as you attach a second punty to the other end cap, you are ready to stretch out the bundle. Remember to firmly attach that punty to the end cap as before by rocking it back and forth and side to side after inserting it. Next evenly heat the bundle out in the far end of your flame. As you may remember, this area has a cooler and softer flame. Make sure that you evenly heat the bundle, applying the flame not just to the barrel of the bundle but also to the ends and the end caps. As it heats up you can monitor progress by wiggling slightly on the punty to feel if it is ready to pull. As you are heating the bundle up, it helps to remove the bundle from the flame occasionally to allow the heat to sink in and prevent the outside from getting too far ahead of the inside. Large thermal gradients in the bundle can result in uneven pulls. Once the bundle feels right, bring it out of the flame and gently stretch it out. If you hold the thick end up as you gently pull and wiggle the bundle, you can use gravity to good advantage. After the stretched cane has hardened, it can be cut up into manageable lengths (1½ to 2") for further assembly. Depending upon the diameter of the pulled cane, you may have to immediately stick it into an annealer to prevent it from thermal shocking. This should probably be done with any cane over one half inch in diameter.

There are time when you may want a variable thickness, or at the very least, sections of different thicknesses to your pull. One place might be letters where you will want to put together ones of similar size to make words. Since it is very hard to consistently pull them to the same size, it is easier to pull variable sizes and the match sections of similar size when you build them up into words. For faces there is also some size relationship between the features that will look more natural looking.

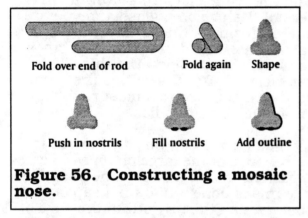

Figure 56. Constructing a mosaic nose.

We are finally ready to move on to construction of the nose. Noses tend to be the most difficult part of the face to get right, mainly just because of their shape. For the simple nose, shown in Figure 56, start out by heating up about an inch and a half of flesh colored rod and fold it over on itself. Heat that up and fold it over again to get a T-like cross sectional shape. Smooth and shape this construction using heat, shapers and mashers to get the basic nose-like shape. Get the bottom hot and use your shaper to push in two indentations to form the nostrils. Lay a thick black line into each of these indentations. Then apply a thin black coating about half way around the nose as shown to get the shadowing effect seen when light is shining on one side of the face. In preparation for pulling this bundle, it will again have to be built up into at least an oval shape by adding extra base flesh color. Then pull as before by adding end caps to punties and heating the bundle up uniformly. Anneal the resulting cane as necessary.

The last major component of the face to be made is the mouth. Begin with a gather of red that you squash and then square up to form the start of the upper lip as shown in Figure 57. After that push in the top of the center with your shaper and marver it some on either edge. Next apply a coat of black or white to the bottom of the lip (or both) depending upon what type of expression you are trying to convey. The white, to represent teeth, is usually applied a little thicker then the black, used to accent lip separation is. Apply another thick coat of red to the bottom of this to represent the lower lip. Marver it together and shape somewhat

Millefiori and Mosaic Cane   121

to a point at either end.
What you really want though
is a sharper end than you
can get by mavering. To get
this sharp edge, heat up one
edge and pull it out to a
point with some tweezers or
a pliers and cut it off at the
appropriate spot. Repeat on
the other side.

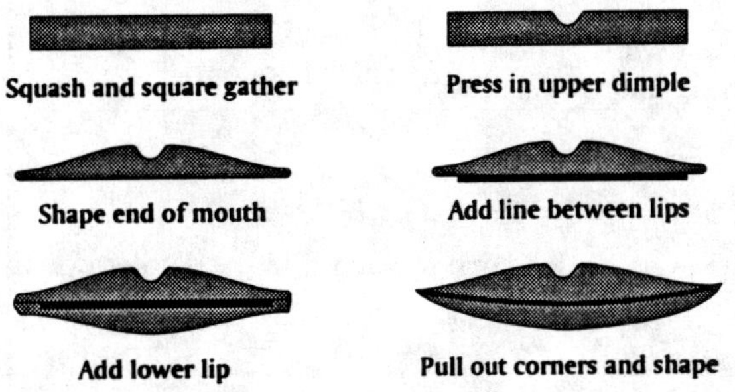

Now you want to shape your
mouth into a smile or a

Figure 57. Making a mosaic mouth.

frown by lightly heating the edges and shaping them with a paddle. In
preparing your bundle for stretching, you have to next cover it up with
surrounding skin color. Start by covering the delicate exposed ends of
the mouth so that they don't melt down as you apply the rest of the
glass. Then fill the valley at the top of the mouth and finally the rest of
the surrounding flesh. Before adding too much flesh, you might want to
consider whether you may be adding a mustache or beard. Once you
have your oval built up around the mouth, again add your end caps,
punties and pull away. When stretching out this bundle into cane, try to
keep in mind the size of the eyes and nose components that you have
already constructed and stretch it to the appropriate size to match.

At this point, you are finally ready to start assembling all of your
components into a completed face. When assembling mosaic
components into a larger image there are a number of things that must
be considered. First, it helps if the component parts are not too small in
diameter — 3/16" or larger in diameter is desired. Otherwise they heat
up too fast when introduced into the flame and are hard to control.
Pieces larger than about a 3/8" in diameter should be preheated in an
annealer prior to assembly to avoid thermal shock. Pieces smaller than
this can generally be successfully preheated on the fly in the outer end of
the flame without mishap. Remember to always start near the center of
your image and work outward. When bringing hot components together,
do not touch them until they are exactly where you want them.
Otherwise they may get stuck in an unintended orientation.

So punty up what will be the center of the face, the nose. Hold the
mouth up to the bottom of the nose and decide if extra flesh or a
mustache is need to space them correctly relative to each other. If so,
add a little to the bottom of the nose. Then heat up this area to soften it
and preheat the mouth. Attach the mouth to the nose by touching them
together at the far edges and slowly closing the two together like the
blades on a scissors until they are attached along their whole length.
This is done in this manner to ensure that they are correctly aligned
down the whole length of the bundle. Any valleys between them now
need to be filled with flesh colored glass. Continue adding this facial
color to build up the shape of the face from the chin to the cheek line —
approximately half way up the nose, as shown in Figure 58. The facial
color layers are added in thin coats applied very hot to keep control of
the shape as you build it up. Marver as necessary, remembering to do
one section at a time.

© 1996 James Kervin

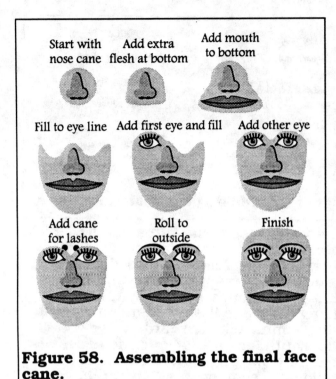

Figure 58. Assembling the final face cane.

Make two grooves with your graphite shaper on the cheek line, one on either side of the nose, in which to set your premade eye cane. Check out the groove to see that they are level and at the correct position. Trial fit the eye cane, without actually touching it to the bundle. Check to see that it looks orientated correctly. If okay, proceed on; otherwise, modify the cheek line and the grooves as necessary to properly position and receive the eye cane. When ready, get the groove hot and prewarm the eye cane. Scissors it into the groove as was done with the nose and the mouth cane. Fill any voids between the eye and the cheek with flesh color. Also apply a thin layer of flesh color over the eye but not too much so that it interferes with where the eyebrow needs to be placed. Now attach the other eye cane in its groove in a similar manner. Shape the face as necessary. Make a slight valley down the center of the forehead to allow for the eyebrows by pushing down in the center with your shaper and rolling it to the outside. In preparation for making the eyebrows, take a second to contemplate their shape. They are thicker near the nose and thinner at the side of the face. To get this effect apply a stripe on the inside of one of the two humps that you just created but not over the nose. Then heat up the stripe and roll over it with your shaper from the inside to the outside to give it this tapered look. Repeat this on the other side of the face. Now fill in the forehead with facial color.

At this point, we can either go on to add hair and other features to the face, or stop and stretch out this basic facial shaped bundle. Stopping and stretching it out to thick cane would allow using this basic face cane to make a number of similar faces with different colors of hair, hats, etc. that we add later. The face could be reshaped slightly each time to give it a little more or less angular appearance. When pulled small, you may not even be able to tell that they were made with the same basic face cane.

Advanced cane techniques

The face cane, whose construction I have just described, has a relatively basic image lacking a lot in color gradation and depth of image. I have already discussed how you can make it a little more complicated by making further more detailed subcomponents but there is another technique that will allow you to add more realism to your images. It will

Millefiori and Mosaic Cane   123

allow addition of things like a rosy color to the cheeks. First you need to blend a number of related facial colors using the techniques for blending colors that was discussed in the chapter on glass. The Moretti palette itself is just too limited to allow developing a gradation of color in your images. What you really need is like twenty different variations of flesh color to be able to develop a more natural looking portrait cane. So go back to that section, review it and blend some colors.

Once you have a variety of facial colors, you are now ready to plan out how you will use them to construct a more natural looking image. As an example, look at Figure 59 to

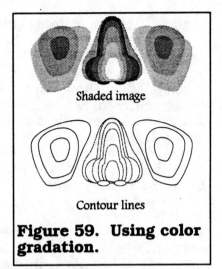

Figure 59. Using color gradation.

see how you might use gradation of color to construct a more natural image of a nose. In this image the top surfaces of the nose are lighter colored flesh and you apply gradations of color as you go from this top surface to lower ones. One way that might help you to understand this is to think of the image like a topographic map with altitude contour lines. The area between lines of adjacent altitudes is colored with the same color. Thus for the image of the nose, you would start with the brightest color being the central bridge and tip of the nose. You would then work your way outward adding thin layers of slightly darker flesh colored glass. Using this approach, you have to keep track of the edge facial color of each construction so that the components will flow well from one to the next. To better understand gradation of color, you might want to go to a museum and examine some of the work of the great masters.

The previous technique is still not the best that can be achieved. By studying the work of the classical mosaic cane master, Giacomo Franchini, Loren Stump came to realize that Giacomo was even going beyond the addition of multiple color layers because he could not see the dividing lines between the different colors as he could with the work of others such as Luigi Moretti. By experimentation, Loren realized the besides developing a large color palette with formulations of many color variations that Giacomo appeared to be blending the colors further as he applied them so that he got gradual color variations such as those seen in paintings. In trying to duplicate this effect, Loren found that if he heated the surface of the bundle as he painted on the next color with stringers and worked it into the surface, that he was able to blend the applied color with that beneath it. Then by doing this with successive color additions, he could get the proper variation that he was looking for. One thing that is necessary though, because you are applying cane to a hot surface, is frequent reshaping of that surface to ensure that you are not distorting your image. This is the type of technique that distinguishes the true master of mosaic cane construction.

Other mosaic cane ideas

There are many other ways that mosaic cane can be used beyond letter and portrait cane. Figure 60 shows some ideas that you could try. Many bead artists are into making aquarium or underwater scene beads because glass lends itself to that look. The fish and other denizens of the deep can be fabricated and embedded into these beads. They can be applied over ocean, coral, seaweed, etc. backgrounds. Build up of multiple layers could allow an increased feeling of depth by applying more fish and seaweed cane. You can also add bubbles coming up from the fish by poking little indentations into the bead surface and trapping air as will be discussed later.

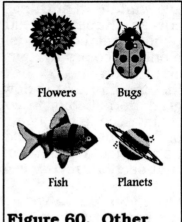

Figure 60. Other mosaic cane ideas.

But why stop with aquarium beads. You could make animal cane of all kinds and build them up to make forest or jungle beads. There you would use rocks, trees and bushes for background and increased depth of image in your beads. You could also use your animal cane to make zoo beads with animals in cages or circus beads with them performing tricks. You could use them in religious themes like having them around a manger or walking up the gang plank of an ark.

Another good image choice would be insect cane that could be applied to beads with internal flowers. Bees and butterfly cane would be the perfect images to go with this type of application.

Of course, once you have portrait cane, why not continue on to make whole figures. Then you can go into comic or story book beads. Watch out for copyright violations. Bible stories might really be popular and you don't have to worry about copyrights there. You could put these figures into other objects like Loren Stump puts people into his cars. Why not people inside of houses, cottages or peeking through portholes.

And why stop with earthly things. Why not go on to build whole new worlds in your beads as Josh Simpson builds them into his marbles. You could make mountains and volcanic canes to add to such images. Or continue on out into space where you can have planet, star, spaceship or constellation cane. Once you have mastered basic cane manufacture, the sky is the limit.

Suggested further reading

Bruhn, Jutta-Annette. Designs in Miniature: The Story of Mosaic Glass, The Corning Museum of Glass, 1995

Sarpellon, Giovanni. Miniature Masterpieces Mosaic Glass 1838-1924 (translated from Italian by Corning Museum of Glass) Prestal-Verlag, 1995

Wound beads

We are now ready to delve into the first of the beadmaking techniques to be discussed in this book, that of mandrel wound beads. This technique is probably the easiest for the novice to master and requires no more than a basic torch setup and the flameworking skills that we have already discussed.

Basic techniques for wound beadmaking

The basic technique of wound beadmaking consists of winding molten glass around specially prepared mandrels whose removal forms the hole in the bead. These beads are shaped using tools and the heat of the torch. They can then be decorated using the constructions that we discussed in the last chapter as well as many other techniques.

Preparing for winding

There are very few special preparations required to get ready for making wound beads beyond preparing a space for flameworking as has been described earlier and possibly making some constructions with which to decorate your beads.

The main thing that needs to be prepared before winding beads is the stainless steel winding mandrels that you are making from TIG filler rod. The first thing that you will need to do is to cut them into about 12" lengths. Next you will want to grind or file any burrs off the ends so that the beads will be able to easily slip off of them. I grind mine all the way around on each end. Be sure to also grind off the stock numbers that can sometimes be found on TIG filler rods.

Now you have to coat the winding mandrels with a separator compound. Many bead makers use a kaolin-based formula similar to kiln shelf separator. Several different formulations are available commercially or you can mix your own. One easy-to-make formula consists of a 40/40/20 solids' mix by volume of kaolin clay, alumina hydrate and whiting. Premix the dry ingredients. They are then mixed with water to about the consistency of thick pancake batter. This mixture should sit for about a day to allow complete rehydration of the alumina hydrate. You may want to always have some mixed up to the consistency of a thick paste that you can then thin down as needed so you do not have to wait for rehydration. Some artists add a couple drops of sodium silicate solution to this mix to act as a fluxing agent. If you find that your beads

© 1996 James Kervin

126   Glass Beadmaking

are not releasing well from the mandrel when using this recipe, decrease the kaolin clay/alumina hydrate ratio or add a little powdered graphite. If on the other hand the release layer is too fragile, increase this ratio. Instead of alumina hydrate, some artists use 200 mesh or finer flint. The Japanese typically use a 30/70 mix of porcelain clay to volcanic ash. Another option is to use commercial kiln shelf mixes. Zircon graphite also works well as a separator compound and is being marketed under the names of "Sludge" or "Super Sludge." It tends to dry quicker than clay based washes. (You can almost go directly into the flame with it.) I also find it to be very durable and produces a lot fewer bubbles.

Mix whatever separator formulation you choose to the consistency of thick pancake batter in a container that you can cap to prevent it from thickening by water loss. One type of container that works well is those long thin olive jars available in grocery stores. They allow more of your mandrel to get coated when you dip one end of the winding mandrel into the separator solution without having to have a large volume of separator mixed up. With a longer coating of separator on your mandrel, you have the option of winding multiple beads on one mandrel as you get better or of making one bead on the end and then a second in the middle at a later time after removing the first bead. This also allows you the option of winding your bead on the center of your mandrel. Some artists like this because it allows them to hold the mandrel on either end so they can come in from all angles as they work on complex beads. The coating on the mandrel should have some visible thickness to it (at least 1/32nd of an inch). Allow the mandrel to air dry before use.

When drying, the coating should not be touching anything. I find that splaying them out, coated end up, in a tin can works well. Other artists I know stick them in sand or polystyrene foam to hold them upright. Do whatever is easiest for you. Preferably you should let the mandrels dry overnight. If you do not have that much time, let it dry for a few minutes and then try passing it through a bushy flame to dry. If you can get it to dry without popping or cracking the separator coating, it should be safe to use. If your coating is not thick enough on the first dip, you can dip the mandrel a second time after the first dip dries. Some artists advocate this, but for most purposes I prefer a smaller diameter hole in my beads and find one dip to be sufficient. If I want a larger hole, I use larger diameter mandrels.

The other thing that you want to do before you get started making beads is to clean your glass rods. They sometimes get an oil film on them that can discolor your work. Use isopropyl alcohol to clean off the oil. A convenient thing to have around is one of those hospital alcohol dispensers where you just push down on the top of the dispenser with a towelette to moisten the towelette with alcohol. Be aware that alcohol vapors can flash into flame if they come into contact with the flame. So if you want something to clean with at your bench you may want to try something like ammonia instead because it is non-flammable although slightly more toxic. Note that as you consume the glass rod with which you have been working, you will reach the area of the rod where you have been holding it and will have to clean it on the fly. For this reason you will want some cleaning material available at your bench even if it is only a dry cloth.

© 1996 James Kervin

Wound Beads

Winding a bead

Start by preheating the winding mandrel slightly. You don't have to get it too hot; just warm it to get rid of water and stick it in the back of your flame. Take a glass rod and develop a gather on the end of it. Then wind the molten glass from the gather onto the mandrel. Do this by adding the glass from the feed rod, which you are holding in your right hand in the pencil mode (assuming that you are right handed), through the flame onto the winding mandrel which is just beneath the flame. Try to make sure that this gather can make a complete loop around the winding mandrel before starting. Wind it onto the mandrel by rotating the mandrel away from you at a rate at which the glass is able to flow evenly from the feed rod onto the mandrel. Start this first wrap going perpendicular to the mandrel.

Once you make it completely around the mandrel, you will have to angle the rod to start a helical spiral of glass along the mandrel. To help ensure a good smooth end it helps to give just a little push at the end, of the first loop to squeeze the air out and push the glass together.

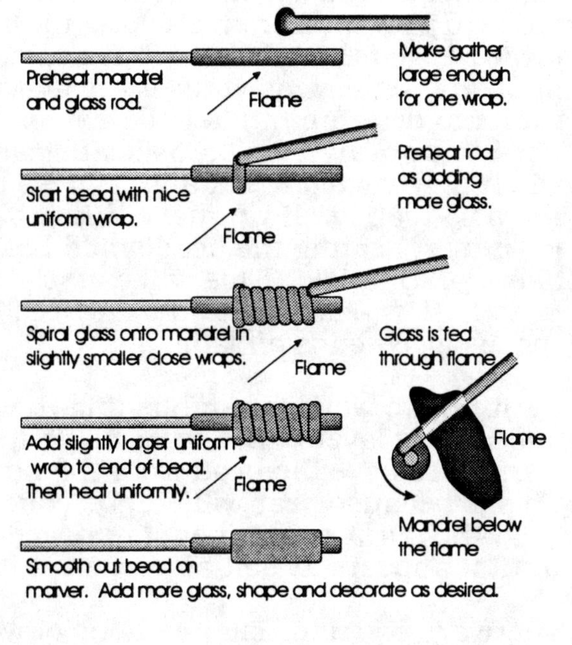

As you add glass to the spiral, remember to keep the bead below the flame and the feed rod in it. Also be sure to rotate the feed rod counterclockwise in your pencil grip to keep uniformly heating the rod around its circumference. Otherwise the feed rod will be less viscous (stiffer) on one side of the rod and can exert enough pull on the bead to break the separator coating. This can also be prevented by rocking the rod back and forth if you find rotating too difficult of a hand motion. Make sure that you do not let the glass touch any bare, uncoated sections, of the mandrel or the glass will stick to it. If this happens, you will not be able to remove the bead without cracking it. A small bead may require only two or three wraps of glass. Others may require many more layers. The wall thickness of your beads should never be less than the thickness of your mandrel (of course this rule of thumb must be used with a grain of salt when you are winding large pieces like bracelets, rings, etc.).

Figure 61. Winding a bead on a mandrel.

When adding glass to the mandrel, pay special attention to the first and last wrap to make sure that you apply a uniform wrap all the way around the mandrel. This will help prevent your beads from getting jagged ends. During the rest of the application apply the glass smoothly in a close spiral as seen in Figure 61 to prevent trapping bubbles between the

128　　Glass Beadmaking

wraps. Push down slightly on the mandrel with the glass to ensure that the glass flows into any undercuts on the previous coil and slightly overlap them. Remember to hold the feed rod no closer than about two thirds of the way out in the flame so that you do not overheat the glass. If you do overheat it, the result will be many bubbles both large and small on your glass rod and subsequently into your bead. Remember also to keep rotating your mandrel just like you did glass rods when gathering so that you keep the bead centered on the mandrel instead of drooping off of it. Although you can also use drooping to good advantage when trying to recenter a bead that may have gone awry.

As you add glass to the mandrel, establish the length of the bead on the first layer. Make this layer slightly shorter than what you want for your finished bead. Also add a little more glass on the ends of the bead for marvering over as shown in Figure 61. Then marver it out to final size to get a nice round edged thread hole. Try not to overheat this first layer in order to prevent it from sticking to the mandrel or forming those dreaded jagged edged thread holes that can cut the bead stringing thread. This happens because as you get the glass hotter, it reduces in viscosity and wants to draw up into a ball, leaving thin ends on the mandrel. Artists used to working with borosilicate glass may have a problem with this when they switch to soda-lime glass because it is so much softer and flows so readily. If you have this problem, don't panic. You can correct for it by reheating the bead while holding the mandrel tilted down at about a 30° angle. This will cause some of the glass in the body of the bead to flow back out to the end. Of course if all else fails you can grind those jagged ends off later.

Continue to work at establishing the general shape of the bead on each succeeding layers. Be aware as you are shaping the bead, that you may want to remove the bead from the heat before it gets as soft as you want. This is because heat will still be conducting into the center of the bead from the surface after being removed from the flame. Thus if you wait until it appears as soft as you want it, it may get too soft on you.

There are two alternate methods of winding beads that insure nice rounded bead ends, not sharp ones, of which I am aware. These two techniques are illustrated in Figure 62. The first consists of winding a disk about your mandrel and then slowly heating the disk so that it gathers in on itself to form a nice rounded bead. Avoid overheating the disk so much that the glass wicks out onto the mandrel. The second technique involves adding glass to the end of your bead up away from the mandrel so that it looks like a disk at the end of your bead. Then through the use of heat from your torch and some light rolling of the bead on your marver, this glass will roll over to extend the body of your bead. This will also leave a nice rounded end.

To aid in holding your winding mandrel steady while heating your bead in the flame, you can fashion a tool to hold the rounded end of your mandrel up. This can be something as simple as putting a small indentation in your graphite paddle in which to stick the end of the mandrel, or you can purchase one of Jim Smircich's "tail stock holders." Here he is making a comparison to a lathe where you have a motor at the jaws and a non-powered holder at the tail. This tool has a ball at one

© 1996 James Kervin

end to slide on your bench and a flat with an indentation on the other end in which to stick the end of the mandrel. The length of the tool is about the height of the flame at the proper working distance from your flame. You can easily make a tool like this yourself.

Sometimes while winding a bead, you may trap air between the wraps and form a bubble. This weakens your bead and is unsightly in transparent glass beads. In order to bring a bubble to the surface to try and get rid of it, get the bead soft by heating the bubble region. Then push on the glass next to the bubble with your tweezers to try and force it to the surface. Once on the surface, chill the top of the bubble by touching your tweezers to it. Then reheat the bubble to get it to pop. To fill in the void left by the bubble, it is best to evenly heat the bead and allow the surrounding glass to flow into the void rather then trying to add glass to the void. Adding glass on top of a popped bubble invariably results in trapping more air to form another bubble.

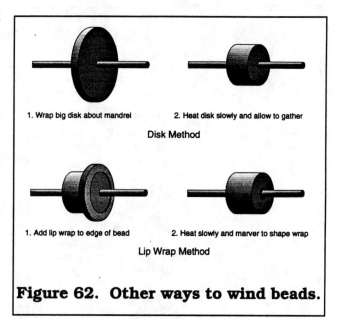

Figure 62. Other ways to wind beads.

Shaping a bead

Beads, unless they are small ones which contract into roughly the shape that you want during a thorough reheating after wrapping, will require some handworking to form them into shape. Appendix A illustrates a number of common shapes for beads that you may want to try making.

Handworking of a bead into a regular shape is accomplished primarily through marvering. As discussed earlier, marvering can be accomplished on a number of different surfaces. What is generally used in beadmaking are small graphite paddles because they will shape and absorb the heat of the bead without discoloring it. There are also specialized paddles made for beadmaking that have grooves and cut outs in them to develop different bead shapes. These include spheres, cylinders, tear drops, etc.

To marver a bead, get it soft but not runny. Remove it from the flame and allow it to cool for a couple of seconds while continuing to rotate the mandrel so the bead does not droop. Then shape it on the marver. Apply very light pressure as you first roll the bead on the marver when the bead is really soft and then increase pressure as the glass hardens. As an example of shaping beads on a marver let's discuss making a torpedo bead (a long biconic shape). As seen in Figure 63, you first roughly shape the bead by adding a few layers of glass. Then heat either the right or the left cone and start shaping by rolling the bead on the marver at the correct angle. Try not to groove the separator compound as this may cause the bead to break free of the mandrel. After this first

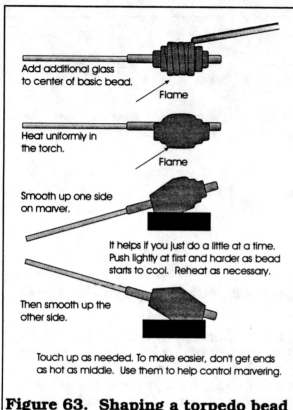

Figure 63. Shaping a torpedo bead on the marver.

rough shaping of the bead, concentrate on refining the shape at the apex of the cone by only heating the top two thirds of the cone. Once you have got this end to the desired shape, concentrate on the base portion of the cone by only heating the bottom two thirds of the cone and rolling the bead on the marver on the apex of the cone. Then repeat this process on the other side.

From this example, you see that part of the trick in marvering a bead into shape is not trying to do it all at once. It is important not to get the bead too soft or it will flow too fast and may tend to form folds as you roll it on the marver. Overheating may also result in a sharp edge around your thread holes as the glass on the ends wicks out onto the mandrel. Instead, try to go little by little for better control of the process. Also as you shape your bead and later as you decorate it, remember to reheat the whole bead every once in a while to prevent one section from getting so cool that it thermal shocks as you move it back into the flame to continue work on it.

Besides rolling of a bead on the marver to create beads with round cross sectional shapes, you can also marver flat surfaces into a bead. Using this technique you can create shapes like rectangular solids and cubes. To do this, just get the bead soft and press it down on the marver with your paddle. This forms two flat surfaces at the same time. Then flip the bead a quarter turn and press again. You can flatten the end of the bead by pressing it on the end of the marver.

Another way to shape beads is to pinch them using pliers. As described earlier, a mashing pliers can be used to mash the glass into a disk shape. Mashing pliers may also have textured surfaces to add another design element to your beads. You can use needle-nosed piers to reach in and pinch fins or ridges into your bead, as will be discussed in greater detail later, or use them to stretch out sections of the bead. Texture can also be introduced onto the surface of your bead by marvering it on a textured surface. Parallel grooved and diamond patterned graphite marvers are commercially available to use for this process as illustrated in Figure 64. You can also use things like files or wire brushes to introduce interesting surface textures.

To get other interesting surface shapes into your beads, you try pressing them into dies that you have carved out of graphite, or press things like leather dies into them while the bead is still hot and soft. This will also be discussed in a little greater detail later.

Finishing the bead

Once you are finished shaping and decorating your bead, flame anneal it and put it in the heated

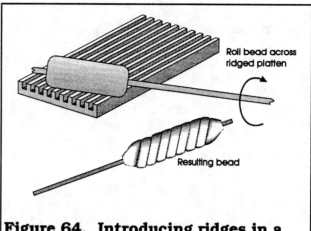

Figure 64. Introducing ridges in a wound bead.

vermiculite to cool gradually. After you are through for the day, turn off the burner under the pan of vermiculite. When it has cooled to the touch (about a half hour), you can remove the beads from the vermiculite and take them off the mandrels. Instead of using vermiculite, some artists prefer to directly insert their beads into an annealing kiln that they have sitting on their bench. This also allows them to be able to preheat rods and decorations prior to use. It alleviates the use of vermiculite which as we discussed, some glass bead artists are starting to worry about because of its close physical structure to asbestos.

To take a bead off the rod, grasp the center of the mandrel with a pliers in one hand and the bead with your other hand. Twist the bead to break it free from the separator compound and the winding mandrel underneath it. Continue to gently twist the bead all the way off the mandrel. You can clean out some of the separator compound by inserting an appropriately sized drill bit into the bead hole and twisting it to remove some of the separator. (There are also bead hole cleaning reamers, twisted wires and brushes being marketed for this purpose.) Be careful as you do this because it is easy to crack your beads if the drill bit is too large. I find that just sliding the bead back and forth on the mandrel before you take it off also helps to clean the hole. Since some of the separator compounds may be slightly toxic, you may want to wear a respirator with a dust cartridge when you are cleaning out the beads. Clean them directly over your trash container and dispose of the powder properly after you are done. Clean up any powder with a wet towelette. Some artists even recommend that you clean out the separator compound under water.

If you have any sharp ends on your beads, they need to be removed so that they will not cut the cord on which you string them. The sharp edges can be removed by using a diamond grinder or by rubbing them back and forth on a file. Dressing tools in the form of a small diamond coated sphere mounted on a shaft and inset into a handle are now commercially available to help with this task. Of course the real solution is not to make any sharp edges in the first place and eventually as your skill level improves, you should not have any more of these sharp edges. Lastly you need to kiln anneal your beads as is discussed later.

© 1996 James Kervin

132　　Glass Beadmaking

Decorating wound beads

There are many different ways to decorate wound beads. We will start out by discussing simple decorations like frit and dots. From there, we will move on to trailing on colors and how to rake and distort these decorations. Remember to rewarm your bead every once in a while to prevent thermal shock.

Frit and enamels

One of the first techniques for the beginner to learn for decorating beads is picking up frit off a marver. This can create interesting random patterns of color and provide instant success to the novice bead maker. For this technique, spread out a single color or a pleasing array of colored frit on your marver. Get your basic bead tacky hot in the flame (just starting to glow) and roll it in the frit on the marver. The bead will pick up some of the frit, more if the marver is being warmed on a hot plate or by your torch. Return the bead to the flame and reheat it to get the surface texture that you want. This can vary anywhere from smooth, where you heat and marver all the frit into the bead, to sandy, where the frit is just barely bonded to the bead.

A commercially available frit that gives a different effect when applied to the surface of your beads is called reduction frit. It is so called because the metal oxide colorants in this frit easily break down in a reducing environment to form a metallized layer on the surface of the glass. This frit is usually made from relatively compatible Kugler glass (COE $\cong$ 90) and should be applied relatively thinly. It is available in different grinds from a fine powder to coarse granules.

Besides frit you can also roll your beads in enamel powders or frit. After all enamels are just ground glass also. Here you will have to ensure that the enamel is compatible with the base glass of your bead. Kate Fowle did a study on the compatibility of Thompson enamels with Moretti glass. She found that some of the opaque window glass series enamels appeared to be compatible and produced nice colors. The enamels are applied like the frit. If you want more information on this you can contact her.

Dots

Dots are added to a bead from a small gather on a rod by touching the gather to the bead and pulling it away. This leaves a small dot from the gather on the bead. During this process, the bead is kept warm just beneath the torch flame to ensure a good joint to the dot. The gather is touched through the flame onto the bead below and pulled back away through the flame. You are doing this through the flame to avoid stringers of glass from forming between the dot and the gather as you pull it away. If you are making big dots which could result in big stringers as you pull the rod away, you may have to wind the stringer up as you pull away with a slight circular motion of the hot rod.

© 1996 James Kervin

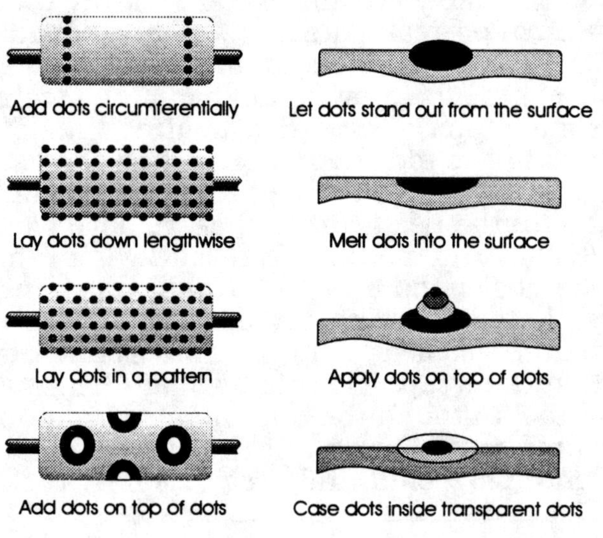

Wound Beads 133

You can control the size of your dots by the size of your gather, how lightly you touch the bead and the diameter of your rod. When using smaller diameter glass rods or canes to dot, you will want to dot the bead through the sides of the flame where the heat is less intense. Otherwise the cane will get fried up by the flame and just curl up into a ball.

You can make all sorts of patterns with your dots. They can be added randomly, in lines, squares, etc. You can control the surface texture

Figure 65. Decorating wound beads with dots.

of the dot by how much you reheat the bead after application. You can even pile dots on top of other dots or encase dots within clear dots as shown in Figure 65. These dots can also be decoratively distorted in a subsequent step as will be discussed later in this chapter.

Check to see that the joint between your dot and the surface of the bead are joined correctly. There should be no undercuts because this will allow the dots to break off at a later time. If there are undercuts, this is indicative of the fact that you are not keeping the surface of the bead warm enough as you add the dots.

Trailing

Trailing is the addition of decorative stripes from a gather onto a bead. To trail on a simple stripe around the circumference of a bead, start by warming your basic bead and developing a gather on a rod of the color that you want the stripe. Pull both up out of the flame and lightly touch the gather to the bead. Then slowly pull the gather away from the bead and spin the bead away from you at the same time. Since you are not pulling away through a flame as you did in making dots, you will get a stringer being pulled from the gather onto the bead. You need to pull away just slightly from the bead and twirl the bead quickly so as not to allow enough time for the stringer to cool so much that it will not attach to the bead. When you have gone all the way around the bead, pull the gather a little further from the bead. Then blow on the stringer and wiggle it back and forth to break it off at the surface of the bead or burn it off in the flame.

You want to make sure that the trailing is well attached to the surface all the way around the bead. Otherwise, when you introduce it back into the flame, it will expand and break off. To do this, lightly heat the trailing in the edge of the flame and marver as necessary to get it to

© 1996 James Kervin

attach. Take your time to do it slowly on delicate trailings because they can burn off really quickly if not attached. You may also have developed a little glob at the overlap of the wrap where the gather left the bead. This can be fixed by using one of two techniques. The first is to remove of some material by gently heating the dot till it starts to glow and touching the rod that you just had the gather on to the dot. The gather should have been allowed to cool some or you will deposit glass from the rod onto the bead rather than remove glass from the bead. When you pull away the rod, material that was in the glob on the bead will transfer to the cooler rod and pull away as a stringer. You may have to do this a couple time to make it look right. The other technique is to use the remaining cooled stringer on the rod left from trailing to stretch out the dot on the wrap. Do this by again heating the dot and using the stringer as a tool to touch the dot and stretch it out to complete the circumferential wrap. At the end of the pull let the stringer rest a second, blow on it and break it off by rocking it side to side.

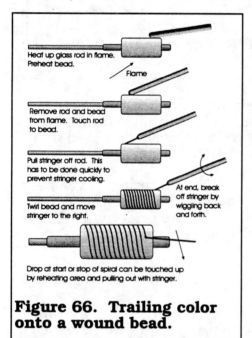

Figure 66. Trailing color onto a wound bead.

Another way that trailing is commonly used is to apply a spiraling line on a bead as illustrated in Figure 66. You do this almost exactly the same way as was done for the circumferential wrap. You start with a touch on one end of the bead. As you then pull the gather away from the bead and twirl it into a trail, you slowly move the gather along the length of the bead. At the end, you pull the gather away from the bead as before and break it off. The initial dot can be handled as before with the exception that if you decide to stretch it, you will stretch it in the direction to continue the spiral in the opposite direction. After application you work the spiral into the bead just like you did for the circumferential wrap.

Trailing can be can be varied in a number of ways. It can be added longitudinally. You can vary the width of the trail by how big the gather is and how fast you pull the trail from it. You can vary the spacing between the lines on spirals. You can apply multiple spirals or wraps of different colors. You can add a second spiral in the opposite direction to make a cross hatched pattern. You can also distort it as we will talk about next.

Distorting the bead surface (raking and twisting)

Sometimes you want to distort a pattern on the surface of the bead to achieve a different effect. There are two ways that a surface is generally distorted: by raking across it or by twisting it. Both of these are achieved through the same general technique. The surface of the bead is heated (note, only the surface has to be heated, not the whole bead down to the core). A tool, made by drawing a fairly sharp point from a glass rod of the same color as the surface feature you are trying to modify, is then used to distort the glass surface. You could also use a tungsten pick or a dental tool but the glass version is easier. If you do decide to use a pick or dental tool, chill it between applications in water to prevent glass from sticking to it. An advantage of the dental tool is that if it gets stuck in the bead, you can heat it up and pull it out without distorting the surface too much. One easy way to make a glass tool after spiraling a trail is to draw a little extra stringer from the gather and save it after breaking it free from the trail. Otherwise you will have to pull a point from the rod.

One thing that you need to be aware of as you distort the bead surface using these techniques is that the size of the effected area varies with the temperature of the glass. If the glass surface is fairly hot, the viscosity of the glass will be low and the tool will easily slide through the glass through only affecting a narrow region of the glass surface. As the surface cools somewhat, the area of the surface that is affected gets larger because the viscosity of the liquid glass increases and pulls more on the surrounding surface. As it cools even more and starts to get hard again, the surface becomes undistortable.

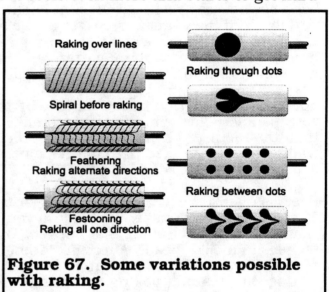

Figure 67. Some variations possible with raking.

The first technique for surface distortion to be discussed is called raking. In this method, you distort the surface of the bead by pulling a tool across the surface of the glass. You can rake though a number of different surface features. When done lengthwise across a trailed spiral a number of times in the same direction, the process is referred to as festooning. When you change direction on every other rake, it is called feathering and creates a distorted spiral as illustrated in Figure 67. Again raking is usually done by drawing a glass stringer of the same color as the surface decoration. Draw the point down the length of the bead and stop. Blow on the surface to solidify it and break the point free from the surface by wiggling it back and forth. It will usually break right at the surface. If not, use a tweezers to break the point off as near to the surface that you can. The rest can be removed by reheating what still remains, removing the bead from the flame, and pulling off the excess material by touching it with a cold rod. If you don't make it all the way down the length of the bead of the bead at one time, don't worry. Just break the point from the surface, rest the bead some to allow it to equilibrate, reheat the surface and finish the rake. The cooling step helps prevent the bead from getting too hot and globby. Figure 67 illustrates the effect of raking on a number of surface decorations like lines and dots.

Besides raking lengthwise down the bead, as shown in Figure 68, you can also rake circumferentially around the bead. This can be used to distort a latticino that has been wrapped around a bead as will be described later. The finished product will look something like that illustrated in Figure 68. When raking circumferentially around a bead, you have to be careful not to pull so hard on the bead that you break it free from the mandrel. This is easier to do when raking circumferentially than lengthwise because there is a shorter length of separator material to react to the force in that direction. The way to prevent this from happening is not to let the bead surface get too cool. Raking through dots can create heart like images. Raking between dots creates a paisley like effect. You also do not have to rake all the way across a surface. You can go just part way across as will be discussed when we make an eye decoration for a tableau bead.

Another way to distort a bead surface is, as was mentioned earlier, to twist it. To do this, get just the portion of the surface that you want to distort hot. Remove the bead from the flame. Then touch a point to the surface and twist it. Again release the point by blowing on it to freeze the bead surface and rocking the point back and forth to break it off at the surface. If it does break free right at the surface, handle the situation as was done for raking. When done in the center of an array of dots this process makes a nice spiral pattern as illustrated in Figure 68. When done on lines it makes the fancy loop pattern as shown.

You can also distort a bead's surface by marvering it with the edge of your paddle. This will give a chevron like effect that is a little different than that achieved by raking. Here you do not get as much of a line trailing behind a raked path to the point where you stop raking. Instead you get more of a zig zag effect because you are not digging into the bead.

Besides distortions created by raking or twisting, you can also create interesting distortions by poking into your bead. One interesting example of this technique that I observed recently was someone making poppies in a clear bead. After embedding a green stem in the bead and covering it with clear, they put a yellow dot on the bead surface. Then by getting the area hot, poking the area in and backfilling the poked in area with clear you end up with a flower. There are probably many variations on this technique that you could develop such as combining poking with twisting or poking into larger dots over smaller dots, multiple dots and pokings, etc.

It is also possible to make slight distortions of your bead surface without using any tools at all. This effect is achieved by using gravity to your advantage. Here you get your bead pretty hot and twirl it in the torch flame fast enough to keep

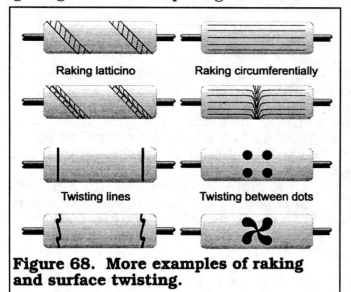

Figure 68. More examples of raking and surface twisting.

© 1996 James Kervin

Wound Beads   137

its shape but slow enough that gravity exerts a slight pull on the hotter side of the bead. This will result in an effect where lengthwise lines will take on a U like shape.

Major distortions of the surface

Sometimes you want to put something like raised ridges or swirls into your bead. These major distortions can be introduced through manipulation of the glass with tools like tweezers or pliers. They can be used to pinch ridges into your bead. After you have all the ridges pinched into the surface of the bead, they can be softened slightly by reheating the bead in the flame. Besides ridges, sharp pointed tweezers can be used to stick into the surface for indented pits or then twisted for spirals. The surface can also be stretched.

Pressing shapes into beads

One interesting technique for decorating simple beads is to stamp them with leatherworking dies. These dies are available in a variety of shapes and sizes. By combining different dies or by multiple stamping with a die, a number of designs can be achieved. When selecting a die, try to ensure that there are no undercuts in it so that you can avoid getting them trapped in the glass. If you are making multiple impressions of a die into one bead, it may be necessary to chill the die in a small container of water between stampings to avoid sticking to the glass. Try backfilling stamped surfaces with clear glass.

When you first purchase a die, it will probably have a rust resistant plating over the surface of the image. With use of this die on hot glass, you will find that this plating will be eroded away. This leaves your stamps open to possible rusting. To prevent this from happening, you should coat the surface of the die with oil by dipping or spraying it whenever they are going to be put away for some period of time. Then before using them the next time, clean off the oil with some degreasing agents like soap and water followed by alcohol.

Applying constructions

Surfaces of beads can also decorated with constructions or images that are made ahead time and are then applied while making the bead. To practice your flameworking skills, you have already made a number of constructions such as canes, latticino, ribbons, and murrine. Let's now discuss how these can be incorporated into your wound beads.

Canes

When applying canes to the surface of your beads, you have to be careful how much heat you expose them to. Because of their smaller diameter, canes heat up much faster than rods. Therefore you want to work them in a smaller flame or at the edge of your flame with just enough heat to soften them up. When applying canes as well as any other construction, you want to make sure both the bead attachment surface and construction attachment surface are both tacky hot as you bring them

© 1996 James Kervin

together. After attaching, check to see that you do not have undercuts, otherwise you may have to reheat the joint some with a sharp flame.

Canes can be applied to a bead in a number of ways. It can be applied circumferentially, lengthwise, spiraled, looped or swirled. A number of these orientations are illustrated in Figure 69. They may be left raised or marvered into the bead surface.

The applied cane can then be modified by raking, twisting, or marvering. Examples of these techniques have already been illustrated Figure 68. The first shows latticino that has been raked down its length. The second illustration shows a bead where cane was applied lengthwise and is then raked circumferentially. The third shows a circumferentially applied cane that was twisted.

Latticino

Applying latticino to a bead is very similar to applying cane. They are also small in diameter and can easily be overheated. They are usually applied on the edges of a flame with the bead slightly below the flame. The flame is positioned to heat the surface of the bead and the side of the latticino. As you touch the two surfaces together, you give the latticino a counterclockwise twist that not only twists the spiral on the latticino a little tighter for an enhanced effect, but it also brings the two preheated surfaces together. You can reheat the bead to get whatever final surface texture

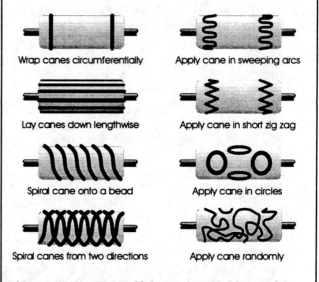

Figure 69. Possible orientations in which cane may be applied.

that you want for the latticino on the bead. I think latticino looks especially nice with some relief to them, so many times I will only lightly reheat them. If you are going to distort them somehow, you may want to marver them into the surface of the bead.

Some beadmakers tell me that they never spiral their latticino during construction but instead just pull it out straight like for compatibility testing. Then they do the spiraling when they apply the latticino to the bead. They claim that this technique gives them more control in construction and application. Try it and decide for yourself which you like.

Latticino are often added circumferentially on the ends of a bead for a decorative finish. It also looks good as spiral wraps on the face of the bead. Latticino once applied can be distorted by raking down the middle for a nice effect as illustrated in Figure 68.

Wound Beads

Ribbed cane floral decorations

Ribbed cane can be used in a number of ways to form floral decorations on your beads. The first, since it already looks like a flower in cross section, is to use large diameter cane like murrine as will be explained shortly. Alternatively for small diameter ribbed cane, you can prewarm the cane and the area to which it is to be applied, touch the cane to the surface of the bead, let it cool slightly, and then wiggle it back and forth to break it off at the surface of the bead. Then heat it to soften its edges. This will also display the cross sectional image of the cane.

Ribbed cane as shown in Figure 70 can also be applied hot in a number of other ways to take advantage of its color variation when viewed from the side. The first way is to get it hot, touch the surface of the bead, swirl the cane, burn it off and marver it to a slightly raised bump on the surface. This gives an appearance of something like a rose. Second, you can heat the end of the cane to form a small gather, touch the surface of the bead, and immediately push forward and pull back. This will give the appearance of a shell-like effect. The third technique is to again form a small gather, then touch the area that will be the center of the flower, pull outward and burn off the excess cane. This creates a flower with a pointed petal.

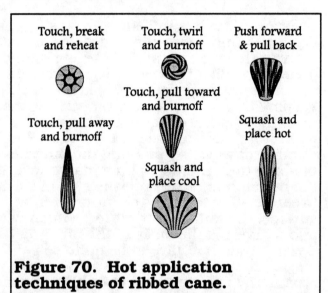

Figure 70. Hot application techniques of ribbed cane.

Alternatively if you touch the gather to what is the outside of the flower, pull inward and burn off the excess cane, you will form a flower with lightly rounded outer petals like a daisy. For the fifth technique, instead of applying the gather right away, squash it first to form a wide petal and then apply it relatively cool to the bead surface with the cane end to the center before burning off the excess cane. This can be used to construct a wide petaled flower like a tulip. Lastly, if the squashed gather is applied hot it can be used to form a more elongated rounded petal.

In all cases, the floral applications described above are then heated and either marvered into the bead surface or sculpted as desired. Then add green foliage as needed. This could also be made with ribbed cane.

Ribbons

Ribbons can also be applied in a number of ways. One is to attach it on end onto a bead, stretched out and shaped like flower petals. (Ribbon is also used in making sculpture beads like the fish beads that will be illustrated later.) Here you heat up the end of the ribbon and the attachment point on the bead. Next press the two together forming a slight bulge. Then gently pull on the ribbon to form a nice smooth joint

© 1996 James Kervin

140   Glass Beadmaking

with no undercuts. Heat up the end of the section to pull it out and shape it.

Another way to attach ribbon to a bead is along one side of the ribbon. This looks especially nice if you spiral the ribbon down the bead as you apply it. When doing this, you heat up the ribbon and attachment point as you go. At the same time, you have to heat up the ribbon some to bend it. Go a little at a time and make sure that the joint between the ribbon and the bead surface is good, otherwise you may find the ribbon rolling some on you as you proceed down the length of the bead. At the ends pull the ribbon down to a point at the surface.

Murrine

Before you apply a millefiori or mosaic cane to a bead, it has to be sliced or nipped into short murrine slices about one eighth of an inch in length. Preheat the murrine slightly before applying them to a bead. This can be done by holding them with your tweezers in the flame, by putting them in an annealing kiln on a steel plate (which is referred to as a ferro), or by keeping them on a heated marver. At the same time preheat the bead until the application area is nice and soft. Then apply the murrina and push it into the surface of the bead. You can apply this pressure in a number of ways: by pushing the murrina into the bead with tweezers, by pushing the bead down on a marver over the murrina, or by squeezing the murrina and the opposite side of the bead between the jaws of your tweezers. Try to push the murrina in at least ¾ of the way into the bead surface. Gradually work it to be flush with the surface by gently heating and marvering the sides of the murrina down. Once it is firmly marvered down you do not have to be quite so gentle with the heating.

Next many murrine tend to bubble or scuzz up when reheated, because of scratched up surfaces or trapped air. Therefore you may want to apply a slight casing of clear glass to the top of the murrina before heating it up too much. Then reheat the area and marver it into the bead surface as desired. You may want to leave it raised so that it acts as a lens. Work slow and not too hot or you will smear the murrina You may have to reapply heat a couple of times to get it worked in right. For murrini that are semi transparent and will be cased with clear for viewing through them, you may also want to really polish them well using diamond belts, as well as felt and cork wheels to make sure that you have no scratches on the surface that will trap bubbles or distort the image.

Some kinds of latticino-like constructions are also applied like murrine and when melted in look like little spiral dots. To make a sample of this kind of latticino make a big gather in the middle of a rod about a half inch in diameter and about an inch long. Draw a few stripes down the side with cane. Thin cane or stringers can be used to get very fine lines. Then heat it all up and pull it out slowly while twisting it a lot. Making it larger and then pulling it out allows you to get much finer lines in your spirals. Pull it slowly to get a fairly thick cane on the order of just under a normal Morreti rod thickness (about 3/16"). Try to twist it a lot to get a really tight spiral. Cut it up into about quarter inch lengths. Apply it like murrine but do not push it more than about half way into the bead

© 1996 James Kervin

Wound Beads 141

surface. When you reheat it to fully attach it, the cane shrinks up on itself to look like a dot of the base color with a spiral on top of it.

Casing constructions

Many times after you have applied decorative constructions to the surface of your bead, you many decide that you want to case part of or the whole bead in a transparent color without distorting the image too much. This will magnify and enhance the image. The secret to doing this is to keep the bead just barely warm enough for the casing to adhere and adding the casing glass as hot as possible so as not to trap air. To do this, make sure that the bead that you are casing is kept below the flame. Apply the casing rod hot through the flame pushing down slightly to squeeze out the air at the bead surface, slightly twisting the casing rod back and forth or rotating it to evenly heat it during application. After you are done, heat the bead thoroughly and lightly marver the surface as desired. Sometimes if your casing is thick and you just have a few bubbles on the surface of a casing, you can reheat that section and pull the bubbles out of the casing.

If you look closely at your casings, you will notice that it will always have some minute bubbles in it. I am not talking about the ones where you trapped air by not applying the casing hot enough or with insufficient pressure. Instead I am talking about the fine bubbles that often scum up the surface of a bead. These fine bubbles are caused by scratches and imperfections in the surface of the clear rods that are a result of handling damage during its manufacture and distribution. Clear is especially susceptible to this damage because it is softer and scratches easily. These scratches can be seen quite easily if you heat the rod to a glowing orange state. These scratches are also why packaged murrine, especially transparent ones, from Moretti form a scum when applied.

Is there anything that you can do to get around this problem? Well you could take your clear scrap and put it all into a crucible and heat it to about 2200 to 2300°F. At this temperature all the fine bubbles from the air trapped in the scratches will rise to the surface and you can skim them off. You could also use clear Kugler with a COE of about 90 or Shott with a COE of about 108 for this. The real adventurous of you could contact East Bay Batch which has a glass batch formulation that is compatible with Moretti and start with it. This will have to be heated longer than scrap glass. Gathers can be taken from the crucibles of hot glass and applied to form bubble free casings.

Most of us lampworkers do not want to get into this and want to work strictly at the flame. So is there anything that we can do to get bubble free casings? One labor intensive answer would be to polish the outside of the clear glass rods prior to use, but this may or may not be successful depending upon your perseverance. A more reasonable alternative is to skim off the outside surface of the glass rod to remove the scratches. This is easier done on large diameter clear rods which have a larger volume to surface ratio. You skim off the scratched surface by heating up the rod, grabbing a section of its outside surface with your tweezers or pliers and peeling it off like a banana. Safely dispose of this skin in container of water, this also serves to cool the tool. After

© 1996 James Kervin

stripping the skin off all the way around the rod, the remaining material will be bubble and scum free. If used in casing something, it will be optically pure.

Inclusions

Besides glass constructions, you can also add some forms of non-glass inclusions to your beads. These are usually completely incased in the interior of beads made from primarily transparent glass. Some of the things that you can use as inclusions in glass beads are metal foils or leaf, mica chips and wire or screen.

Foil and leaf

Foil and leaf is available of a number of different metals: gold, silver, platinum, palladium, etc. Foils are easier to handle than leaf because they are thicker, less likely to fly away on you, and more resistant to getting burned off right away. Silver is one of the better foils to work with because it is reasonably priced, looks good, and stands up reasonably well under the torch. It does react somewhat differently with the different colors of glass — sometimes remaining silvery, sometimes diffusing into the glass to give it a yellow tint. This is what silver stain was all about after all. Gold and platinum don't have this problem but are a lot more expensive. Platinum actually ends up looking more like gold than gold. You can try practicing with copper foil but it tends to turn an ugly brown.

To use foil, start by cutting the foil to the size of the bead. You may want more than one wrap around the bead for richer color with some foils. Heat the bead to a tacky hot. Apply the foil. Roll it on or crinkle it on. Burnish the foil onto the bead with your tweezers real well. If you don't burnish well, the foil will quickly burn off in the regions where it does not make good contact with the bead as soon as you hit it with the torch flame. Next you have to case the foil in a transparent glass casing for durability. To help avoid burning off the foil when you reheat the bead, reheat it only lightly. You have to reheat the bead some or the casing glass will not stick. Now apply an overcoat casing of glass to those areas where you want the foil to remain when you are done, all the while keeping the bead out of the direct flame. You can use the casing to provide decorative foil regions by applying it in dots, lines, spirals or over the whole bead. The overcoat should be as hot as possible so as not to trap any air next to the foil. After you have applied whatever decorative casing you want, then thoroughly reheat the bead to burn off whatever exposed foil remains and fix the casing. Add whatever other decorations you desire to the bead or finish casing it for a uniform surface. This whole process is illustrated in Figure 71.

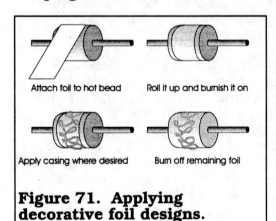

Figure 71. Applying decorative foil designs.

© 1996 James Kervin

Wound Beads   143

Some higher melting temperature foils like palladium don't have to be cased over if you do not want. Just make sure that you secure the edges of the foil with some glass to prevent it from unraveling. Be a little careful when doing this because palladium may change to a silver color if overworked in the flame

Mica

Colored mica available for fusing, can also be used successfully for decorating beads. It is usually applied by getting the bead tacky and rolling it on some mica that has been spread out on your marver. You should then gently marver the mica into the surface of the bead. If you decide to reheat at this point be careful because the color on the mica burns off even faster than do foils. You should case the mica in transparent glass as soon as possible again trying to avoid heating the bead.

Powdered colored mica is also available. It is sold under the trade name of "Pixie Dust". It is also applied by getting your bead tacky hot and rolling it in the mica. If this is your last step the mica does not need to be cased. Extra material will rub off of your bead.

Wires and screen

You can also use wire and screens as inclusions in your transparent beads. They should be of a very fine gage so as to be easily deformed by the glass and not to exert much stress on it. They are applied to a hot tacky surface and must be cased if you expect them to stick.

Dichroic coatings

The use of dichroic glass can add wonderful color effects to your beads. Because its use is a little tricky, it requires some discussion. First of all, as mentioned previously, the compatibility of this glass is dictated by the base glass on which the coating was plated. Therefore since most of the high temperature dichroic is on COE 90 compatible glass, you will be working with that as your pallet. Dichroic coated Moretti glass is also available but in more limited supply. Remember also to make sure that the coating is high temperature compatible otherwise you may see it burn off in you torch. Even if high temperature compatible, you have to treat it right or you will ruin it. As you apply and work the coated glass, don't be surprised to see the coating break up, crack or wrinkle as you move the base glass around, after all it is only a thin coating and will not flow like the base glass.

The first thing that you have to understand about working with dichroic glass in making beads is that you want to avoid directing your torch onto the dichroic coating. If you do, you will very likely burn it off. This can also happen if you get the bead too hot. What happens in this situation is that the coating material goes into solution in the glass just like the silver in a silver foil if you overheat it. This is especially a problem when using a propane-oxygen torch where much more heat is available. The coatings prefer a cooler reducing flame. So to add dichroic glass, turn

© 1996 James Kervin

144   Glass Beadmaking

down the oxygen on your flame and heat the dichroic glass on the side opposite the coating.

If you are adding dichroic glass that has an opaque base, you will have to add this with the dichroic coating side up. To do this keep your bead just below the flame and add your dichroic glass by preheating the bottom as you feed it onto the bead. In this process you are rotating the bead as you normally do with the glass being added to the top and being rotated away from you. Then marver it in as best as possible. To marver it any better heat it way out in the end of your flame and do not get it too hot. What you really need to do to protect the coating is to case it in clear glass. As in most cases you want to keep the bead relatively cool as you case it. The casing glass is hot and fluid as you add it. Press down as usual to try to avoid trapping air. Then reheat the bead and marver into shape.

If your dichroic is on a clear base glass, you have the option of adding it coating side down. It will usually be applied over a solid color core for contrast. So again have your bead below the flame and feed the dichroic through the flame with the dichroic surface facing away from you. You attach the strip to the close surface and rotate the bead so the dichroic goes under the bead. This is reversed from the normal direction. After a full wrap pull off the extra dichroic and lightly heat the bead out in the end of the flame. If you heat too much now, you will find that the end of the glass will roll up and expose some of the coating which will then get discolored. To avoid this, lightly heat and marver out the edges of clear base glass to get it to spread out and seal in the coating.

If you decide to add more than one layer of dichroic glass, do not try to put the coated side of one to the coated side of the other. They just don't want to bond that way. The only way you can get it to work is if there are enough cracks or holes through the bottom coating.

Bubbles and cracks

Sometimes you just want to break the rules and have bubbles or cracks in your beads for effect. Bubbles can be achieved in a number of ways. Very fine bubbles can be simulated by rolling a bead in a light dusting of sand or silica flour on your marver and then casing it in a transparent color. Because of its crystalline properties these inclusions will look like fine bubbles.

To include larger bubbles into your beads, you can try distorting the bead surface to create depressions and then casing these depressions with a transparent color to trap air. To distort the surface, you can shape the bead on things like files or wire brushes which will leave indentations on the bead surface or just poke holes in it with a sharp pointed tool. If making multiple depressions with the same tool be sure to chill it between applications in water so that the glass will not stick to it.

Now reheat the bead and case the depression with your transparent color. When doing this there are two things that you have to watch out for. If the bead is too cool, the rapped air may expand more than desired

© 1996 James Kervin

Wound Beads 145

upon reheating. The other is that if the casing glass is too hot, it may fill in some of the depression. After placing and casing all of your depressions, you may want to strongly reheat the bead. Doing so will give the glass and the air enough mobility to reform into their lowest surface energy interface configuration, a sphere. When doing this be aware that large bubbles may try to migrate to the hottest or least viscous portion of the bead which is usually the surface. To avoid this, heat the bead slowly in the outer region of the flame and repeatedly chill the outer surface by gently rolling the bead on a marver. For information on making a tool to make multiple indentations at one time see the article on "Bubbles and Droplets" from Glass Line that is listed at the end of this chapter.

The other rule that you may want to break occasionally is to introduce cracking into your beads. To do this, get your bead real hot and then dip it into some water. You will get a lot of cracks. Reintroduce the bead into the flame to refuse the outer surface of the bead. You may want to try multiple dips and temperatures to play with this effect. It should be obvious that these beads will not be quite as strong as a normal bead. Playing with this technique will also give you a feel for how the heat is penetrating into your bead as you watch the cracks vanish upon reheat. When you do this you will not be able to marver the bead larger because the water washes away much of the exposed separator compound

Examples of more complex wound beads

There are an infinite number of variations possible using the decorative skills to which you have been exposed. You have already seen some examples as these skills were introduced. To peak your interest a little more let's go over some examples here to give you ideas of what can be achieved with practice.

Tableau beads

The first bead we will discuss is a tableau bead. This is a simple flat disk shaped bead with a picture of some sort on it. It works very well as a central pendant on a string of beads. The basic bead is constructed by winding an ellipsoidal shaped glob on the mandrel. When you then flatten this glob out by pressing it between your marver and your paddle or by squashing it with a set of squashing pliers, you will get a circular disk. As you squash the bead, you should not make it thinner than about three times the thickness of the mandrel.

For this example we will apply the image of an eye to the face of the tableau. Start by applying a fairly large dot of black to the center of the flat side of the bead. Flatten it out with your marver. Add a white dot on top of the black dot and marver both into the surface of the bead. Pull a small black point to use as a tool. Heat up one side of the circle and stretch it out to an eye shape by raking a short distance with your glass tool right at the junction of the white and the black dot outward to the edge of the bead. The surface of the glass should be hot enough that you affect too wide an area as you rake out the eye shape. Remember to stop at the end of the rake, blow on the end of the point, and break it off.

© 1996 James Kervin

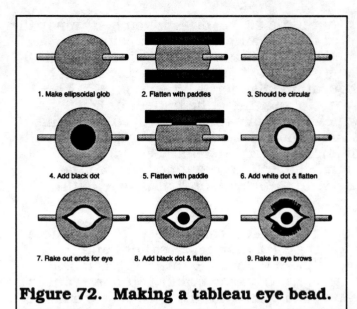

Figure 72. Making a tableau eye bead.

Next heat up the other side of the black circle. Stretch it out as was done with the other side to complete the basic eye shape. Again break off the tool, reheat the bead and marver the surface flat. Add a black dot to the center of the white to serve as the iris of the eye.

You can decorate the eye further if you want by raking eyelashes from the top and the bottom of the outer black ring of the eye. Here you would heat these areas with a small sharp flame before raking. Further decorations can be added to the bead in the form of latticino on the edges, looping circles around the eye, or whatever else you may come up with.

Hollow wound beads

One form of wound bead that many artists are not aware that they can make are hollow beads. This technique allows making a larger bead without greatly increasing the weight of the bead.

This bead is constructed very similarly to the technique for making clay bowls that you may have learned when you were younger. That consists of building up the shape of the bowl using coils. You start by making two small thin disk shaped beads as far apart on the mandrel as the bead is to be wide. From there you build up the shape of the hollow bead by wrapping coils of glass around the two original beads as shown in Figure 73. It is easiest to coil in a little at a time from both ends switching back and forth from end to end as you go. This allows you to be able to build up the bead without having to try to lay a coil inside of the last coil. This also helps to prevent from thermal shocking the bead because you have worked entirely on one side and the other side has cooled before you can get back to it. The secrets to the success of this type of bead are not to break the seal of the separator compound underneath the small beads and make sure that each wrap is completely attached to the one below as you build up the bead. This is especially critical on the last wrap where you have to ensure that

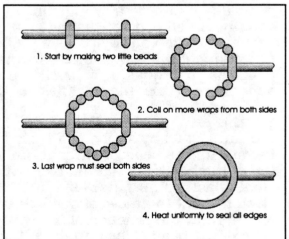

Figure 73. Making a hollow wound bead.

the wrap seals on both of the hollow cups that you have constructed.

After you have completed all the wraps, heat up the bead uniformly to seal all the edges. If you did not get a good joint between some of your coils, they may separate at this time and start to collapse. If this starts to happen, try to patch the hole with a little dab of glass over the hole and heat it up again. If you did get a good seal between the wraps, the bead will stay inflated as you heat it from the expanding air inside the bead. As you continue to heat the bead the glass will flow and even out the wall of the bead. With this technique it is also possible to do things like making a bead that can roll around inside the other bead.

With practice you will be able to shape the bead at this time. This may be something as simple as rolling or pressing it hot on a paddle, to as complex as pulling points out from the surface of the glass. This is also a good time to decorate the surface of the hollow bead with color or constructions. Some artists will not heat up the glass to the flow point and instead prefer the look of the coils. This gives the bead much more texture.

Sculptural beads (fish, heads)

As a beginning sculptural bead that also uses many of the decorative techniques that have already been discussed, let's fabricate some tropical fish beads. The finished bead will look like the one shown in Figure 74. The first step is to choose the rough color scheme that you want for your bead. You can make your fish with the color scheme of real fish or be creative and makeup one of your own. Next in preparation for making your bead, you need to make some ribbon with the color scheme that you propose for the fins. With that completed, you are ready to start construction of the bead proper.

You start by making a pear shaped bead of the base color for the body. Then you trail on a spiral of a contrasting color over that. After thoroughly heating up the bead, flatten it as shown in the figure. Using a point drawn from the same color as the trailed on spiral, festoon each side of the bead by raking a number of times in the same direction (head to tail) to give the appearance of scales.

Now you are ready to start adding features to the fish. To make the mouth, add a ring of red to the head of the bead and then rake it back. For the eyes, start out with

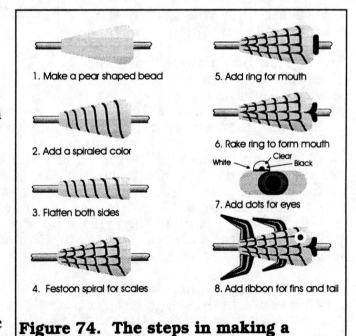

Figure 74. The steps in making a sculptural fish bead.

© 1996 James Kervin

a dot of white and flatten it out. Then add a small dot of black to the center of the eye. Finally for that bulgy fish eye look, you overcoat it all with a layer of clear as illustrated in the figure.

Lastly you have the sculptural element of this bead to do, adding the fins. They are made from the ribbon that you constructed ahead of time. Proceed by working your way from the larger fins to the smaller ones. Start with the tail fins. Heat the attachment point of the ribbon and the body. Get a good attachment by pressing them together so they bulge lightly and then pull them out slightly to get a nice smooth joint. Apply a little heat to shape and draw out the tip of the fin as desired. Repeat this procedure next with the other tail fin, then the dorsal fin, and finally the two belly fins.

Another example of a sculptural bead is a head bead as illustrated in Figure 75. Start by making an ordinary cylindrical bead. Flatten slightly on two sides of the bead. Then add extra material to shape the chin. Shape the flattened cylinder into a head shape. Now add two small black dots to the surface of the bead to form the outline of the eyes. These two dots will probably not be the same size but that does not really matter because you are going to shape them to the same size before fusing them into the face. You do this by gently heating only the dots and then marvering them out to the desired size that you want even though that may result in them being different in thickness. They you heat up the dots to sink them into the surface of the bead. Next add a white dot and repeat the heating pressing to size and melting in — being sure to leave as thin and equal a lip of

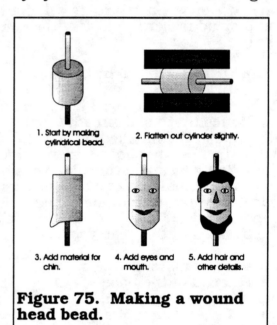

Figure 75. Making a wound head bead.

black all the way around the white as you can. Heat up the eye and pull slightly at either end with a tungsten pick to get the basic eye shape.

Next move on to the mouth. First add a thin line of black or white for the color between the lips. Don't worry if it is just a little bit too big because you will make it more narrow by covering it with the red of the lips. Do this now by adding a thin line of red to the top and the bottom of the mouth. Shape them into the general lip shape by pinching the ends and pulling down the center of the top lip. Stretch out the corners of the mouth.

Now it is time to sculpt depressions into the face. One of the best tools for this is one of those tungsten picks with a curved point. Push in the corners of the mouth into the surface of the bead slightly. Push in laugh lines at either end of the mouth by rolling the pick hook on the U of the hook on either side of the mouth. Push up under the lips to raise them

Wound Beads 149

slightly and create the upper part of the chip. Make the groove between the lips. Push in on either side of the place where the nose will be to form the shallow between the nose and the cheeks. Roll the hook around the edge of the eyes to inset them and form the edge of the eye socket.

The last step is to add raised details. Add eyebrows by touching a dot to the brow over the inside of the eye and immediately lift up and stretch it out along the area over the eye to form a tapered eye brow. Burn off any remaining stringer and marver it into place. Add a small dot to the eye for the iris and another for the pupil of the eye. Add glass for the nose and shape it with your hook. Add a little blob for an ear and shape it. Add hair and/or beards. Sculpt them with pick or use a razor blade to add fine lines. With that the bead is done and placed into the annealer.

Part of the secret for making sculptural beads is in planning out the order of build up. First sculpt the general shape of the piece. Next paint on the larger features that are worked flush into the surface. Then do all inward sculpting since valleys are less vulnerable to heat than protrusions. After that add the smallest most vulnerable protruding features so that they do not get melted while doing work on another feature. Lastly add the finishing feature and detail sculpting. Try to work in different sections of your bead at a time but keeping it all warm.

These are just a simple start into the many possibilities available in sculptural beads. You can move on to any of a number of things animals, flowers, people, etc. For examples, you may want to see Louis Wilson's video on sculptural beads.

Suggested further reading

Beadle, The Venerable. "Bubbles and Droplets" in The Bead Column of Glass Line Vol. 9 No. 5 (February/March), 1996

Mickelsen, Robert A. "Flame On! The Soft Touch Part Two: Beadmaking", Glass Line Vol. 5 No. 6 (April/May), 1992

Reynolds, Gil. "What's Hot? -- Glass Beads" Glass Art Vol. 8 No. 1 (November/December), 1992

Waggoner, Shawn. "Beadmaking II: The Wound Bead Artist" Glass Art Vol. 8 No. 2 (January/February), 1993

© 1996 James Kervin

150   Glass Beadmaking

© 1996 James Kervin

Blown beads

Another way to make hollow beads is to blow them. They can be blown either on a blow pipe or from tubing. The more common technique and most easily accessible to the beginning lampworker is to blow them from tubing. This technique is a little harder than winding because you don't have the solid mandrel to help stabilize your work. The glass of choice for blown beads is borosilicate glass because its low coefficient of thermal expansion does not require the entire bead be kept hot all the time. It even allows you to put down the bead while you are working, let it cool off, then pick it up and start working again. This is something that is almost impossible to do with soda-lime glass. The price that you pay for this benefit is the higher temperature and heat input required to get borosilicate glass into its working range. To do this you definitely need a fuel-oxygen system and even a minor bench burner is barely adequate for this work. Other disadvantages of borosilicate glass are that its higher viscosity requires more effort on your part to move material around and colors are fewer as well as being more costly.

Tubing skills

Before we get into making blown glass beads from tubing, let's discuss how manipulation of tubing differs from those flameworking skills that we have already learned about for working with glass rods. Glass tubing is a little harder to work with than glass rod just because it is hollow. This gives it less mass, causing it to heat up and lose heat faster than you expect. It will buckle and collapse if not kept moving constantly. You have to develop a whole new feel to work well with it.

Tubing, like rods, is usually referred to by its diameter, in particular its outside diameter (O. D.). Since it is not solid, its complete specification requires an additional descriptor; either inside diameter or wall thickness. Of the two, specification of wall thickness is the most common. Wall thickness may be specified by an actual dimension or a qualifier such as standard wall, medium wall or heavy wall. Table 14 lists some common sizes of standard, medium and heavy wall tubing. The heavier walled tubing tends to be more uniform in wall thickness. In working with tubing, the heavier the wall thickness, the easier it is to control the glass when it starts to get soft. Increasing the wall thickness also increases the period over which the glass will remain soft once heated. Doubling the thickness more than doubles the working time.

© 1996 James Kervin

152   Glass Beadmaking

Table 14. Common glass tubing sizes.

Standard Wall Tubing		Medium Wall Tubing		Heavy Wall Tubing	
O. D. (mm)	Wall (mm)	O. D. (mm)	Wall (mm)	O. D. (mm)	Wall (mm)
2	.5	6.3	1.2	9.5	2.0
3	.6	12.7	1.6	12.7	2.4
4	.8	15.9	1.6	15.9	2.4
5	.8	19.0	1.6	19.0	3.2
6	1.0	25.4	2.4	22.2	3.2
7	1.0	31.7	2.4	25.4	4.0
8	1.0	38.1	2.4	31.7	4.0
9	1.0	44.4	2.4	38.1	4.0
10	1.0	50.8	3.2	44.4	4.0
11	1.0			50.8	4.8
12	1.0				
13	1.2				
14	1.2				
15	1.2				
16	1.2				
17	1.2				
18	1.2				
19	1.2				
20	1.2				

Cutting tubing

Cutting smaller diameter tubing up to about 30 mm in diameter is done exactly as with rods. However, as tubing gets larger, it is harder to break uniformly. In this case, what works well to propagate a crack around the circumference of a tube, is the judicious use of some heat. Make a score with your glass knife all the way around the outside diameter of the tube. Next apply a little saliva to part of the crack. Then bring the cold tube up under the flame and just barely touch the tube to the end of the flame. This should initiate a crack at the base of the score which you can lead around the tube with more heat (rotating the cracked edge toward you) or by pulling lengthwise on the tube. If you do not get the crack to initiate right away, it is often better to move to a new spot around the circumference of the tube and start over. Continued application of heat will just cause the crack at the bottom of the score to blunt.

An alternate technique of applying heat to run a crack, is to make a wrap of resistance wire around the circumference of the tube over the score and to run electrical current through it. This heats up a narrow region in the vicinity of the score all the way around the tube. After heating it up, the current is turned off and a damp cloth is applied to the score to initiate a crack by thermal shock.

© 1996 James Kervin

Blown Beads 153

Gathering or shrinking

In the case of tubing, what we mean by gathering is heating up the tubing in such a way that the tubing starts to shrink in diameter and increase in wall thickness from the surface tension of the glass as seen in Figure 76. This can be continued, if desired, all the way until the tubing completely closes up. This exact thing is done to get a round closed end like on a test tube at the end of some tubing.

The way you develop a gather on a tube is very similar to the way that we did a gather on a rod. You introduce the tubing into a medium flame at the place you want to make the gather (end or interior) by waving it through the flame as before. Be careful in doing this because tubing tends to be more sensitive to thermal shock that solid rod but since the tubing is borosilicate glass it is not as sensitive as it would if it were made of soda-lime glass. Once in the flame, you rotate it with a steady regular motion using the tennis grip that we talked about earlier. This applies the heat uniformly all the way around the tubing, which may be larger than the flame, and prevents it from drooping. If you get tired of rotating it in one direction all the time you can vary that off with rotating back and forth. Peek over the top of your glasses to check out the color of the flame. As the tubing starts to get hot, the flame will become more intensely yellow. Watching the color of the flame as you spin the tube can help you tell if you are heating the tube uniformly. The important thing in getting the glass to thicken and draw down uniformly is to apply your heat evenly around the tubing. To facilitate this process, it helps to use a softer flame. Like with solid glass rods, if your gather droops just rotate the tube and it will straighten itself out.

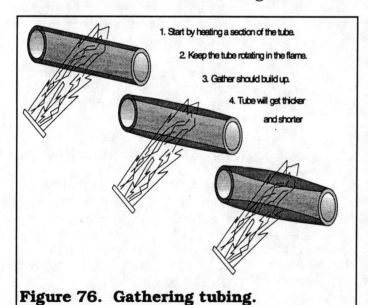

Figure 76. Gathering tubing.

When you first start making gathers in tubing, you may find it hard to keep the cross section of your gathered tubing uniform and circular. As you make your gather, you may lose control of the gather and have it twist out of shape. For gathers at the end of a tube, this is usually the result of not heating uniformly around the exterior circumference of the tube. For gathers away from the end of the tube, this is usually the result of not rotating the tubing at the same speed on both sides of the gather or not keeping them in line. One hand may just be slower than the other. If you have this problem, notice that it does not happen until the glass gets quite soft. This points out the secret to successfully working with tubing, don't let it get too hot. Working a little slower at a cooler temperature accomplishes the same objective while keeping the glass stiffer so that it is easier to handle.

© 1996 James Kervin

Pulling points

When making blown glass beads, you will need a way to hold the bead as you are working on it. This is usually done by pulling points at the ends of the section of the tube with which you are working, as shown in Figure 77, and using them as handles. As before, when you pulled points or cane from rod, you first have to make a gather in the center of the tube which you subsequently pull out into a point. The difference here is that the point will be hollow. So start by making a gather a couple inches in from the end of the tubing and about an inch and a half long. Keep both ends of the tube rotating and remove it from the flame. Begin to draw it out while simultaneously bending the main part of the tubes down at a slight angle and continuing to rotate until you pull it out about 12 inches long and about 1/8th inch in diameter. Then straighten out the tube and pull it straight. Once it stops moving, continue to hold it in tension for a few more seconds to allow it to solidify. Make sure that the glass has completely set up before you release the tension on the point, otherwise it can bend on you. With practice, this will become one smooth easy rhythm. The tricky part is to keep the point on center relative to the tubing. You should practice gathering and pulling points a number of times until you get the hang of it.

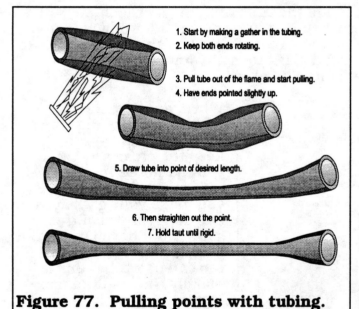

Figure 77. Pulling points with tubing.

You can then separate the point at the center by reheating a short section of it which should now be about an eighth of an inch in diameter. Because of its smaller size it will heat much faster. Heat a short section of the point and pull it out in the flame to allow it to separate. You may find it easier to do this final flame cut if you pull out a small section of the point a second time first.

Points can also be pulled from the end of a tube. To do this, start by closing off the end of the tube with a gather. Use pliers if you have to on larger tubing to help close off the end. Then attach a punty to the center of the closed off end. Next reheat the gather just in a little from the end until it starts to close in (remembering to rotate all the time of course) and pull it out into a point. The tapered end of a well made point will be circular in cross section and in perfect alignment with the center of the tubing. If you roll it between your thumb and forefinger the central tubing section will run true.

If your point is not centered, and they probably won't be when you just start trying, it can be adjusted enough to work. To accomplish this,

Blown Beads

apply a small flame to the region where the tube narrows down into the point. Gather this region in slightly by continuing rotation while heating and possibly pushing the point back into the tube slightly. Then remove it from the flame and slightly pull on the point to straighten it out. You may also find that your points are not be as circular in cross section as you would like. This is usually the result of not heating the gather uniformly around its circumference before pulling. The cooler side does not pull out as well and therefore will be flatter. The cure for this is simple, keep the tube rotating evenly whenever in the flame.

Inflation/reinflation

One skill that you have not practiced up until now in working on beads is inflation of a bead by blowing into it. With blown beads, you may shrink and reinflate a bead a number of times until you get the shape right. Usually all you will have to do is to give a slight puff into the bead via a hollow point to reinflate it. If you do not like the result, you can just slowly heat the bead out in the end of the flame, let it gather back in on itself and try again. So let's start by pulling two points on a short section of tubing. One point should be open and one should be closed. Then shrink down your tube. One of the ways to tell when the tube is hot enough for inflating is when it becomes hard to keep it on center and its wants to droop on you. Pull it out of the flame while continuing to rotate. Put the open point into your mouth while still rotating. Then gently inflate the tube. You will find that you may have to blow a little harder initially to get the glass moving, then you can ease up some as it starts to move and finally you have to blow harder again as the glass chills. A common mistake with beginners is to blow too hard – resulting up in a paper thin bubble. Take it easy.

Blowing it out

Sometimes you want to create a hole in the side of a blown bead as illustrated in **Figure 78**. The easiest way to do this is to chill the bead slightly, spot heat the area where you want the hole very locally with a sharp flame, and then blow into the point. This will cause the heated portion of the wall to pooch out like a balloon until it breaks. Heat up the jagged edges and use a small tungsten rod to pick off the extra glass. Use a graphite or brass reamer to get a nice uniform hole.

This can also be used as another way to cut tubing. In this method we heat a narrow area all the way around the tube and pull it into two pieces by pulling a point and breaking the two pieces apart. Gather the point to close up the end of the tube. Then heat the very end of the closed end, take it out of the flame and blow it out. Break the paper thin glass off the end of the tube. Then smooth out the edges of the hole with your pick as above and you are ready to go.

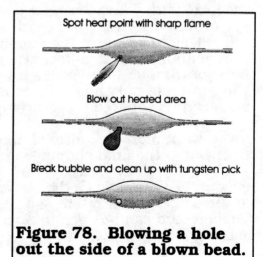

Figure 78. Blowing a hole out the side of a blown bead.

© 1996 James Kervin

Borosilicate tube beads

As a way of practicing a few of the skills that I have discussed, let's talk about how to make beads from borosilicate tubing as practiced by Don Schneider. He starts with borosilicate tubing 6 to 10 mm in diameter which he cuts into workable lengths of 1 to 1 1/2' long and fire polishes the ends. After preheating the last couple inches of the tube to a temperature just before showing color, he then cases most of the outside of the soon to be bead in a solid color. Colored borosilicate glass is manufactured by Northstar and Colrex and tends to be quite expensive in comparison to that available in soda-lime glass. For this reason it is usually used sparingly as in this case where it is applied as a casing to the clear tubing rather than making the whole body of the bead from colored borosilicate.

After winding on the casing, he works it into the surface of the tube by heating it up and rolling it smooth on the marver. To assist in maintaining its tubular shape while marvering, Don uses a graphite rod down the center of the tube. The graphite rod should be mounted in a handle to keep from burning yourself and getting your hands dirty. He uses a pin vise to hold his, but you could also used doweling.

To decorate his beads, Don adds murrine pieces that he cuts from millefiori that he has made from colored borosilicate using techniques like those described previously. He also uses latticino. You could actually use many of the other decorative techniques that we have talked about like frit, dots, cane, etc. The only thing that you have to remember is that you are working with borosilicate glass and have to work slightly hotter than soda lime glass.

After you are done decorating your bead, you are ready to flame cut it off from the end of the tube. To do this turn your flame down to a pinpoint. Then quickly heat a thin ring around the tube where you want the end of the bead to be. When hot and soft remove the tube from the flame and grab the other end of the bead with your tweezers. Then pull out this ring into a thin thread and break it free from the tubing. While holding the bead with you tweezers, break off the thread and use a flat file to smooth up the end of the bead where any clinging glass should be pretty thin. These edges can then be fire polished in the flame by holding the bead with a hot fingers tool rather than your tweezers to allow you to roll it in your hand. If it needs a little more shaping you can slide it onto your graphite rod and use a graphite paddle to marver it. Afterward the ends can be squared on your marver.

If you want more free form shapes than cylinders, you can evenly heat up the bead in the final shaping step on the graphite rod and let gravity start to stretch it. Once it starts to stretch, the process can be encouraged and modified by inserting a second graphite rod into the hole in the center and stretching it further, possibly even inserting twists. This method can be used to turn your tubular bead into bolo tie beads or scarf slides.

© 1996 James Kervin

Blown Beads

Blowing beads

Now with these basic tubeworking skills behind us and with the practice you had in using them to make tube beads, we are ready to discuss how to make a blown bead.

Basic blown bead

For blowing beads, 3/4 to 1 inch (20 or 25mm) tubing works best. If you don't want to waste any tubing, close off an end with a gather and then pull it out into a point with a punty as discussed previously. Then go in from the end of the straight section of the tubing about 2 inches from that point, make a gather and pull another point. The amount you move in depends on the size of the bead that you want to make. Break off the bubble in the middle of the second point (you can use your glass knife if you want to avoid a gagged edge). At this point you should have something that looks like the first step in Figure 79. If you did not care about wasting a little glass in trade for slightly increased speed, this same thing could have been made from two internal gathers on the tube.

At this point you want to be sure that one of the two points is closed off at the end. Otherwise, when you blow into the bead to reinflate it nothing will happen. Now, add any decorations that you want to the bead (more on this in the next section). After you have the bead decorated to your satisfaction, shrink the bead down to the desired shape through a combination of uniformly heating it followed as necessary by reinflation. You can also roll it on a marver to get the correct shape. It is important to work slow and not to blow too hard. Remember to keep it spinning to prevent it from sagging or buckling and to keep you points centered. All that is necessary to get a point back on center usually is to slightly heat the bent area and give it a slight tug. Sagging can also be handled by removing the bead from the flame and using gravity to bring things back into shape. Doing this outside of the flame, allows more control over the process. Buckling of a point can be handled with a slight reinflation. After you are done shrinking the bead down to about half of its original size and increasing wall thickness to about twice its original thickness, shape the bead.

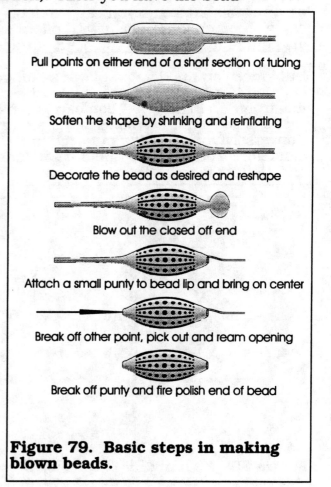

Figure 79. Basic steps in making blown beads.

© 1996 James Kervin

When you get the desired shape of the blown bead, melt off the closed point at the edge of the bead. Then blow open the melted off end, pick off the extra glass and use a reamer to properly shape the opening on that end of the bead. A reamer is used by inserting it into the hole as you heat it and spinning the reamer or the bead to get the desired shape. You may have to reheat the hole a few times before you get it right.

Now slightly chill the bead to stabilize it. Spot heat a small section of the bead lip that you just finished and attach a small punty. Heat the punty and bend it on center so that you can work the other side of the bead. Alternatively you could use a hot fingers tool to hold the bead on the completed end while you finish the other end. Now burn off the other point and pick it open. Use the reamer to shape the hole. Chill slightly and use a tweezers to grab the bead by this newly formed end. Break off the punty (if you used one) and touch up the punty mark with the flame. Then bury your bead in the heated vermiculite.

Shaping blown beads

Blown beads can be shaped in a number of different ways some of which are identical to what has been discussed for wound beads. Generally though they tend to be simple in shape (spheres, ellipsoids and such) relying on their clear colors and translucence for their beauty. But if you do want to shape one, you can roll it on your marver to shape it. You can also pinch it or poke it with pliers to collapse and distort it. You can also pull out sections of the bead surface.

But since you are doing a blown bead, you may want to try some of the shaping ideas that can only be practiced in that medium and are illustrated in Figure 80. You can you use your flame to shrink down sections so that it is smaller in diameter and thicker than other sections. Conversely you can blow out sections to make them thinner and larger in diameter. You can also pull out sections like points to make them long and slender for dangles on ear rings. You can twist your beads to make them collapse into spirals.

For something more interesting, make a small mold with a unique shape and blow the bead into the mold. With this technique, you can get beads in all sorts of interesting shapes from simple rectangular solids and bipyramidic solids to complex non regular shapes like birds and simple animals.

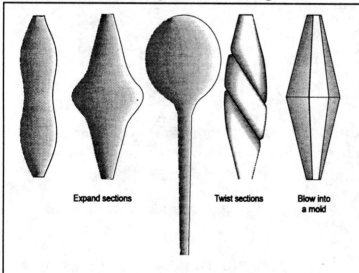

Figure 80. Shaping ideas for blown beads.

Blown Beads   159

Decorating blown beads

Many of the decorating techniques discussed for use with wound beads also work well with blown beads. You can decorate them by rolling in frit; adding dots; trailing on color; surface distortion in the form of twists, pokes or pulls; applying canes, latticino, murrine or ribbons; or by sculptural lampworking techniques. One of the tricks in adding decorations to blown beads is to have the pieces that you are adding to be hotter than the bead. This is because the bead tends to heat up faster and get out of control if you are not careful. You have to keep the bead warm enough to make a good joint between the decoration and the bead. If not, your decoration could fall off later. You accomplish this by feeding your decorating rod though the flame onto the bead while applying slight pressure down onto the bead. If applying cane, try to keep the rod rotating slightly as you apply it to heat the glass uniformly. If you find this hard to do, try twisting it back and forth instead.

One way to make sure that your decorations are properly fused onto the surface of the bead is by slightly gathering and reinflating the bead after applying all your decorations. Another thing to be aware of when applying decorations to blown beads is that areas with large changes in wall thickness can be locations of localized stress that will need flame annealing to prevent cracking.

An important thing you should be aware of when trying to decorate your blown beads is that not all the techniques that you have learned for use with wound beads work as well for blown beads. This is the result of not having the stabilizing influence of the mandrel and the much higher viscosity of borosilicate glass. One of the most notable of these techniques that does not work well is raking. To rake properly you have to get the surface of the bead really hot to some depth. Blown beads are generally too thin to do this properly and attempts to do so result in major distortion or tears to the bead surface. It is possible once you develop a good feel for working with blown beads to be able to rake, but don't expect this any time soon.

To get an effect similar to raking, you instead have to take advantage of one of the shaping techniques available for blown beads, twisting. This process is illustrated in Figure 81. Start by applying longitudinal stripes down the axis of the bead. Spot heat one circumferential section of the body of the bead being sure to keep it rotating quickly to prevent it from drooping. When hot, twist one end of the bead one direction and the other end in the opposite direction as if you were winding a latticino. This will produce a spiral like effect. Next spot heat the circumferential section of the bead next to this spiral and then twist in the opposite directions to get a spiral in the opposite direction. Back-to-back, these two steps will result in an effect similar to circumferential raking. If you do a number of these in the same direction but slightly separated, then you will get an effect similar to festooning. If you switch directions every time, you will get an effect something like feathering. The only thing that you need to be aware of is that this process is harder to do near the ends of the bead where the wall is thicker.

© 1996 James Kervin

Glass Beadmaking

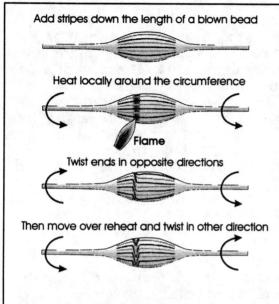

Figure 81. **Raking-like technique for blown beads.**

Another technique that is only possible with blown beads is to partially blow out decorations. Dots on the surface of your bead can be heated up and blown out a little so that they become hollow. You can also gather and blowout circumferential decorative rings. If you wanted you could also go all the way and blow a hole out of the side of a bead. This might be good for a necklace to which you want to add a pendant. If you want more than one additional hole out of the bead, just do not break any of the blown-out bubbles until they are all formed.

Surface decoration suggestions that can done with borosilicate blown beads to give them color include the possibility of letting it cool and then decorating them with compatible enamels or lusters. To decorate them with high temperature enamels roll them in the enamels and then uniformly heat the bead to a light cherry red to fire the enamel. You can also try mixing up some lower temperature enamels with a liquid binder such as Thompson's Klyr-fire, painting them on and firing them in the kiln. Alternatively paint lusters on your beads, let them air dry and fire them up in the kiln. Try this with any of the four types of lusters: metallics, iridescents, coloreds or halos to develop a feel for how to work with them. Be sure that you have adequate ventilation when working with these materials because some of the vapors released in firing these products can be toxic.

Another nice decorative technique to use with blown beads is to mirror the inside of the bead. Silvering is not too difficult a process and can easily be done by an individual artist. To silver you first clean the glass if it is not fresh. Next you sensitize the glass surface by pretreating it with a tinning solution. The silvering is a three step process. First the silver solution is applied, next the silver surface is activated and then reduced. Finally all chemicals are rinsed off the glass. For more information see either of the references listed below from "The Independent Glassblower" or Homer Hoyt's book.

Another process that you might want to try to do with your borosilicate blown beads is to irridize them. Iridizing a glass surface can be achieved by spraying a metallic solution on the glass surface while it is hot (1100° F to 1150°F) to form a thin layer of lustrous color. The most successful of the solutions to use is 1 part by volume stannous chloride with 1 part muriatic acid and 2 to 4 parts of water. This is the solution that Bullseye Glass Company uses to irridize their glass. The solution can be sprayed after heating either in the torch or in the kiln. The solution is toxic so

Blown Beads   161

this must be done with adequate safety measures both to protect you from the fumes as well as the solution. A plastic or glass siphon sprayer is necessary for application as the acid will attack metal. The solution should be sprayed in a hood and washed down which is neutralized afterward. After spraying put the bead into an annealer. For more information see Boyce Lundstrom's article from Glass Line.

There is also a Mother of Pearl thermoluster manufactured by Engelhard. It has 1,1,1-trichloroethane tetraisopropyl titanate as its active ingredient. (I dare you to try and say that three times in a row fast.) It still requires good ventilation (paint hood is suggested) and protection from contact with your eyes and skin, much less ingestion, but it is supposed to be much less toxic although more flammable than the stannous chloride solution reported on above. It is the same chemical that Spectrum Glass Company and Armstrong Glass Company use to irridize their glass. It is non-corrosive to metals but I would not advise using an expensive air brush to apply it. Your bead should be warm, over 800°F, when applying this product but not hot. It will burn off if you heat the bead over 1200°F. Be sure to ask for an MSDS with it.

How about combining surface treatments. You could first add flameworked decorations and then apply lusters, iridizing or mirroring. It might also be interesting to apply lusters like on those small Murano bottles or vases and then mirror the inside.

Another thing that you might want to consider trying with when making hollow blown beads is to fill them with things. Shari Hopper uses this idea with some of her blown beads. You can filling them with just about anything. One idea is food. You could make a dried bean necklace and fill each bead with a different kind of dried bean. You could also make a grain necklace and put in things like rice, wheat, oats, etc. How about flowers that you then let dry inside the bead. Small figurines might also be an interesting idea. Or how about a ship in a bead. I am sure that with a little imagination you will be able to come up a lot of ideas. Play with it and let your mind run wild. Of course, I bet you are wondering how to get those things into the bead, I sure did the first time I saw them. The trick is to put them in after pulling the first point but before pulling the second point while you still have a relatively large opening. If the object is relatively large, you may have to inflate the tubing and cut it in the inflated section to have a big enough opening. Then gather it in some and pull a point. Try to work a little cooler than usual if you have something really delicate or flammable in your bead.

Suggested further reading

Carberry, Edward. Glassblowing, An Introduction to Artistic and Scientific Flameworking, Second Edition, MGLS Publishing 1994

Gruenig, David. "Silvering Glass" The Independent Glassblower Issue # 26 (June/July/August) 1992

Hasluck, Paul N. Traditional Glassworking Techniques, The Corning Museum of Glass, 1988

© 1996 James Kervin

162 Glass Beadmaking

Hoyt, Homer L. Glassblowing An Introduction to Solid and Blown Glass Sculpturing, Crafts & Arts Publishing Co. Inc., 1989

Lunstrom, Boyce. "Iridizing Pyrex Glass At The Bench" Glass Line Vol. 4 No. 5 (February/March) 1991

Schneider, Don. "Lampworked Beads" Glass Studio No 35 (repeated and updated in Glass Line Vol. 7 No. 4 December/January 1994)

Drawn beads

Basically drawn beads are made by collecting a gather of glass at the end of a blowpipe. Air is blown into the gather to form a small bubble. Next the bubble is decorated. Then the bubble is blown out some. An assistant attaches a punty to the end of the bubble and then draws it out into a tube. After cooling down, the tube is cut into short sections and the ends are smoothed out. This is the basics of the process, let's now examine it in greater detail.

Preparation

This technique is really borderline on being achievable using a torch and lampworking. If you are doing it this way, you will be doing it on a small scale or you will need a much larger torch than a minor bench burner. As an alternative to a torch, this technique works even better when done using a glory hole.

For this technique, you need to use a couple new pieces of equipment besides the glory hole; you need a blowpipe and a punty. Like the mandrels that were discussed for making wound glass beads, you want your blowpipe and punty to be made from stainless steel. As you may remember, the reason for this is that stainless steel has low heat conductivity. This allows you to have a relatively short piece of pipe or rod glowing cherry red on one end but being cool enough to hold on the other end. The size of the blowpipe and punty that you will use depends on the size of the flame you are working with. For a minor bench burner, you will be working fairly small, say on the order of a quarter inch in diameter for your blowpipe and one eighth inch in diameter rod for your punty. Ed Hoy's carries a cute little small blowpipe that can be used for this purpose or you can use small diameter tubing. Always work with the largest diameter tubing possible because this requires more air be blown into the tube to pressurize and shape the bubble. This gives you greater control and feel for the expansion process. With a small glory hole you will be working with slightly larger equipment, a blowpipe of about a half inch diameter and a punty about one quarter inch in diameter. Tools of this size are available from a number of glassblowing suppliers. If you want, you can also use pyrex tubing for your blowpipe. Just be sure that you remove all the pyrex when you are done or you will have compatibility mismatch cracking.

© 1996 James Kervin

Forming and decorating the bubble

In a hot glass studio, you would take the gather on your blowpipe directly from a crucible of molten glass. For a smaller studio without a furnace, a couple of options are available.

First, you can lay up your glass sheet or rods in a kiln and bring it to a temperature slightly over tack fuse where it is soft and pliable. Then roll your blowpipe over the glass to gather it onto the pipe. Initially you will want to use a single color glass so that if it does not wrap perfectly around the pipe you will have not messed up any pattern you may have tried to achieve. As you get practice wrapping hot sheet glass around your blowpipe, you will come to realize exactly how much glass to lay out in the kiln so that it will wrap completely around the pipe. (To do this you want the length to be about 3 1/4 times the blow pipe outer diameter depending on the thickness of the glass.) The width of the glass is controlled by the size of the bubble you want-about 2" is a good place to start. When you have reached this point, you might want to start thinking about laying some patterns up with the glass on the kiln shelf that will then be contained in your final bead.

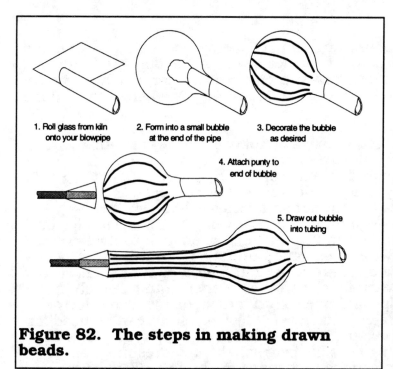

Figure 82. The steps in making drawn beads.

Alternatively you can wrap hot sheet glass around the end of your blowpipe or punty as if you were making wound beads and it was your mandrel. Obviously you will be working out at the end of your blowpipe and will actually wrap out over the end of the hole. This is hard to do for glass rods on a small pipe but easy using a glory hole.

In doing this in a glory hole it helps to have an assistant. (You will need him or her when pulling the tube anyway.) The assistant's job is to sneak the sheet glass slowly into the glory hole by holding it with long handled (one to two feet) pliers. (These can be made by adding some pipe on the handles of some ordinary pliers.) The glass is first held off to the side outside the mouth of the glory hole and slowly introduced to the flame. Try to look for changes in color or of rounding of the edges to use as indicators of how fast to feed the glass into the flame. Be careful not to introduce it too fast or pieces will break off and fall on your glory hole liner. Hot glass is very corrosive to the ceramic fiber liners and can eat its way though them. Once the sheet glass starts wholesale drooping, pull it out and wrap this hot section around your

Drawn Beads 165

blowpipe which has been kept warm by moving it in and out of the glory hole as necessary.

The glass will wrap only part way around the blowpipe. To complete the wrap, stick the blowpipe back into the glory hole such that the transition of the region of where the glass wraps around the tube to the still flat section is up. Allow the heat of the glory hole and the force of gravity to help complete the wrap. Use the marver to help as needed to close the wrap.

For those of you working in a torch, take a few wraps around the end of the pipe for attachment. Then gather more and more glass on this. As you get enough start building it up like one half of the hollow wound bead I discussed in the wound bead chapter. Then as you have enough roll over the top of this to build a glob handing on the end of the pipe. Then wind on more and more glass.

Introduce a small air bubble into the center of the glass as soon as you are able to. You then as needed keep picking up more glass from the kiln (or wherever) and winding it on as before, making sure that you do not let your bubble collapse. As you add more glass to your bubble you want to get it and keep it pear shaped with most of the glass off the end of the blowpipe because only the glass off the end of the pipe can be drawn into a tube.

Once you have a fairly good thick starting bubble, you can decorate it as you want. This can be done in a number of ways. You could add other colors by hand in the torch flame. You could roll on other colors of glass from the kiln. You could roll it on decorations laid out on your marver. Alternatively you can pick cane up that is arranged around the inside of a bucket or on a grooved marver. After picking up additions to the outside of your glass, they can either be heated up and marvered into your bubble or they can be just lightly heated to retain texture. This can be done either in your glory hole or large torch.

When adding different layers of colored glass, you may want to vary their thickness around the bubble. When doing this you have a couple of options open to you. You could add the glass directly with varying thickness or you can add it uniformly to your bubble and then distort it. There are a number of ways to distort it. The first would be to rake it as you did for wound beads but here the idea is to leave creases running down the length of the bubble. This suffers from being hard to control both in the depth of the creases that you leave and in how uniformly spaced they end up around the bubble.

A second choice is to use a marver with a series of parallel grooves cut into it to put in the creases. Rolling the bubble on this marver will result in uniform grooves around the bubble. The problem with this technique is that if you do it on successive layers, you will find that the ridges will not line up from one layer to the next. First because it is hard to line up the starting point from one layer to the next. Second because the angle subtended by a constant length circular arc decreases as the radius or size of the bubble gets larger.

© 1996 James Kervin

To form distortions of constant angular orientation, optic molds are used. Optic molds as explained earlier are conical molds with interior variations of a given shape. The shape is constant but of decreasing size as you go deeper into the mold. This prevents having any undercuts that could trap the glass in the mold. Common cross sectional shapes include: triangles, squares and multi-pointed stars and they are now being manufactured for lampworkers by Steiner. A simple optic mold for shop use can be constructed as illustrated back in Chapter 5 by marking equal angled arcs drawn on the top of a piece of wood. Finishing nails are then driven into the block of wood at the marked locations. The nails should be driven in a slight angle leaning away from the center of the circle to avoid trapping the glass. For uniform distortion you must try to control the angle you drive the nails in so it does not change.

With an optic mold, the number and angular orientation between the grooves in the glass are constant from layer to layer because they are controlled by the mold. All you have to be concerned with is how deep you insert the bubble into the mold. These techniques will allow you draw the bubble out to make the multi-colored chevron beads (also known as Star or Rosetta beads). Of course you have to then back fill the distorted areas to get back to a circular cross section for this.

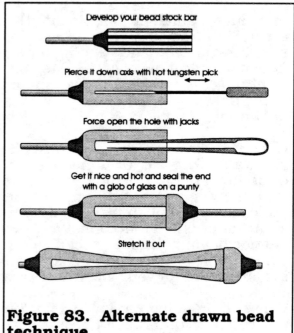

Figure 83. Alternate drawn bead technique.

Sometimes you also want your drawn beads to have a cross sectional shape other than circular. To achieve this the bubble can be shaped with a marver and paddle into a triangular, square or some other cross section. It can also be blown into a mold of the desired shape or pressed into an optic mold. By being careful as you draw out the tube, this shape can be retained in the final bead. If you add more glass to one side than the other, you can force the hole in the bead to be off center for a different effect.

An alternative method of forming the initial bubble which is then drawn out into tubing is illustrated in Figure 83. This can be done on pieces using the kilnforming methods that we discussed for manufacture of mosaic cane or for rod built up using optic mold techniques. Make a cylinder a few inches in diameter and in length. Attach it to a punty. Then get the cylinder hot and poke a hole down its center with your tungsten pick. Smooth up the hole and enlarge it as necessary with glassblowing jacks. Size the hole that you put into the cylinder with the knowledge that as you pull the tubing that the wall thickness to hole diameter ratio will remain approximately constant. Then attach a second

Drawn Beads   167

punty with a small gather of glass over the open hole trapping a bubble down the center of the cylinder. Then draw out the cylinder as described in the next section. This is another good way to try and make chevron beads.

Drawing out the tube

As you prepare to draw out the bubble into a tube, there are a few things that you need to remember. First is that the initial diameter of the tube is controlled by the area of the punty attachment to the bubble. Therefore you will want to keep the punty attachment about the size that you are looking for in your finished bead. This attachment is made by getting a small gather of glass on the end of the punty and forming it into a cone. The base of the cone is at the end of the rod and the point of the cone is pointing toward your hand. The base should just barely cover the end of the punty. If the base gets out too far from the end of the punty, it becomes hard to control and will stretch during pulling.

Second is that, as in drawing out points, the continued diameter and thickness of the tube is a function of the speed with which you draw out the bubble into a tube and the initial temperature of the bubble. The slower you draw it out, the larger and the thicker the resultant beads. Your bubble should have fairly thick walled as we discussed before to help keep the bead thicker. Also the size of the air pocket that you want in your bubble depends on how much you are going to draw it down. The more that you are going to draw down the bubble into tubing the larger an air pocket you will need to get the appropriate size hole down the middle for your bead. If you want, you can also twist your tube as you draw it out. This will cause you surface decorations to spiral up the length of the bead. This also creates an interesting effect if your bead has a non-circular cross section.

So at this point you may want to extend the bubble out further into the gather. To prevent the bubble from blowing up uncontrollably instead of traveling down into the gather, you need to lightly chill the sides of the bubble on a marver or paddle. This makes the sides more viscous than the center.

Once you have the bubble to the desired size, attach your punty and pull away.

Finishing the bead

After your drawn tube has cooled, you can cut your beads from it. The beads can be cut by any of a number of techniques. You can use the same techniques that we have already discussed for cutting rods (scribe and break, nipping, etc.) Another method is to use any of the many diamond saws now available (wire, band and cut-off.) Lastly tungsten chipping hammers and anvils are available to chip off beads. These are some of the subjects that will be discussed in the chapter on finishing your beads. That chapter will also discuss mechanical grinding and polishing the ends of your beads. They could also be fire polished in the torch flame or a kiln.

© 1996 James Kervin

Glass Beadmaking

Suggested further reading

Waggoner, Shawn. "The Talismanic Glass Jewel Techniques of Blown and Fused Jewelry" Glass Art Vol. 4 No. 4 (May/June), 1989

Waggoner, Shawn. "The Drawn Glass Bead" Glass Art Vol. 8 No. 3 (March/April), 1993

Pressed and Pierced Beads

Let me start this chapter off with the admission that I don't know a lot about what I will call pressed beads for short. This is because I have never worked with them, nor have I observed them being made. What I do know about them comes by way of reading and some excellent lectures presented by and subsequent discussions with Shari Hopper on her travels in Czechoslovakia where pressed and pierced beads are part of a cottage industry. I am also indebted to Andy Magisano and George Darveaux of Gypsy Dragon Bead Company who let me examine some of the vintage tools that they were importing from Eastern Europe although I hear that they have sold them all.

Modern development of the process came from a desire to satisfy the costume jewelry industry's desire for cheap gem-like stones with which to decorate clothing. This led to the simple pliers tooling to make cabochons, shaped pieces of glass with one flat side. The flat side made for easy attachment to a metal backing which was then sewn to the fabric. This process is easily extended to two sided jewels which could be enclosed by a ring of metal, but as we will see it took some ingenuity of design to develop tooling that would put in holes for stringing these glass jewels.

Basic techniques of pressed and pierced beadmaking

Basically the process of pressed and pierced beadmaking consists of heating up a glass rod to a semi molten state using a small furnace, kiln or glory hole. The molten glass is then fed into a pliers-like press where two jaws with dies on them come together to form the exterior shape of the bead. At the same time, a needle is pushed through the molten glass to form the hole in the bead. The needle can be pushed through either perpendicular to or parallel to the face of the jewel. The glob on the rod is usually big enough to make a couple of beads before having to be reheated. The rough beads, which at this point have some flashing on them where the jaws of the pliers meet, are fed down a funnel into a can where they await post processing. This can may be kept warm but there is no real effort to make it hot enough for annealing. (In general, Shari says most East European beads are not annealed.)

Post processing of the pressed and pierced beads consists of breaking them apart and screening the results to separate the bead from the flashing. Beads may then be tumble polished to get rid of the rest of the

© 1996 James Kervin

flashing marks and to smooth the bead. Alternatively rough faceted surfaces of the bead may be polished by cold working the bead.

Equipment used in pressing beads

As mentioned earlier, this equipment was derived from tools that look like a big set of pliers. Figure 84 illustrates what one of these devices looks like. The basic construction of the tool is from steel for strength and durability. The patterned dies on the jaws may either be fixed to the tool or be removable to allow for interchangability with other dies of different patterns. To use them you just stick a blob of glass between the dies and push down on the tool to make the jewel. Bringing the dies together shapes and chills the glass at the same time. The handles may be spring loaded to quickly open the jaws for the next jewel. This allows one-handed or one-footed (if hooked up to a pedal) operation of the tool. With this tool you can quickly turn out jewels. The next question is how do we put in holes to turn them into beads?

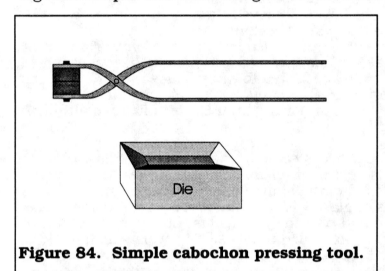

Figure 84. Simple cabochon pressing tool.

The easier of the two examples that I will present on how the holes are put in is for the case of a hole parallel to the face of the jaws of the die. Before we get started into this explanation, let's think about some of the requirements to do this. It requires, first, that the rough shape of the jewel be established. Second, the relative fragility of the needle requires that it plunge straight in and out to prevent it from becoming jammed in the hole or bent. This is what the device illustrated in Figure 85 does.

In the this tool, linkage *a*, which consists of the bottom handle and the top die is held stationary. First of all, you can see from our previous discussion how the basic shape of the bead is established as before by pressing the jaw dies together. So, because of tension on the spring on top of the tool, initial downward motion of the end of the top handle (linkage *c*) results in closure of the dies by clockwise rotation of linkage *b* about pivot point #1. After the dies close, further motion about pivot point #1 is not possible. This means all further downward motion of the top handle results in motion of the T shaped linkage *c* about pivot point #2. This in turn pushes linkage *d* forward on the pin slider through motion of pivot point #3 on the bottom of linkage *c*. The pin block is restrained by the guide rod to motion parallel to the face of the bottom die. Thus the pin is forced through a slot in the face of the bottom die and the glob of rapidly chilling molten glass contained therein. This forms the hole in the bead. As pressure on the upper handle is released,

Pressed and Pierced Beads 171

the spring pulling on the top of linkage c causes the pin to be withdrawn first through counterclockwise motion of linkage c and resultant pulling on linkage d. As more pressure is released the weight of the lower jaw causes the dies to come apart exposing the finished bead. Then the feed rod is pushed further into the jaw, pushing out the finished bead and supplying more molten glass for the next cycle. The cycle can be accomplished a few time before the feed rod has to be reheated.

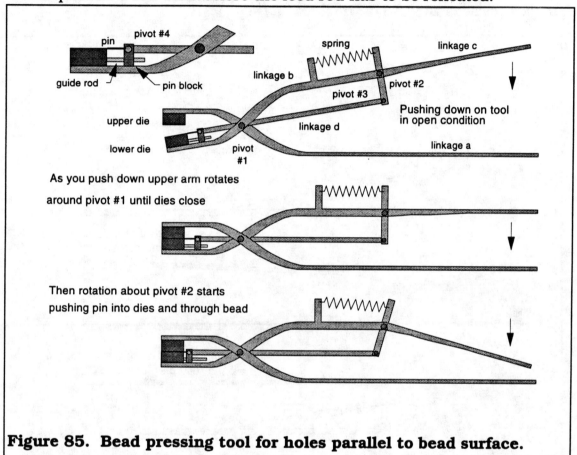

Figure 85. Bead pressing tool for holes parallel to bead surface.

Hopefully now that you understand the operation of the first pressed beadmaking tool, the next one will be easier to understand. This one makes holes in the bead perpendicular to the face plane of the dies. It is illustrated in Figure 86. As before, linkage a is fixed to a base. In this tool as you press down on the handle of linkage b both the dies are pressed together and the pin gets pushed through the dies simultaneously. The dies close as before by clockwise rotation of linkage b about pivot point #1. At the same time this causes sliding pivot point #2 to push down upon linkage c. This in turn causes rotation of linkage c about pivot point #3. This rotation drives sliding pivot point #4 downward, which results in pushing the pin block along the guide rod. This sliding pushes the pin through a hole in the top die, the rapidly cooling molten glass and another hole in the bottom die. Pulling up on the handle on linkage b then causes the pin to withdraw and the dies to open for more glass to be fed in. This final release could be made easier by adding a compression spring between linkage a and b to the right of

© 1996 James Kervin

pivot point #3. This would help force the linkages apart on the return stroke.

Linkage c and the sliding pin block are slotted at sliding pivot points #2 and 4 respectively because the pivot point pins move relative to each of these components. Sliding pivot point #2 moves backward toward the handle end of the slot as the jaws close, while sliding pivot point #4 moves towards the end of the jaws as they close.

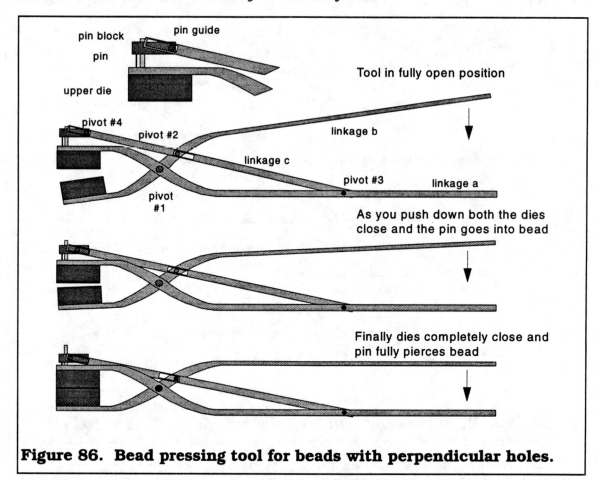

Figure 86. Bead pressing tool for beads with perpendicular holes.

I hope that you understood the explanations of how both of these tools work. There are many variations on each of these themes with different geometries and linkage organizations. Some of these themes have also been mechanized to turn out many beads a second. With this explanation and a little engineering know how, it would be possible for you to go out and build one of these tools. Alternatively if you are interested you could call Andy and George to see if they might still have one left.

Decorating pressed and pierced beads

As you can probably guess after reading the explanation of how these tools work, there is not a lot that you can do to decorate beads that are made this way. Once they are done, they are done. There is not much that you can do in hot working these beads. One thing that you can do

Pressed and Pierced Beads   173

is change dies on the jaws to get different shaped beads. Of course this is not something that you will be able to do on the fly in that the dies have to be rugged and made out of something hard like steel. You will have to go to a machine shop to get new dies made.

The other thing that you can do is play with the glass that you feed into the tool. Shari tells me that the glass used for this purpose often has variations in color that go through it much like that commercially available stained glass. These variations in color act as accents within the bead. So you can mix glass colors before feeding it into the tool. The other thing that Shari points out about the operation is that there is no real mixing of the glass in the pressing operation. The glass doesn't really have to be as hot as we get it during winding to press a bead from it. This means that colors and patterns in the feed stock will not diffuse as much and complex patterns could possibly be fed into it. Because of the rapid chilling, chill marks are also put into the bead that could serve as decorative accents.

Another possibility for decorating these beads is that they could be cold worked. They can be carved, polished, plated, etc. By making beads of multiple colored layers they could be carved to have cameo like images. I am sure that if you think about it you can come up with more ideas how to decorate pressed and pierced beads.

Suggested further reading

None that I am aware of

© 1996 James Kervin

174   Glass Beadmaking

© 1996 James Kervin

Fused Beads

Fusing is a kilnworking process where layers or pieces of glass are heated up together to temperatures where their surfaces become soft and flow together to form a permanent bond. The degree to which the layers of glass flow together, as illustrated in Figure 87, will vary with temperature and the hardness of the glass. (Hardness refers to how easily the glass flows under heat.) When heated to the lower end of the fusing temperature range, commonly called tack fusing, the glass layers will stick together and there will be very little change in the shape of the layers. Edges will just barely be rounded. Heating to a slightly higher temperature, commonly called full fusing, the glass layers will start to sink into each other and edges will become very soft and will flow into each other in smooth transitions. Finally heating again to just a little higher temperature, commonly called flat fusing, the layers will all collapse down into one another to form one flat fused mass of uniform thickness. I find that these different fusing temperature regimes for more most soda-lime glasses are about 100°F apart. Thus Bullseye glass tack fuses at about 1350°F, full fuses at about 1450°F and flat fuses at about 1550°F.

In making fused glass beads you have two basic options. The first is that you can make the beads as individual fused pieces. The second option is to make large fused bead stock pieces that you then cut apart into individual beads which are either fire or grit polished. In either case, unless you work to overcome it, you end up with beads that tend to be flat rather than cylindrical. The first part of this chapter will mainly focus on the fusing process after which we will focus in more on how to use this process to make beads.

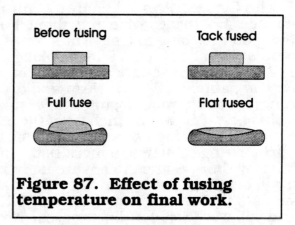

Figure 87. Effect of fusing temperature on final work.

Choosing your glass

The process of making fused glass beads is a fairly simple one. It starts with choosing your glass palette. As you can guess, the glass in your palette has to be compatible. As we discussed in the chapter on glass properties, this means that they all have nearly the same coefficient of

176   Glass Beadmaking

expansion. Glass is now available that has been tested at the factory to ensure its compatibility. Bullseye Glass Company for example maintains a continuous testing program to ensure the compatibility of its fusing glass. Other companies have also started doing this and some have developed formulations that are compatible to Bullseye. Wasser and Uroburos are examples of these. As we have discussed, all your Moretti glass is pretty much compatible to itself (some of the alabasters may be an exception) but not to Bullseye glass. Moretti is now also making flat glass that can be fused to the rods.

We have discussed how you can test the compatibility of your glass by pulling threads and watching how they bend. This will work fine for small handmade wound beads but not for all fused beads. The reason for this is that in mass producing of fused beads you often make large fused logs of bead stock as an interim step. The thread test is not sensitive enough in measuring compatibility to ensure that stress will be kept low enough to prevent these larger logs from cracking. The variability is partly a result of the quick heating and cooling of the glass in doing this test. It is also partly a result of the variability of how proficient you are in doing the test.

Measuring glass compatibility for fusing

The most accurate way of ensuring that two glasses are compatible is to fuse up a test strip. To run a test strip requires a clear compatible base glass against which to test. What you are really doing is testing the compatibility of each of the other glasses to this base glass. Then by using the Transitive Property of Glass Fusing (i.e. if A is compatible to B and C is compatible to B then A must be compatible to C) we can presume their compatibility.

To run the test strip you start by cutting a strip of the clear base glass about 1 1/2 inches wide and about 1 1/2 inches long for each specimen that you are going to test. Thus if you are going to test 6 specimens, the strip should be at least 9 inches long and 1 1/2 inches wide. Next cut 1/2 by 1/2 inch square specimens of each of the glasses you want to test for compatibility. Wash, clean and dry the glass carefully to prevent contamination from biasing your results. Space the specimens on the strip of clear base 1/2 inch from the edges and 1 inch from each other. Keep track of which glass is which since sometimes they change color during firing. It helps to mark both the original glass sheet and the glass strip by the specimen to ensure no mix-ups. Some marking pens are available (Steel Paint marking pens made by the Alton Company are one version) that have a metallic-based ink that will fire into the surface glass and will work well for this process. Now fire the test strip as will be described to a flat fuse. This will require a processing temperature somewhere in the range of 1450 to 1650°F depending on the hardness of the glass. After this firing, the thickness of the strip will be almost constant all the way down the strip.

Now that you have fired the test strip, it is time to examine it for signs of incompatibility by looking for stress in it. To do this we use polarizing filters like those on expensive sunglasses. You will need two of these filters to conduct the test. These filters have fine parallel assemblages of

© 1996 James Kervin

crystals in them that only let light through that is vibrating in one direction, say left and right. If you rotate these filters relative to each other over a light table, you will see that they will get dark and light periodically. They are dark when the filter on the bottom only lets light vibrating left-to-right through and the second filter only lets light vibrating top-to-bottom through. As you rotate the top filter 90° relative to the bottom filter the crystals on both are now aligned such that both filters now allow only light that is vibrating left-to-right through. This configuration allows the maximum amount of light through. As you turn the top filter further, they will again get darker until at another 90° the light is again at a minimum.

You are probably wondering how these filters are going to be used to measure stress in the glass. To understand how this works, you have to know that light which passes through stressed glass is twisted so that the direction of its vibration changes. Light that passes through unstressed glass is not twisted. With this in mind, put one filter below the test strip on the light table (or over a light bulb) and the other filter on the top of the glass. Rotate the top filter to the position that lets through the minimum amount of light. Any signs of incompatibility that exists in the test strip will be visible as a halo of light around the test

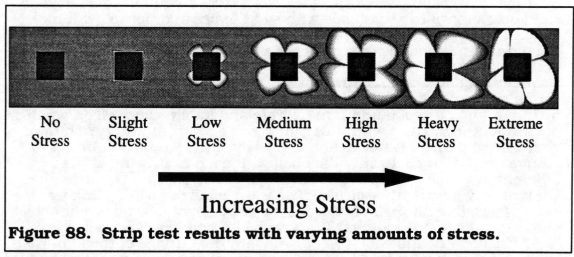

Figure 88. Strip test results with varying amounts of stress.

specimens where the light has been twisted by stress in the glass. Figure 88 illustrates what this will look like for varying amounts of stress in the glass. The bigger the halo the greater the amount of stress. The only exception to this rule is for strips that have cracked. Stress will be relieved in the vicinity of a crack. Of course developing cracks should also give you a clue that something is wrong. Specimens that show only slight stress or less are compatible with each other.

Color stability

The other thing that you have to be aware of in choosing and mixing glasses in projects is that some glasses will change color when they are fired. This is caused by the metal oxides changing oxidation state from the atmosphere inside the kiln. It is usually better to steer away from using such glass. Also some colors seem to interact and will form a third color along their common boundary. This could be used as a design

178 Glass Beadmaking

element but it is best avoided. These are just things that you will only become aware of as you work with fusing different types and colors of glass.

Fusing glass with your kiln

We have already discussed what makes up a kiln, how a kiln works, how to maintain it and some basic kiln safety rules. Let's now discuss the procedure for using your kiln in the process of making fused beads or other objects.

Preparing for a firing

Before firing the kiln, you have to prepare a kiln shelf to put your work on. Kiln shelves are made from clay and mullite and are designed to withstand the high temperatures inside a kiln but they must be treated to prevent your glass beads from sticking to them as the glass gets soft. For this reason, the kiln shelf has to be coated with kiln wash like you did for the bottom of your kiln when you tempered it. If there is any residual kiln wash on the shelf, you will have to scrape it off with a paint scraper. This kiln wash dust is an irritant so make sure that you wear a dust mask or respirator. If the shelf is scratched you may also have to sand out some of the scratches with sand paper in order to get a nice smooth surface. Now it is ready to coat with kiln wash. If your shelves are new, it is a good idea to temper them also as you did the kiln.

Commercial kiln wash mixtures are available from most glass or ceramics stores. If you can not find any, you can make your own from a 50/50 dry mixture of aluminum hydrate and kaolin clay. Mix a small amount of the mixture with water until you get a thin watery solution; about three parts of water to one part of dry mix. Use a soft brush to paint several thin coats onto the shelf with each coat being applied in a different direction. It should not leave visible streaks as you brush it on. Let it air dry overnight, if possible, as this seems to form a stronger coating possibly through chemical reactions. If you are impatient to get started, you can put it directly into your kiln and heat it up slowly to 200 °F. After it is dry and cool, you can smooth the surface of the kiln wash layer by rubbing your hand across it. If not overfired, the coating should last a number of firings. Once it starts to develop pull outs, it should be replaced.

Next, clean your glass. Any dust or body oils can cause spotting of the glass during firing. I use Windex. Alcohol is also a good choice. Handle the glass by the edges once it is clean. Cover it with a clean paper towel to keep the dust off. Lay out your work on the "washed" kiln shelf. Different fusing projects should be positioned on the shelf so that they are not touching each other, otherwise they might become fused together. Find three or four 2" or longer ceramic posts from your collection of kiln furniture and place them on the bottom of the kiln in the locations where the corners of your shelf will be. These posts will raise the kiln shelf off the bottom of the kiln for more even heating. Place your thermocouple through the hole in the peephole plug into the kiln. It

© 1996 James Kervin

Fused Beads   179

should end up just above (within a couple of inches) your project on the kiln shelf. You are now ready to go.

Some glasses have a tendency to crystallize or devitrify on their surface through loss of some of their fluxing agents when heated in a kiln. This is something that again you will only learn from experience in using each type of glass. Sometimes you will only get a touch of it on the first firing cycle and it will get progressively worse with subsequent firings. Some glasses don't seem to do it at all. There are a couple of ways to handle this problem. The first is to live with it. I know some artists who like the look and actually try to find ways of inducing it. Personally I don't like the look of it. Once it has developed, you can sandblast it off and fire that bead again to restore surface luster. The other technique to control devitrification is a preventative one.

Devitrification comes from reactions at the surface of the glass and not in the bulk of the glass. So one way to deal with the problem is to cover that surface up. The way that this is usually done is, as Dan Fenton would say, to spray it with your favorite "devit medicine" prior to firing. The "devit medicines" that he is referring to are clear overglazes or clear enamels. These mixtures of micron sized particles of low melting temperature glass are actually formulated as additives for enamels that serve to modify both their firing temperature and their expansion coefficient. They are not cure-alls for devitrification though, because they will interact with the agents used in iridizing glass. (Although this can also be used as a way to selectively remove an iridized surface or to selectively fire-polish a sandblasted surface.) They also have the problem that they will stick tenaciously to kiln wash which you now have to figure out how to remove.

When choosing an overglaze there are a couple factors that you should take into consideration. They include: how hot you want to heat the glass in your next step (you may want to keep the temperature low to avoid glass flow), their lead content (are you going to eat off of or suck on the glass) and its compatibility to your glass (does it have the right coefficient of expansion.) There are fluxes available commercially that match Bullseye expansion 90 family ("Spray A", "Super Spray" and "Standard Ceramics Flux-92") and some for borosilicate glass (Reusche & Co. 32). The lead free formulations generally require higher firing temperatures (1300°F) than a high lead one.

To use most dry powder overglazes, mix them with 50/50 mixture of alcohol and distilled water. Then apply it by either painting it or by spraying it. To spray it use nice even strokes with a small airbrush from a distance of 6 to 10 inches trying to get the edges also. It is important to get a nice uniform spray that is not too thick as thick coatings will fire hazy. Also coatings the are too thin will look blotchy. (These problems have led some of the fused bead artists that I have talked to, to swear off all use of overglazes entirely.) If you only want the overglaze on one part of a stack up, spray that part individually, allow it to dry and move it over to the kiln self by handling it only on the edges. If you are having problems with overglaze sticking to the kiln wash on your shelf try covering the shelf with a non-rigidized ceramic fiber paper such as Fiberfrax™ 970-J. This is a paper made from alumina fibers that have

© 1996 James Kervin

been woven together and is held together using organic binders. Prefiring burns out the organic binders which otherwise could leave unsightly residues on your bead.

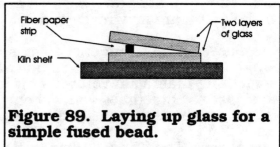

Figure 89. Laying up glass for a simple fused bead.

Overglazes can also be used to shine up the edges of beads cut from a larger fired piece. Here you cut the beads off and grind the edges flat. Apply the overglaze to the bead and fire it to a temperature that correctly matures the overglaze. The overglaze that you choose will depend on the effect you are trying to achieve. If you want nice sharp corners, then you will choose a low-fire one. If you want more rounded corners, then you will choose a high-fire one. Of course if you are trying to fire both ends of the bead at once while suspending it on a ceramic bead rack, you have to use a low fire overglaze to prevent slumping.

Let's lay-up glass to make simple fused glass designs using a hole former in the space where you want the bead hole to be. For this initial bead we will just sandwich a strip of fiber paper between two layers of glass as shown in Figure 89. The best pore former for making beads is prefired rigidized ceramic fiber paper cut into strips or cord. The yarn or paper is rigidized by soaking unfired paper in a hardening solution of 15% colloidal silica followed by air drying and firing it in a kiln to about 1300° F. If your beadmaking process is a multi step one with cutting and grinding steps between firings, you may find that you will need to replace the fiber paper between firings.

Before starting a firing, you should take a second to reflect on the size of the pieces that you are working on. This will determine the rates at which you can change temperature and the time you will have to soak at process temperature. You should also reflect on what you are doing to decide whether you will have to vent the kiln as you increase temperature. If you are applying overglazes or lusters, then you will need to vent the kiln during heat up. With these considerations in mind, you can plan how you will carry out the

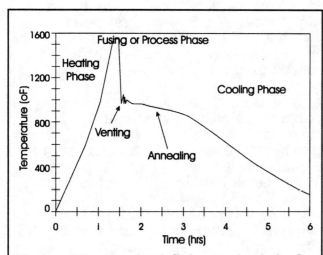

Figure 90. Typical firing schedule for fusing.

three main phases of the firing cycle: the heating, the fusing and the cooling phase. The basic firing cycle is illustrated in Figure 90. Plan out your run on a worksheet like that shown on the next page.

Then record actual run measurements as you go along so that you have a record of

© 1996 James Kervin

Fused Beads 181

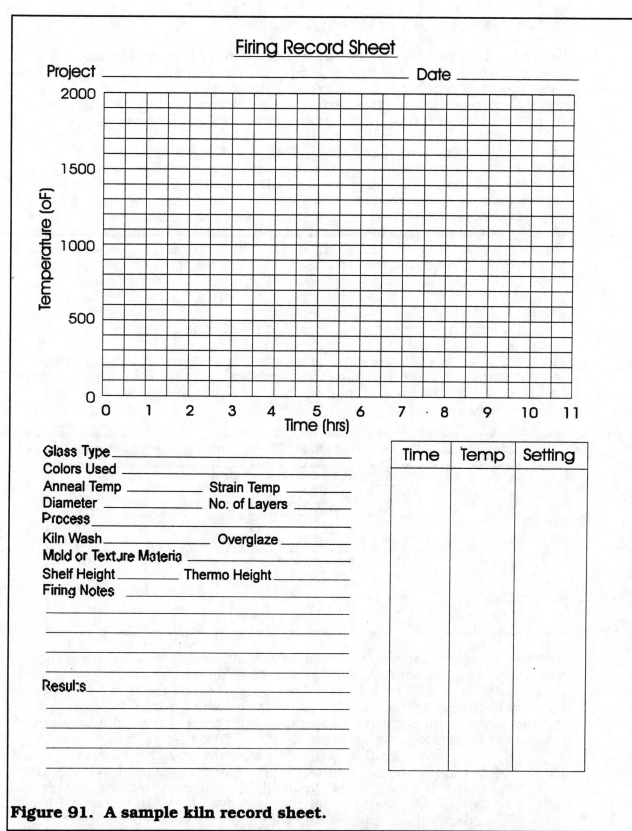

Figure 91. A sample kiln record sheet.

what you did and will be able to keep track of what works well and what doesn't. This will save you a lot of time and money in the long run.

182   Glass Beadmaking

Phase one of the firing cycle: heating

In the heating phase, you are raising the temperature of the kiln from
room temperature to the fusing temperature. The speed with which you
raise the temperature is measured in degrees per minute. So if you are
going to go from room temperature (or 70°F) to a low temperature flux
polish temperature of 1100°F in one hour, you will be heating at a rate of
17.2°F/min. That is actually pretty fast unless your pieces are very
small. The maximum speed with which you should increase the
temperature of your kiln depends upon the size and thickness of the
project that you are working on. The larger or the thicker the project, the
slower that you should to raise the kiln temperature. The reason that
you have to go slower is that you develop large temperature differences
through the glass cross section. The areas that are hotter expand more
than the cooler areas. These temperature distributions stress the bonds
between the atoms in the glass. If this stress becomes too large, the
bonds will break leading to cracks in the glass. This is not much of a
problem with beads but may be a problem with beadstock or larger
projects. The first 700°F of temperature rise seems to be the most
sensitive region since the glass is in the brittle solid regime. You can
then go faster as you move into the non-brittle solid regime. Table 15
gives some suggested rates for various thickness projects through both
regimes. If your project is of the same order of magnitude in length or
width as the thickness, you can probably double these rates without
encountering problems.

Table 15. Maximum heating rates for various glass thicknesses.

Glass Thickness	Maximum recommended heating rates			
	Side Fired Kiln		Top-Fired Kiln	
	Brittle Zone	Non-Brittle	Brittle Zone	Non-Brittle
(in)	(°F/min)	(°F/min)	(°F/min)	(°F/min)
1/8	7.5	11	8	12
1/4	6.5	9.5	7	10
3/8	4.5	7.5	5	8
1/2	2.5	5.5	3	6
1	1.5	2.5	2	3

In order to determine how your controls will have to be set during the
heating phase, assuming you do not have a kiln controller, you will have
to get practice with your kiln and keep good records using record sheets
such as those suggested earlier. Start from room temperature, set your
infinity switches at a given location (say 50% power) and time how long it
takes to reach various temperatures. If you plot this data out as in
Figure 92 you will notice that it is not a straight line. Notice how it heats
faster at low temperatures than at higher temperatures. This is because
more heat is lost through the walls at higher temperature. From this
data, you can plan the various settings required to get different heating
rates. With data on a couple of different settings you will be able to
estimate heating rates for other switch settings. Be aware that heating
rates will also depend on how full the kiln is. So you will want to do this

© 1996 James Kervin

testing with at least one kiln shelf present in the kiln or better yet a project. You might want to combine it with testing of what happens to stacks of glass taken to different processing temperatures. As an example, try taking Bullseye glass to 1150, 1250, 1350 and 1450°F. Or you could distribute cones around the kiln to check for uniformity of heating.

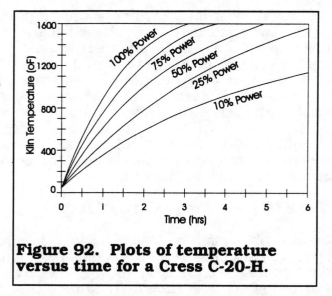

Figure 92. Plots of temperature versus time for a Cress C-20-H.

Phase two of the firing cycle: fusing

The details of the next phase of a firing, the fusing phase, is a function what kind of glass you are using. Because of their different hardnesses, the temperature at which different soda-lime glasses soften and start to flow will vary. This temperature also is a function of the color of the glass. Darker colors absorb radiant energy more efficiently than lighter ones and thus get hotter faster and at slightly lower temperatures. Thus a black Bullseye glass which is nominally a harder glass, will soften at similar temperatures to that of the softer Wasser glass. The following table should give you a feeling for temperatures required in fusing different types of art glass.

Table 16. Fusing process temperature ranges for different glasses.

Glass Type	Annealing (°F)	Slumping (°F)	Tack Fusing (°F)	Partial Fusing (°F)	Full Fusing (°F)
Bullseye	980	1050	1250	1350	1450
GNA		1200	1350	1450	1550
Moretti	970				
Pyrex	1040				
Spectrum	950	1100	1200	1300	1400
Wasser	950	1000	1150	1250	1350

During the fusing phase, you want to hold the temperature as steady as possible to accomplish the process without overfiring. It requires time for the glass to flow. Unfortunately it is also not always possible to tell if the desired result has been achieved by peeking into the kiln because there is so much light coming off and your glasses have to be so dark to protect your eyes. You just have to trust your pyrometer or cones to correctly record the temperatures. Glass flow increases with higher temperature, so for better control you can usually trade off a little lower temperature for a little longer time at that temperature and still achieve the same amount of heat work. This may be the desired way to go because overfiring can ruin many effects.

© 1996 James Kervin

184   Glass Beadmaking

Holding at a particular temperature requires much less heat input than was involved in the heating phase because the heat is just being added to make up for that lost through the walls of the kiln, which hopefully is not much. You will find that you will have to turn your infinity switch way down to prevent further rise in temperature and should keep close tabs on the kiln. The ideal thing to maintain a constant temperature is a set point controller. It is a device that automatically holds a kiln temperature constant. It does this by using a thermocouple to measure the kiln temperature and cuts off power when the kiln temperature rises over the set temperature and turns the power back on when the temperature falls back down.

Phase three of the firing cycle: cooling down

The last phase in a typical kiln cycle is the cooling phase. The first part of the cooling phase usually consists of venting the kiln to rapidly drop in kiln temperature to about 1000°F. Venting is done to prevent too much time at high temperatures. Too much time at high temperature is not desired because it might result in crystallization of the glass. This crystallization appears a dull haze on the glass surface commonly referred to as devitrification. It typically occurs when soda-lime glass is held for long periods of time in the temperature range of 1300 to 1400°F. To vent the kiln, don your dark glasses and your non-asbestos gloves, and open the kiln door. Watch the kiln temperature on your pyrometer. As soon as it drops down to about 1000°F, close the door and allow the inside of the kiln to reequilibrate. You may need to vent the kiln a number of times to get it down to the right temperature range. Be careful in your venting that temperatures in parts of the kiln do not drop so low that you thermal shock your glass. Better to take it easy and vent a number of times rather than thermal shock your beads. Some people advocate any further venting after the first vent be done by propping open the door about 1" until the kiln equilibrates to the proper temperature. This is fine unless you are like me and always doing about three things at once causing you to lose track of what is happening in the kiln. For those of you like me, stick around and hold the kiln open.

The next portion of the cooling phase, going through the annealing range, is where you must cool the kiln fairly slowly to allow all the stress that was just frozen into the glass (to get it through the devitrification range safely) to flow out. The annealing range for a glass occurs in its non-brittle solid regime (which for soda-lime glasses is in the range of 800 to 1000°F) where the glass is solid but the atoms are still pretty mobile and can twist and stretch around one another to relieve stress. Annealing temperatures for common art glasses are given in Table 17. It is important that you go through this range at a slow enough rate that the stress in your glass can get out and that no new stress develops in the glass. If you cool too fast, you will have to reheat the glass to get the stress back out. That process is referred to as annealing and is discussed elsewhere in great detail in this book. It is something that has to be done for all lampworked beads

© 1996 James Kervin

Fused Beads   185

Table 17. Annealing zone temperatures for common glasses.

Glass Manufacturer	Strain Point (°F)	Annealing Point (°F)
Wasser	650	950
Spectrum	700	950
Moretti	680	970
Bullseye	750	980
Pyrex	950	1058
Window	850	1150

During the controlled portion of the cooling cycle, you first soak the project at the annealing point for a given amount of time. Then slowly cool it down to the strain point. This is the temperature at which atomic motion is now so much slower that stress can not be released in a reasonable amount of time. Lastly you cool from the strain point to room temperature at a rate that is slow enough so the bead cools relatively uniformly. The time that you soak at the annealing temperature and the rate at which you cool both through the annealing range and on to room temperature is determined by the thickness of the glass in your project and suggested values are given in Table 15 for expansion 90 glasses. Values for Morreti glass are given in the chapter on finishing of beads where I discuss annealing. If you want to calculate values for other glasses consult some of the references at the end of that chapter.

Table 18. Annealing schedule times and ramps for Bullseye glass.

Glass Stackup Thickness (in)	Number of Glass Sheets	Anneal Soak (min)	Annealing Cooling Rate (°F/hr)	Final Cooling Rate (°F/hr)	Annealing Cooling Ramp (min)	Final Cooling Ramp (min)
0.125	1	20	153.8	615.0	273.7	24.6
0.25	2	30	38.4	153.8	68.4	6.2
0.375	3	45	17.1	68.3	30.4	2.7
0.5	4	60	9.6	38.4	17.1	1.5
0.625	5	90	6.2	24.6	10.9	1.0
0.75	6	120	4.3	17.1	7.6	0.7
0.875	7	150	3.1	12.6	5.6	0.5
1	8	180	2.4	9.6	4.3	0.4

Fusing considerations

There are a number of things to consider in making fused beads that differ from other beadmaking techniques. They must be understood in order to have control in making fused beads and to allow different techniques for shaping your work.

Slumping

When you heat glass up in the kiln above its softening point, it will start to sag and stretch under the effect of gravity if not completely supported underneath. This can be used to your advantage to shape the glass to your liking. Molds can be made from a number of different materials such as ceramics, ceramic fiber paper, stainless steel or plaster. We will discuss making plaster molds for Pâte de Verre beads in the next chapter. This process could also be employed for making small slumping molds for beads. If you want to know more than this about making your own molds, check out one of the general fusing references at the end of this chapter or the next. There are also a number of small ceramic molds commercially available for making small glass jewelry that can be used in making beads.

There are two types of molds: external and internal, which before the age of politically correct speech were referred to as male and female molds. External molds are used to drape objects over the mold and support the glass in the center. Internal molds on the other hand support the glass on the edges of the piece and the glass slumps down into it. In either case, the mold has to be first coated with a layer of kiln wash to prevent the glass from sticking to it. The glass also has to be cut so it fits correctly on the mold and does not drape over the edges. This would cause the glass to crack from pinching down on the mold as it cools. This is not a problem with an external stainless steel molds as the COE of stainless steel is larger than glass and the mold will actually shrink away from the glass during cooling. For a similar reason, internal molds are usually made from ceramic materials. These materials have a lower COE than glass, allowing glass to shrink away from the mold as it cools.

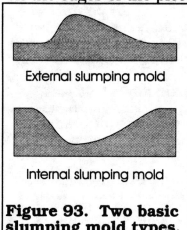

Figure 93. Two basic slumping mold types.

If you use internal molds, you will find that they will usually have an air hole in the bottom. This allows air to escape as the glass slumps into the mold. This hole will have to be kept clean of kiln wash and the mold has to be raised off the kiln shelf to ensure air egress through the hole and under the bottom rim of the mold. Cleaning of the hole is easily accomplished by running a pin or a wire through the hole after application of the kiln wash.

In slumping large pieces, you have to heat up the kiln very slowly, especially during the early stages of the firing to ensure that the glass is heating up evenly. The unsupported portion of the glass does not have the mass of the mold beneath it to slow its temperature rise as the other sections do. Also on external molds you are getting heating from both sides of the glass. Both of these effects can lead to higher thermal gradients in the glass than are encountered in fusing on a kiln shelf. Once the glass is up in the region of the strain point, this is no longer of concern. Rate of temperature fall is also not as much of a concern (beyond normal fusing concerns) during the cooling phase, assuming that you have fully slumped the glass onto the mold.

Slumping starts at temperatures just above the strain temperature and is quickly fully matured at temperatures about 50°F below the tack fuse temperature for that particular glass. As the glass reaches the strain

Fused Beads 187

temperature, you will start to see it slowly sag. As the temperature increases, the glass will start to stretch faster and soon come in contact with the rest of the mold. Then at the upper end of the slumping temperature region, it will begin to pick up the finer detail of the mold. Don't expect too fine of detail though. If you proceed higher in temperature, the glass will start to flow and those portions over raised sections of the mold will start to thin. If you reach this point, you have overfired the slumping run. After slumping, anneal and cool the glass as if it were an ordinary fusing run.

Slumping can be used to achieve a number of effects in beadmaking.

Volume control

When you fuse glass at higher temperatures, it will gradually change its shape and volume in seeking its ideal thickness as dictated by the surface tension of the glass. This ideal thickness is about a quarter of an inch or just slightly over the thickness of two standard sheets of glass. Thus if you are fusing layers thinner than this, they will pull in on themselves to try and achieve this ideal thickness; first at the edges and then in the interior. This process is illustrated for a series of squares singly and placed on top of each other in Figure 94 below. Again this can be controlled somewhat by firing at slightly lower temperature for a longer amount of time.

The existence of this effect leads to a couple of design concepts that you ought to consider when you are developing your ideas. The first is that for objects that you are going to fully fuse, you should have a thickness of two layers of glass. Second try to keep the largest design additions of glass away from the edges of the piece as this will generally lead to variations in the border. This is something that you will develop a feeling for.

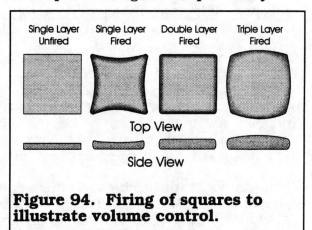

Figure 94. Firing of squares to illustrate volume control.

What happened

Sometimes even though you think that you did everything right, your fused bead project will turn out to be a disaster. Here are some of the most common problems experienced in fusing beads.

Cracking

Cracking is most likely due to thermal shock. You can get an indication of when the cracking occurred during the firing cycle by looking carefully at the cracks. Soft partially refused cracks occurred during the heat up phase, while sharp cracks occurred during the cooling phase. This logic is based on the fact that edges get rounded at the fusing temperature. Thermal shock results from heating or cooling your work too fast. In

188   Glass Beadmaking

heating, the outside is trying to grow faster than the inside. In cooling, the outside is trying to shrink faster than the inside. In either case, if there are large temperature gradients through the glass there is a large amount of stress present. If your projects are small, they may be able to accommodate the stress because its magnitude will be smaller, but when you try to do a larger project with the same firing schedule you may run into trouble. Instead use the rates that are given here as a guide for larger projects. They are probably slightly conservative, but if you have a lot of money or time (doesn't time really equate to money anyway) involved in a piece you may want to be conservative.

Another possible source of cracking is in the piece being restrained somehow during the firing process. There are a number of ways that this can occur. One of the most common of which is when you are trying to slump your bead or bead stock project over a ceramic mold of some kind and the project is larger than the mold. In this case the project will fold a little over the edges of the mold. Then as you cool down, the glass wants to shrink more than the mold since its COE is larger. In this situation, the mold always wins and breaks apart the glass.

The other common source for cracking is from glass sticking to something and getting pulled apart during cool down. If you place your projects too close together on the kiln self and they stick together from spreading during the fusing process, this can result in cracking. Another common cause of sticking initiated cracking is breaks in the wash on the kiln self that allow the glass to stick to the shelf during the fusing process. Make sure that you have a good uniform coating of kiln wash before each firing and that the coating is thick enough.

Bubbles

In making fused glass beads, you may at times discover bubbles in your beads. If small this may not really be a problem, except aesthetically, and even not that. You may like the look of the bubbles and even try to introduce them at times. Bubbles may come from a number of sources: the glass itself, air trapped between glass layers or from other sources.

If you do not want bubbles in your beads, look closely at the glass that you are using. Many art glasses contain bubbles as a decorative feature to help break up light and to give an antique look to the glass. These bubbles are called seed bubbles and cannot be removed by kilnforming. You do not get the glass hot enough to reduce the viscosity enough to let them rise to the surface and pop. This process in glass preparation for blowing is called fining and requires temperatures in the neighborhood of about 2000°F for soda-lime glasses. So be selective in choosing your glass to avoid this source of bubbles.

The next source of bubbles is from air trapped between the layers. This is generally a result of texture on the surface of the glass that you are using that can trap air during fusing. This is more of a problem the larger your project is. There are three things that can be done to try eliminate this problem. The first is easy, if possible. Just use glass without texture. The reason that this in not always possible is that much of the glass that is made as the standard of the industry for fusing

© 1996 James Kervin

Fused Beads   189

(i.e. Bullseye) is textured. The second way to get around this, suggested by Dan Fenton, is to prefire the glass, sandblast the backside clean and look mom – no texture. The next and last technique will probably not eliminate the problem but may help reduce it. Air gets trapped inside the piece when the edges of the piece fuse a lot sooner than the center. Slower heating will allow more of the bulk of the glass to slump before the edges get fused and seal the air in. If you do get air bubbles in your work do not proceed higher than the flat fuse temperature or they may rise to the surface and you can get bubbles thin enough at the surface that the glass can crack.

The last common source of bubbles is from moisture getting trapped beneath your glass. The most common source of this moisture is kiln wash that has not been dried properly. This can be overcome by proper drying of shelves before use or by using ceramic fiber paper on top of the shelf.

Shelf marks and wash sticking

When fusing glass on a kiln shelf, you will sometimes get a lot of unwanted texture in or kiln wash sticking to the bottom of your project. Besides being undesired, it can be a nuisance trying to clean the kiln wash off the back of a project.

There is really not too much that you can do to prevent some texture on the back of your fused project because the whole idea anyway is to get the glass soft enough to flow, stick together and develop smooth edges. It is just normal then that it will assume whatever texture exists on your kiln self. So the only thing that you can do is to make that texture as smooth as possible. If the wash has had areas of pull out from previous firings scrape it off and replace it. If there are too many "pebbles" on the surface of the wash think about looking for a new source of wash. Washes formulated specifically for glass rather than ceramics should have finer particles. Check the surface of the washed shelf before reusing it by running your hand over the surface. If you still don't like the surface, you can try firing over prefired unrigidized fiber paper. This will be really soft though and will have to be replaced quite often. Hey, if you have the bucks go for it.

The other thing that both increases the texture that you see on the bottom of the glass or causes the kiln wash to stick to it is overfiring. If you take the kiln temperature higher than it really needs to be, then the glass gets softer than it needs to be and causes it to stick to whatever it is sitting on – kiln wash or fiber paper. This also results in sharp edges around the bottom of your piece. The mechanism for this is that the glass is sticking to the shelf while trying to contract in volume at the same time and thus thins out along the edges. The way to alleviate this, is not to go to as high a temperature. If you really need that much heat work, get it by spending longer times at lower temperature. Think of glass as maple syrup. When hot it is really running and will get all over the place making a big mess. When slightly cooler it will still pour but it will pour slower so that you have more control over where it goes.

© 1996 James Kervin

Making fused beads

Now that we have discussed the fusing process in a fair amount of detail, let's focus on how to apply it to making beads.

Simple layered beads

You have already seen how you can make a simple bead by layering two pieces of glass with a piece of ceramic fiber paper between them. As you heat this glass sandwich, the top piece of glass slumps over the fiber paper and fuses to the piece below it. Since you used two full layers of glass, it will more or less retain its shape and not shrink much. This type of bead will have one good face that you can decorate as you see fit with the techniques that we will discuss shortly.

There are many variations possible with simple fused bead techniques. The first is the shape of the bead. They can be circles, ellipses, squares, rectangles, diamonds, triangles, etc. The second is that both pieces of glass do not have to be the same size. As shown in Figure 95, you get different effects if you put a larger piece on top of a smaller piece than you do for the reverse. Placing a smaller piece on top allows you to see a decorative background piece beneath it. The second variation, where you insert some filler rods beneath the top piece on either side of the ceramic fiber paper helps balance the smaller piece over the hole former so that it does not move. It also assists a little in volume control by helping to minimize thinning of the upper layer over the hole. The other lay-up orientation, that of putting the larger piece over the smaller, allows the larger piece to wrap around the smaller piece with one uniform color. This is nice for those cases where the side of the glass is a different color than the top of the glass (as in the case of Wasser glass), because the side will usually roll under the piece onto the kiln shelf.

As an alternative to sheet glass, the top or bottom layers could be made of frit sprinkled in place. (We will discuss using and making frit in much more detail in the next chapter on sculptural Pate de Verre beads.) Basically using frit rather than sheet glass allows a number of additional possible choices. It allows developing a gradation of color through the bead. You do this by using a mixture of two colors of frit and changing the ratio of the two frits over the length of the bead. Then when the frit fuses, the bead will have sort of a granite-like appearance where the ratio of the colors varies. I like the effect that this achieves when using transparent colors. Another thing that you can do with frit that is kind of interesting is to only tack

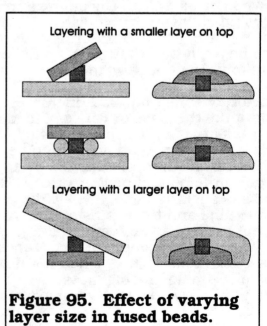

Figure 95. Effect of varying layer size in fused beads.

Fused Beads 191

fuse it together. This gives the bead an interesting pebbly texture.

With simple fused beads you have the option of the fusing process temperature that you use. As discussed earlier, if you only tack fuse your glass, you will barely round its edges. While at flat fuse, it makes one flat bead. You can adjust the process time and temperature to get anything in between these two options as was illustrated back in Figure 86. Also why have just one hole or a straight hole. You can have more holes or different effects by changing how you lay out your fiber paper. Bolo tie beads anyone?

A technique for making glass jewelry that I like, is to lay up larger fused bead stock pieces in a sheet orientation which have a pattern running across them and a bead hole along one edge. Then after fusing the piece, you can cut the sheet up into strips perpendicular to the hole to make a dangling bead necklace where the pattern flows from one long dangling bead to the next. These beads as will be discussed, could be refired to fire polish the edges or tumble polished.

Decorating simple fused beads

You can decorate your kiln-made beads with many of the same design elements that we used in making lampworked beads: murrine, canes, latticino, frit, inclusions, etc. The only difference is that the elements are placed on the stackup of glass cold and are fused onto the glass in the kiln. This change has its benefits and its problems. It is beneficial in that it allows for more precise placement. If you don't like the position of the decoration, you can move it, as long as you have not fired the piece. The problem with placing decorations cold for a fused piece is that, unless you have a real light touch, you can move them when you don't want to. This is especially a problem when moving the kiln self, set up with your project, from the work table into the kiln. Some people try to get around this problem by working with the shelf already in the kiln but I find that this gives me backaches. The other option is to try to hold the decorations in place. The most common way used to hold pieces in place is through the use of glues. A cheap glue usually suggested for this is a little white Elmer's glue. It is applied sparingly with a toothpick. There are also other commercially available formulations like Thompson's Klyr-fire that are made to be used in a kiln and burn off clean without any residues. If you are gluing down fairly large decorations, it is suggested that you apply the glue near the edges because it can cause bubbles during firing if trapped in the center of a piece of glass. Be aware that even glued decorations may move during the firing process as the adhesive burns off.

Using glue, decorations can be arranged in many variations. They can be stacked on or draped over one another. Then by controlling the fusing temperature you can have them blend into one another or just tack fuse and retain their individuality. You can use frit and canes to "paint" images on your glass beads. To really get the a feel for the possibilities available to you, look at one of the suggested references that has a lot of pictures.

© 1996 James Kervin

192   Glass Beadmaking

If you are adding inclusions (like foils, wires, screens, etc.) to fusing projects, these are usually not placed on the upper surface of the glass. This is because they can get burned off or badly oxidized there. It is better to place them between layers of glass as this protects them from the oxidative effects of high temperature air.

There are also many other things that can be done to decorate the surfaces of kilnworked glass. They include: lusters, paints, enamels, and decals. I am going to declare them beyond the scope of this work and am listing several suggested references for reading to find out more about these topics.

Making tubular bead stock

If you want your fused beads to have patterns on all sides, you will have to use a slightly different technique from that we have talked about to this point. You will have to use molds to form beadstock patterned on all sides which you then cut up into individual beads. The bead stock can have any of a number of cross sectional shapes: squares, triangle, circles, etc. For this discussion I will illustrate how to do the easiest cross section type, squares. For illustrations in how to manufacture circular cross sectional beads, see the article on Molly Haskins' work from Ornament Magazine listed at the end of this chapter.

Prior to starting the fabrication of fused glass beadstock, you have to make or develop molds in which to fuse them up. They can be made from many of the same materials that slumping molds are made from. For making square cross sectional beadstock, I use rigidized fiber paper formed in the shape of a U that I then supported along the sides with slices taken off of an old kiln shelf. For triangular beads, a V shaped trough could be similarly constructed. For her circular cross section beads, Molly Haskins uses mullite kiln stilts which had been manufactured with a circular hole down the center. She cuts them in half down their length to make two beadstock molds. These molds have to be well kilnwashed to prevent the glass from sticking to them.

Next depending on what you are trying to achieve in your fused beads, you may want to prepare patterned or decorated sheet glass from which you will make your beads. Molly uses mainly Wasser glass in making her fused beadstock because all the different colors and patterns are about the same hardness. In other words, their viscosity curves are about the same, resulting in the fact that they soften at about the same temperature and rate. This is not true with most other glass manufacturer lines. They will vary in hardness from one color to the next. Wasser is a very soft glass, meaning its viscosity tends to be lower at a given temperature allowing it to flow at lower temperatures. It seems to match the properties of Bullseye's black. For your beads, you may want to fuse strips, dots, latticino, etc. onto the sheet glass prior to cutting it up to make strips to lay in the molds.

Now you are ready to start laying up the glass and the hole former into the mold. What you do here depends a little upon whether you are after disk shaped beads or longer beads. The difference is whether you only decorate the outside of the beadstock or you also try to decorate

© 1996 James Kervin

throughout the thickness. For disk beads, since more of the inside of the beadstock slice shows than the outside, you want to have lots of color and decorations coming up through the beadstock. For longer beads, you may want the inside to be a uniform color. Black seems to be a good color for that purpose. Usually the cross sectional dimension for the different cases will be different also. For disk beads, you will tend to have beadstock cross sectional dimensions that are larger than for normal longer beads. So start cutting up strips and laying them into the mold. Use one of the glues that I talked about in the last section to help hold things in place if needed. Don't forget to position the central hole former down the center of the stack up.

Now fire the stack up, like any other fusing project, paying particular attention to the ramp rates and annealing to avoid thermal shock as well as to keep the final stress in the beads low. You will want to keep your process temperature down in the low full fuse region to prevent too much flow. Let time at temperature do some of the work for you. Some cross sectional shapes may require multiple firings with rotation of the beadstock bar between firings to get the cross sectional shape to look right. This appears to be the case with circular cross sections. Castings of this cross section might be facilitated by use of a mold top that settles down on the stackup to shape the top portion of the beadstock bar as it gets hot.

After the final firing run, your beadstock is ready to cut to length for the desired bead shape. Then you can either grind and fire polish the cut surfaces or tumble polish the whole bead. We have already discussed the use of low melting-temperature glazes for fire polishing. The procedures for slicing of beadstock and tumble polishing beads are discussed in the chapter on finishing of beads since they are applicable to a number of beadmaking techniques.

Individual mold beads

If you want beads of shapes other than disks or tubes, you have to resort to a different type of mold use. One type that we have already discussed is slumping. Here you can take a simple flat fused bead or a thin slice from a beadstock bar as discussed above and then slump them into an internal mold or onto an external mold to shape it. Alternatively you can cast the beads individually in molds that you purchase or make. This technique is described as Pate de Verre beads in the next chapter.

Suggested further reading

Elskus, Albinas. The Art of Painting on Glass, Chas. Scribber and Sons 1980

Fenton, Dan. "Clear Overglazes for Glass", The Firing Line, Orton Firing Institute, Vol. 3 No. 4 (July/August) 1992

Fenton, Dan. "Luscious Lusters", Professional Stained Glass magazine, Vol. 8 No. 4 (November) 1988

Glass Beadmaking

Lundstrom, Boyce and Schwoerer, Daniel. Glass Fusing Book One, Vitreous Publications, 1983

Moorman, Shar. Warm Glass - Kiln-fired Glass Forming Techniques, CKE Publications

Reynolds, Gil. The Fused Glass Handbook, Hidden Valley Books

Ross, Anne L. "Kiln Formed Glass Beadmaking", Ornament Magazine, Vol. 18 No. 1 (Winter) 1994

Pâte de Verre Beads

Pâte de Verre, which is French for paste of glass, is a kilnworking technique where a paste of powdered glass is packed into a refractory mold and fired until the glass is fused. Different colors of glass are combined together to achieve different effects. By varying the firing temperature, you can manipulate the amount that the individual grains fuse together from a full density bead to a sugary texture as in African priest beads. After annealing, the beads are removed from the mold.

Using Pâte de Verre techniques, you can make intricate one-of-a-kind beads with an alabaster like quality or production line reproductions of simpler beads all depending on where your interest lies. Multiples of complex shapes are possible using lost wax casting techniques. In this section you will learn the basics of this process. If you would like to learn more on this process such as making multiples of a particular bead, I suggest that you consult one of the books on the subject, such as "Pâte de Verre and Kiln Casting of Glass" by Dan Fenton and myself (which we hope to have available in 1996), "The Technique of Glass Forming" by Keith Cummings or "Glass Casting and Moldmaking - Glass Fusing Book Three" by Boyce Lundstrom.

To get started in Pâte de Verre beadmaking will require a few items. The first is a kiln. You should already have a kiln in order to properly anneal all the lampworked beads that we have been discussing throughout most of this book but it may not be big enough to do much in the way of Pâte de Verre beadmaking. The next item, a pallet of compatible glass, is one that you should also have at this point from your other beadmaking techniques. A new requirement unique to Pâte de Verre beadmaking is refractory mold making materials. The two materials that we will be discussing here will be fire brick and plaster-based refractories. For simple bead shapes, you may also be able to purchase molds from a fusing or ceramics supply store. You could also make them from many of the materials that are conventionally used for slumping molds: rigidized fiber paper, refractory mixes, clay, etc. These reusable types of molds will have to be kilnwashed prior to use.

Lastly you will need materials to act as hole formers for the beads. These can be made from ceramic fiber strips as was discussed for the fused beads, metals coated with separator compound or wood for low temperature beads.

© 1996 James Kervin

196 Glass Beadmaking

Frit preparation

Fully fused Pâte de Verre work has a unique alabaster appearance that results from microscopic air bubbles trapped between the grains of glass. This leads us into a discussion of the first step of the process, making glass frit. Frit is another name given to small granules of glass. There are a number of ways that you could use to produce frit. The easiest might just be to just put on a pair of safety glasses and grab a hammer. The problem with this technique is that glass flies everywhere. This can be controlled somewhat by wrapping the glass in newspaper first. I put small pieces glass in a paint can and beat on it with something long like a capped piece of pipe. A side benefit of mechanical frit production is that you get a chance to work out all your frustrations without making enemies. This technique produces a wide variety of frit sizes, from fines to fairly large chunks. You can strain out the size range that you are most interested in and continue to mash the large chunks until you are satisfied with the final result. Although if you are trying to make castings of beads from patterned glass as Molly Haskins does, you may want to keep your chunks fairly large or you will lose all of the pattern.

A second method that produces a roundish frit slightly larger in size than most mechanical impact methods is to heat glass in the torch and then chill it in water. In fact you probably have already made a bunch of frit in your attempts to make lampworked beads without even realizing it. How many times have you introduced glass into the flame only to have it thermal shock into pieces. Hey, save those pieces. To do this a little more purposefully heat up your glass strips or rods and stick them into a cup of water. This quick chill will results in tremendous thermal stresses throughout the glass that literally tears it apart.

To speed up this process, you can use your kiln to heat up the glass in bulk. Then turn off the kiln, reach in using heat resistant gloves and tongs, pull some of the glass out, and immerse it into a bucket of water. If your buckets are made of plastic, hold the glass up off of the bottom of the bucket until it cools (which it is doing as it cracks up). Standing unexpectedly in a puddle of water is not a smart thing to do next to an electric kiln and can prove to be quite a shocking experience. If you are making multiple colors of glass in one kiln run, it makes it easier to sort the frit afterward if you frit each color into a separate bucket. To make the kiln fritting process a little faster, you might want to take the kiln all the way up to tack fuse before you shut it off so that the glass can be picked up as fused lumps rather than individual pieces. The hotter the glass is when put it into the water, the smaller will be the resulting frit. If you have crucibles, you can pour molten glass directly into the bucket (slowly though so as not to melt the bucket). If your frit is not small enough for you, the thermal treatment makes it easy to mechanically break it up into smaller frit.

In determining what size frit to use, you have to decide what you want your final project to look like. The finer the frit, the more air that gets trapped in the Pâte de Verre process and the more opaque will be the resulting bead. Donna Milliron likes to use a Bullseye #2 frit to get the translucency and density that she likes in her beads.

© 1996 James Kervin

Pâte de Verre Beads

Bead mold construction

The size and intricacy of your bead will dictate how much work you have to put into making your mold. I will discuss two main methods for making molds: carving them from fire brick and casting with plaster based investments.

Simple brick molds

The easiest bead mold would be one for columnar beads as was used in antiquity and continues to be used today to make powdered glass beads. These beads have traditionally been made in Africa using clay molds. The molds are round pancake affairs with multiple bead holes. The bead holes are made by poking sticks into the wet clay and making a smaller hole in the bottom to center the hole former. These molds are then dried and fired.

You can make an easy mold to try the same technique using fire brick. Just take the brick and drill holes part way down into it. You can make them all the same size or of many different sizes. Then in the bottom of the hole, you drill a slightly smaller sized hole to hold your hole former. For the low temperature African beads, leaf stems are used as the pore former. For higher temperature processed beads other materials will be substituted.

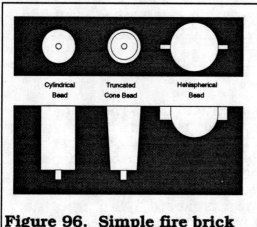

Figure 96. Simple fire brick mold.

The depth to which you make the holes in the mold depends upon two factors. The first is obvious, you can make longer beads in deeper holes. The second is not quite so obvious. For low temperature beads with a texture like sugar, the bead pretty much is the same size after firing as before. For higher temperature fired beads, a lot of shrinkage occurs. This shrinkage occurs primarily in the length of the bead as the individual pieces of frit get soft and settle down deeper into the mold. In going to a full density glass bead, you will get up to about 30% shrinkage in volume (which equates to length in a constant cross section mold). Thus if you want a final full density bead about 3/4" long, your hole will have to be about an inch deep.

You will have to kilnwash these molds prior to use to prevent the glass from sticking. This also allows them to be reused. When cutting the shapes into the mold, you might want to consider having draft or taper in this as seen in the second hole of Figure 96. This makes removal easier after firing of the bead. Also avoid having any undercuts in the mold or it will have to be sacrificed to remove the bead.

198 Glass Beadmaking

Plaster based molds

For beads more complicated in shape than ones you can carve into firebrick, you will need to use the techniques illustrated Figure 97 to make sacrificial plaster based molds. To start, make a model of the bead. There are many materials from which an original bead model can be made. The traditional material used in Pâte de Verre is wax. The beauty of wax is that it is easily removed after casting the mold by melting it out over a pan of hot water in the kiln. Alternatively the model could be made from any object that is combustible, like a nut. In this case, the object is burned out of the mold during the cure cycle. Lastly, the model could be made of clay. This is an excellent choice if you are making flat beads like a medallion with a minimum of under cuts. After investing the mold around the clay, it can just be pulled out and the mold cleaned with water to remove any clay residues. Once you have your bead design, you are ready to start thinking about making the mold.

You have to consider how you will get the hole in your bead. If you are making something like a flat medallion the hole former will run parallel to the mold surface in slots cut into the mold. For this situation, mount your model directly onto a piece of cardboard. Then you will cast your mold around it leaving the backside open. Next remove the model from the mold and cut two slots a little deeper than half the thickness of the model and about a quarter of an inch long on either side of the model impression. Into these slots you will lay your hole former so that it lays across the model volume. Then use a little prefired fiber paper to fill in the top part of the slot above the hole former and prevent glass from filling this area. The right bead hole in Figure 96 is setup for this technique.

For other bead shapes, the hole former may extend down the funnel which you will build into the mold for adding the glass frit. So you will need to orientate the model with the hole running up and down in the mold. In this case the first step in the mold making process is to mount a small funnel of wax or clay about 1" long onto a piece of cardboard. The small end of the funnel should be at least about 3/8th" in diameter and the large end about 1" in diameter. Then mount your model to the funnel at one end of where you want the hole and have the other end where you want the bead hole pointing up.

Now you want to construct a mold frame around your model in which to cast the mold. I find making round frames to be easiest. To construct round frames, I use old strips of linoleum. Remnants can usually be obtained cheaply, if not for free, from a flooring contractor. Good sizes to prepare ahead of

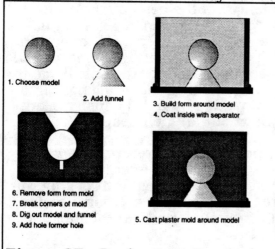

Figure 97. Basic steps to plaster mold making.

Pâte de Verre Beads   199

time are strips varying in width between 1 to 3 inches and in lengths ranging from 8 to 24 inches. (The length is so long because I make molds for casting multiple beads at once.) When needed, these strips can be coiled to size with the ends held in place by duct tape or rubber bands. The bottom edge is hot glued down to your cardboard.

Next coat the inside of the box with a separator compound. Products such as liquid dish washing detergents, cooking pan coating (Pam) or light machine oil (WD-40) sprays are suggested. It is easiest if this coating can be applied as a spray. Depending on what you used for your original model and how you plan to remove it from the mold, you may want to coat it also. For materials that you are going to burn or melt out, this is not necessary. If you use the separator on the original model, be aware that some surface detail will be lost – so apply it sparingly. Leave about a inch separation between your models and a half inch between the model and the side of a mold.

It is now time to mix the plaster mold material. I recommend a mold made of a 50/50 solids mix of Hydrocal plaster and 200 mesh silica flour. Mixing plaster can sometimes be a little tricky. Don't expect to necessarily get it right the first time. With a little practice though, you will soon become a pro. Mix enough to completely fill your mold in one pour to make the strongest possible mold. If this is not possible, allow the previous batch of plaster to set up before adding the next batch. In mixing any plaster-based material, there are a number of suggested rules that should be followed to achieve best results:

1. Always use cool, about 70°F, clean water to make up your mix. Likewise keep your mixing bucket and tools clean. The presence of old hardened plaster will cause the new plaster to set up faster, in as much as one half the expected setup time

2. Add the plaster mixture to the water, not water to the plaster. Slowly sift the plaster out onto the surface of the water. The plaster will absorb water and sink. Keep sifting mix onto the water until it no longer sinks and the surface stays slightly dry. This indicates a good plaster to water ratio. Your finished mix will have approximately twice the volume of the original water.

3. Next, allow the mixture to sit undisturbed and rest for about 3 minutes. This time can be varied from as short as one minute to as long as 10 minutes. It is called "slaking" and is necessary for the plaster to set properly. During this time the plaster is starting to chemically adsorb the water.

4. Now stir the plaster trying to avoid whipping any air into it. Stir from the bottom to the top to allow any air to rise to the top. The mold mixture should appear to be creamy at this point, not thin and watery, but sort of opaque on the stirrer. Do not overstir because this will cause the plaster to set faster.

5. After mixing, apply the plaster to the model by slowly pouring it into the mold. Try not to trap bubbles. It works best if you pour the plaster into an empty corner of the mold and allow it to flow around your models. Afterward, gently vibrate the mold by tapping on the edge of the container or shaking the work table to free any trapped air and allow it to rise to the surface.

© 1996 James Kervin

200   Glass Beadmaking

6. Lastly clean your plaster coated tools and bucket in water right away. Start by pouring off extra plaster mix into some disposable trash container such as a plastic bag in a cardboard box. Do not clean your equipment in your sink or any other plumbing fixtures (i.e. toilet.) The mold mix particles will settle out in your pipes, and since plaster can set up underwater, will eventually harden. This practice could eventually lead to complete blockage of your plumbing. Instead always wash them off in another large container of water. Let the heavier plaster particles sink to the bottom of the bucket. Then dispose of the water at top in some appropriate manner like giving a tree a drink. Put the plaster sludge at the bottom into your plastic bag for disposal.

7. When first poured, the plaster will look shiny and have a slight water film. As the shine goes away and the plaster starts to get mushy, you will want draw a flat instrument like a metal ruler across the top of your pour to form a nice flat bottom for your mold to sit on the kiln shelf. This should be done in a number of light passes to avoid ripping up the smooth plaster surface and is complete when your mold is flush with the top of your box. Clean the plaster off your screeding instrument after each pass.

Your mold should start to harden up in about 20 to 30 minutes. If not, you may have gotten a bad batch of plaster or have somehow done something drastically wrong. Once the plaster has initially set up, remove the mold frame from around the mold and any hot glue. (Setup for plaster-based molds generally takes about two hours to develop the proper interconnective chemical bonding.) Next you should scrape all the edges of the mold with a sharp knife trying to remove any sharp edges or divots along the edge. These may serve as a points for cracks to initiate as the mold dries and is cured.

After your mold has completely set up, it is time to remove your models. Since plaster mixes expands upon curing this should be easy. (Assuming that you don't have a lot of undercuts in your models.) You may be able pry the model out with a sharp tool. Injecting compressed air under your model is also helpful in breaking the suction between it and the mold. If you used something like clay, you can carve out the bulk of it from the mold and wash out any residual clay with warm water. All the clay must be removed or it will contaminate your final work. If you used wax, you can melt it out over a pan of water in your kiln after you dry your mold. (Don't let the water all evaporate out of the pan or you may start a fire.) After you have melted out all the wax you think possible, you will have to burn out the rest during curing of the mold in the next step.

For best results the mold should be air dried before putting it in the kiln. Drying reduces the amount of water in the mold so that it does not turning to steam when in the kiln. If you used wax or organic models, you will need to burn organic residues out of the mold after drying. If not, you can cure to mold during the frit casting step. To do this, place the mold in your kiln with the funnel opening up. Slowly heat the mold to drive out any remaining water, but not too fast or steam could be produced. Of course slowly is a relative thing. It is relative to how much time you have already put into this mold and how willing you are to take

© 1996 James Kervin

Pâte de Verre Beads 201

chances. You can use an initial temperature rise rate in the range of 100°F per hour per inch thickness of the mold. Soak the mold for about an hour per inch of thickness, first at 225°F to remove physically adsorbed water and again at 350°F to remove any chemically bound water. Then continue to slowly heat the mold up to 1200°F to burn out any residual organic materials. Here the heating ramp rate should again be in the range of 100°F/hr. The slower you go, the stronger the mold will remain.

At about 900°F, the mold will start to turn black and will smoke as organics begin to burn out. For your protection, keep the kiln well ventilated. As it gets near 1200°F, the mold will turn white again because all the carbon will have been burned out. After it is burned out, slowly cool the mold back down to room temperature.

Filling your mold

The first step in filling a bead mold for casting is the insertion of the hole former into the mold. What type of material you choose for a hole former depends upon how dense you want to fuse the bead. If you are looking for a lightly fused sugar-like bead, then you are going to do a low temperature fusing run. In such a situation the frit does not move around much and just fuses in the spots where they are touching each other without filling in the voids between them. In such a case a material that burns away like the leaf stems that the Africans use is adequate. A more current material might be something like tooth picks. Be aware though that the carbon may stain your bead.

For the case where you want a full density bead, where the frit will pack in and fills voids, you have to use a hole former that can survive the high temperatures of the full fuse firing cycle. In this case there are a number of high temperature hole former options available. You could use short sections of winding mandrels or copper tubing coated with separator. Rigidized Fiberfrax® alumina yarn (available in 3/32nd and 1/8th inch diameters) or fiber paper strips are also a good choice. Most artist use fiber paper strips rather than yarn because it is cheaper. The yarn or paper can be rigidized by soaking it in a hardening solution of 15% colloidal silica followed by air drying and firing in a kiln to about 1300°F. These hole formers may or may not then be coated with separator compound. It is not really necessary to rigidize and prefire the paper unless you are trying to save it. Let the hole former stick up out of the funnel for easy removal after firing. For medallion flat molds, fill in the top parts of the slots with unrigidized fiber paper as was discussed earlier.

Now slowly pour the frit into the mold. You can use one single color, layers of color or pack different colors into specific places. Try not to bend the hole former or it may be hard to remove after firing. When using large patterned glass chunks instead of frit in simple shaped reusable molds, you may find that use of a little glue in holding the pattern together in the desired orientations as you pack the mold helpful.

© 1996 James Kervin

Firing your bead

The bottom of your mold that you screed with the ruler should sit flat on your kiln shelf. If not, the weight of the mold may cause bending and cracking. Also check to see that your kiln shelf is level. Otherwise whatever you are making will vary in final thickness. This may not be apparent on small beads but it certainly is on larger medallions. Use sand to level under your mold if you have a problem with either of these.

Once your mold is filled and in the kiln, it is time to cook. The basic firing schedule is sketched out in Figure 98. Slowly bring the mold up to the Pâte de Verre temperature for your glass (about 1300°F for Bullseye.) Ramp rates have to be controlled in order to prevent thermal shocking your mold and should be in the range of 100°F/hour/inch of plaster thickness. If you have not prefired your mold ahead of time, you will have to go slower and dwell at both 225 and 350°F for at least an hour per inch of mold thickness to remove water bound in the plaster as was described earlier. It is during this rise to process temperature that your mold is most likely to crack, if at all. Here your glass is still fairly rigid and your mold starts to shrink fairly quickly once it reaches about 1200°F.

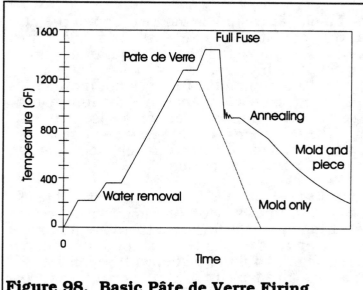

Figure 98. Basic Pâte de Verre Firing Schedule.

Upon reaching Pâte de Verre temperature for your glass, you will need to hold the kiln at that temperature until you are sure that your glass has equilibrated inside the mold. The mold insulates the glass causing its temperature to lag behind that of the kiln. You will have to hold the temperature at the control point for 1 to 2 hours per inch of thickness of the mold depending on how fast you heated up the mold. You will then want to continue on up to full fuse point and hold for another hour per inch of mold thickness to get full fuse. Check to see if you need to add more frit as it consolidates itself.

After you have finished your hold at process temperature, vent the kiln to rapidly drop its temperature down to the annealing point as was done for fusing. Then close your kiln. You will have to hold at this temperature to allow the glass to equilibrate again for the same 1 to 2 hours per inch of mold thickness. You now want to slowly lower the work from the annealing point to the strain point for your glass. You will want to do this over a time period of 4-8 hours per inch thickness of casting.

© 1996 James Kervin

Pâte de Verre Beads 203

Lastly you want to slowly cool your casting to room temperature. You want to do this at a rate of about 100°F per inch of mold thickness. Then allow the mold to remain undisturbed at room temperature for a few hours before you even think of demolding. After it is completely cooled off, slowly break away the mold from the glass. Use a small hammer and chisel if necessary to slowly break plaster molds apart. (For properly constructed fire brick molds, you should just be able to slide the bead out of the mold.) If it starts to feel hot, stop and let it cool some more. After you have the casting free from the mold, don't stick it in water right away to wash off any remaining mold material. Let it sit for a couple more hours before you clean it. The key to the whole firing process is patience.

Most artists find that some work on the beads is required after firing to clean them up and polish them. This is usually done using sanding belts, grinding wheels and polishing felts. Final polish can then be done by tumbling as will be described in the next chapter.

Suggested further reading

Cummings, Keith. The Technique of Glass Forming, B. T. Batsford Ltd., 1980

DeCamp, Lane. Inspired Beads, Artistry at Arrow Springs, Bead & Button Magazine Num. 8 (April) 1995

Fenton, Dan and Kervin, Jim. Pâte de Verre and Kiln Casting of Glass, work in progress

Francis, Peter Jr. West African Powder Glass Beads, Ornament Magazine Vol. 16 Num. 4 (Summer), 1993

Lundstrom, Boyce. Advanced Fusing Techniques - Glass Fusing Book Two, Vitreous Publications, Inc., 1989

Lundstrom, Boyce. Glass Casting and Moldmaking - Glass Fusing Book Three, Vitreous Publications, Inc., 1989

© 1996 James Kervin

204   Glass Beadmaking

© 1996 James Kervin

Finishing Beads

After the initial manufacture of your beads, there are often some finishing adjustments that need to be made. They may need to be cut to length in the case of kiln cast or drawn beads. The ends of these beads may then need to be smoothed. Wound beads may need the ends ground slightly to take sharp edges off. Pate de Verre beads may need to be polished to give them shine. Wound and drawn beads will all need annealing to remove stress introduced in the forming process. Some artists also like to etch their finished beads to give them a matte finish. This chapter will discuss these processes and possible techniques to achieve them.

Cutting beads to length

There are a couple different ways to cuts beads to length. They vary in speed, accuracy and cost of equipment. We will discuss them in order of increasing expense.

Chipping hammer and anvil

The simplest and cheapest method to cut long kiln cast or drawn beads to length is unfortunately also the least controllable. It is to use a chipping hammer and anvil similar to that used in Dale de Verre. The anvil is a piece of steel bar with a 45° angle cut on the top surface. It is usually fastened to a working surface like a sawhorse. The chipping hammer is probably more commonly known as a tile setter's hammer. The head has a square shaped face on one side and the other side comes to a sharp edge like on the anvil. The glass is cut by placing it on top of the anvil and striking it directly on top of the sharp edge of the anvil. The process works best if you try to swing past the end of the anvil with the hammer. The tools will also last longer and cut better if they have tungsten cutting surfaces. This will make them more expensive though. For obvious safety reasons, you should wear goggles to protect your eyes from flying debris and gloves to prevent getting cut if the bead stock breaks in an unexpected manner.

Glass rod cutters or nipper

Round bead stock can be cut into beads using tungsten glass rod knifes or files. This is done by scoring a groove around the circumference and breaking it with your fingers. Likewise you could use tile nippers to cut

© 1996 James Kervin

206 Glass Beadmaking

the stock to length. See the previous discussion on cutting glass rods for more details.

Sawing to length

The most accurate way of cutting the bead stock to length is to saw it with a glass saw. Glass saws use diamond embedded blades to grind their way through a piece of glass. They come in three main configurations: a band or wire saw, a cutoff saw and a table saw. In all cases, the saw will use a cutting fluid to keep glass dust out of the air and to keep the blade cool so that the diamonds are not melted out of the blade's binding matrix.

A band saw has a blade made of a continuous loop of metal banding or wire that runs between two drive pulleys through a table that has a slot in it. The back of the blade is supported by a guide to react the push of the glass against it. Water is fed onto the blade from a reservoir above the blade or by passing the blade through a water-filled reservoir. If water is fed from above, you will have to be sure that the feed reservoir is full and the feed valve is adjusted properly. If the blade picks the water up from a reservoir below, then you just need to make sure that the reservoir is filled to the proper level. To cut the glass, slowly push it up against the front of the blade and feed it in as the glass gets ground away. One of the disadvantages of a band or wire saw is that the blade tends to wander a little as it cuts through the bead stock leaving a rougher surface.

The cutoff saw configuration is similar to that of a radial arm saw. In this configuration, you pull the saw blade toward you and it cuts off a slice of the glass bead stock that is being held on the table. Cutting fluid feed will again either be from above or from a blade picking it up from the reservoir. The same lubricant adjustment requirements as above apply.

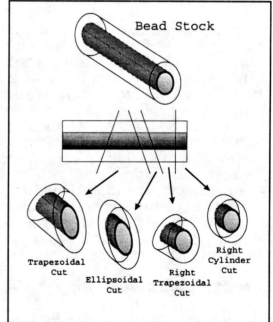

Figure 99. Some of the different ways to cut tubular bead stock.

The table saw configuration has the spindle of the blade mounted below the table and cutting fluid is picked up by the blade from a reservoir below the table. To cut glass, just push it up against the spinning blade.

The table for all three of these configurations will usually have a guide to help feed the bead at the desired angle into the blade. You may not always want to have the ends of the bead perpendicular to the axis of symmetry of the bead (i.e. its hole). You may want to cut circular cross sections at an angle in order to get elliptical beads. Alternatively you

© 1996 James Kervin

may want to give your beads pyramidal shapes by cutting at an angle and then flipping it over and cutting again at the same angle. Figure 99 illustrates some of the possibilities for cutting bead stock.

Even though the cutting fluid helps keep glass dust down when sawing, it is recommended that you wear a respirator with a mist cartridge or at the very least a dust filter when using any glass cutting or grinding equipment. This is because small cutting fluid droplets with glass dust are thrown into the air and can be inhaled. For the same reason you should also wear goggles to keep glass out of your eyes. Be sure to read the equipment instruction manuals for more complete details.

Kiln annealing your beads

From our earlier discussion on the properties of glass, you can understand how a lot of stress probably still remains in them. Even though you may flame anneal a bead as well as you can, the temperature on the outside of the bead drops very rapidly relative to the inside of the bead. The inevitable result of this is residual stress. The larger the bead, the more stress contained inside of it after flameworking. You may be able to get by without annealing small beads but you can never be sure. Therefore it is best to kiln anneal them and remove as much stress as possible. The basic idea behind the annealing process is as follows. You heat the beads up to the point where the atoms are mobile enough to

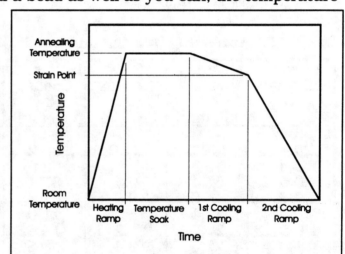

Figure 100. Typical kiln temperature cycle during an annealing run.

move around and relieve any strain, but not so mobile that the bead loses its shape. Then we cool the bead back to room temperature at a slow enough rate that temperature variation, and thus the shrinkage through the bead, is uniform enough that large stresses are not introduced.

To anneal your beads, lay them out on a kiln shelf and put them into your kiln. You then heat up the kiln to near the upper region of the non-brittle solid zone. The rate at which you heat up the beads depends on their size. The larger they are the easier it is to develop considerable temperature gradients within the bead and thus stress that could crack the bead as you are heating it up. The temperature to which you heat the beads will be below that which you will see any droop over the time you stay at temperature. You now soak the beads at this temperature, commonly called the annealing temperature, to allow the stress to flow out of them. After this you slowly lower the kiln temperature through the rest of the non-brittle solid annealing zone where the stress can still flow

208   Glass Beadmaking

fairly easily. The lower limit of this zone is referred to as the strain point. The limits of the annealing zone varies with the composition of the glass. Moretti glass has a strain point of about 670°F and annealing point of about 970°F. For the proper temperatures of other glasses see the chapter on fused beads. Lastly you slowly lower the temperature of the kiln through the brittle solid zone to bring the beads back to room temperature. This basic annealing temperature cycle is illustrated in Figure 100.

The heating and cooling rates that you use in the annealing cycle are determined by the physical properties of the glass and the size of the bead. Table 19 gives appropriate rates for Morreti glass beads of various sizes. For other types of glass, rates can be adjusted by multiplying by the ratio of the coefficients of expansion. So for Bullseye glass the rates would be 104/90 times faster or the ramp lengths would be 90/104 shorter. If you would like to develop a better understanding of how annealing cycles are determined see "Contemporary Lampworking" by Bandhu Scott Dunham.

Table 19. Annealing heating and cooling rates Moretti beads.

Bead Diameter (in)	Heating Rate (°F/min)	Slow Cooling Rate (°F/min)	Fast Cooling Rate (°F/min)	Heating Ramp Time (min)	Slow Cooling Time (min)	Fast Cooling Time (min)
0.3	249.5	37.4	149.7	3.5	3.6	4.9
0.4	140.3	21.0	84.2	6.2	6.4	8.7
0.5	89.8	13.5	53.9	9.7	10.0	13.6
0.6	62.4	9.4	37.4	13.9	14.4	19.6
0.7	45.8	6.9	27.5	18.9	19.6	26.7
0.8	35.1	5.3	21.0	24.7	25.7	34.8
0.9	27.7	4.2	16.6	31.3	32.5	44.1
1.0	22.5	3.4	13.5	38.7	40.1	54.4
1.1	18.6	2.8	11.1	46.8	48.5	65.8
1.2	15.6	2.3	9.4	55.7	57.7	78.3
1.3	13.3	2.0	8.0	65.3	67.7	92.0
1.4	11.5	1.7	6.9	75.8	78.6	106.6
1.5	10.0	1.5	6.0	87.0	90.2	122.4
1.6	8.8	1.3	5.3	99.0	102.6	139.3
1.7	7.8	1.2	4.7	111.7	115.8	157.2
1.8	6.9	1.0	4.2	125.3	129.9	176.3
1.9	6.2	0.9	3.7	139.6	144.7	196.4
2.0	5.6	0.8	3.4	154.6	160.3	217.6

Of course these are recommended times and rates only. You can be more or less conservative in your annealing cycles. Larger beads definitely need to be annealed. Ideally you would have a kiln with an electronic control system and would just program in the desired annealing cycle and forget about them. Most of you will probably not have this equipment though because of its expense. You should at minimum have a pyrometer to monitor the temperature. By doing trial runs while monitoring the current settings on your kiln, you should be able to develop a feel for the proper settings to get the desired rates of

© 1996 James Kervin

temperature rise and fall. This will allow you to determine approximate settings and times for the different portion of the firing cycle. Probably one of the most important things to be careful about during annealing is not to go to too high a temperature or your beads will slump and lose their shape.

After you have annealed your beads, they are ready to sell, string and wear. Unless you are going to polish them to remove rough edges as will be discussed next. This is usually done after annealing.

Grinding and shaping of beads

After cutting drawn beads to length or sometimes your wound beads may have a sharp edge or a rough surface that you want to grind off. For this job diamond grinders are suggested. They use diamond embedded tools like the saws. They come in a number of configurations: cylinders, wheels or flat disks. In all cases they will have to be lubricated with cutting fluid as discussed for the saws. This process is very similar to that used in stained glass to grind the edge of the glass or in beveling of edges. In all cases wear goggles and a respirator like when sawing. Read your instruction manuals so that you understand how to operate your equipment correctly.

Polishing beads

The final polishing of cut edges has been traditionally done by tumbling of the bead. You can tell if a bead has been tumble polished by looking at the edges of the bead. If they are rounded, then there is a good chance that the bead has been tumble polished. If instead of being rounded, the edges are sharp then your bead has most likely been polished on a lap or wheel. I will briefly discuss tumble polishing. If you want to learn about lapping, I suggest you consult a reference on beveling.

The theory behind tumble polishing

Nature has been practicing tumble polishing for eons. You have only to go to the beach, look at all the smooth pebbles and realize that at one time each of these was probably a sharp, jagged rock to realize the scale on which she has been practicing this art. The soothing sounds of the waves breaking on the beach is the sound of her tumbler in action.

Tumble polishing of beads was done traditionally by putting the beads in a pear shaped barrel of beaten iron filled with a mixture of charcoal and clay or sand. The drum was then suspended over a fire and rotated by your apprentice. The charcoal mixture would pack the inside of the bead holes preventing them from collapsing. It also kept the beads from adhering to each other as the heat softened their surfaces. The mixture combined with the friction of the beads hitting one another, rounded their edges and smoothed their surfaces.

These days apprentices want a lot more for their time, so we grind our beads cold in electric driven lapidary tumblers. The type of tumbler that

© 1996 James Kervin

210 Glass Beadmaking

you are most likely to buy is a simple drum that lies on its side on a pair of rollers. One of the set of rollers is powered by an electric motor and the other runs free. The motors are one speed and have been set by design to run at the right speed for tumbling gems. The drum will most likely be of molded plastic and round in cross section. The inside wall of the drum has low ridges that cause the load to circulate inside the tumbler as it rotates. The lid will either screw on or be fastened with nuts or clips. You can get tumblers in either single or multiple barrel designs. In the multiple barrel designs, the barrels just hook on to one another end-to-end and ride on multiple rollers. This allows you to have beads in the different stages of polishing going at all times. The size of the barrels you want, depends upon your bead throughput and their size. A one and a half inch long bead is too big for a quart barrel and when you run a batch, the barrel should be 2/3 to 3/4 full of beads. Since each step in the grind takes about a week, use these factors to gage how large a tumbler you need. If you produce about 1/2 gallon of beads a week you could get either a triple 1/2 gallon tumbler or a single 1 gallon one. Generally speaking, the larger the barrel the more efficient it will be, but I also prefer a smaller multiple barrel tumbler because I can use a different barrel for each different grit. This makes it less likely to contaminate a fine grit tumble run with coarse grit from a previous run.

The other type of tumbler that is very good for beads is a vibro-tumbler. This piece of equipment has plastic drums that polish by a vibrating action instead of a rotating one. This is accomplished by mounting the container on a spring base and driving vibrations into the base by rotating an unbalanced weight. This causes the base to vibrate back and forth just like an unbalanced fan. This vibration grinds the beads using the relative motion of the fluid and the beads. This type of tumbler costs about the same as a rotating tumbler but is felt by some to work faster and to reduce breakage of delicate beads. The operation of this type of tumbler is very similar to that which I will describe for the rotating tumbler, although the times may be different.

The grit that is used in tumbling is the same that you may already use for sandblasting, silicon carbide. It is the material of choice because, except for diamond, it is one of the hardest materials known. It also has the property that when a silicon carbide crystal breaks, it forms another identical sharp fracture edge regardless of particle size. These two properties combined to make it an excellent grinding agent second only to diamonds. In theory, you could just load up your tumbler with the glass beads and a coarse grit, walk away for a long, long time and return to find your beads all polished. But since most of us want to get our beads off to market as soon as possible, we choose instead to tumble in a number of stages proceeding to finer and finer grit in each stage.

Grits are graded according to their size which is measured by passing the particles through wire mesh or screens. The mesh size of the screen is the number of openings per inch in the screen. Your first tumbling run will use a coarse grit of about 80 mesh. This would be followed by a run with a medium grit of about 220 mesh, one with a fine grit of about 400 mesh and lastly a polishing run using cerium oxide polishing compound.

© 1996 James Kervin

Finishing Beads   211

Some artists prefer using a finer grit in the 500 to 600 mesh range before moving on to polishing.

The practice of tumble polishing

After cutting your drawn or kiln made beads into sections, flatten them out just a little on a roughing wheel or flat grinder if you have one. Now you are ready to ready to start tumble polishing out the sharp edges. If the beads are kiln made ones don't worry about removing the fiber paper before the first tumbling but do so before subsequent ones. If you know anything about tumble polishing, treat the beads as if they were soft rocks or Apache tears. Open up the barrel and fill it between 1/2 and 2/3 full with glass beads. If you do not have quite enough beads to fill the barrel cut up some sheet glass or glass rods to about the same size and give them an equivalent smoothing as you gave the beads. It also helps to mix a number of different sized beads. Next add your coarse grit (if you have done a good job smoothing your bead on a flat grinder with an 80 grit you can proceed directly to a medium grit). Lastly add plastic pellets to fill the barrel 2/3 to 3/4 full (about 10 to 20% pellets). These pellets slow down the action inside the barrel some so as not to crack or chip the beads. You can buy plastic pellets from lapidary shops. You can also slow down the action more if necessary by adding sugar to the water but this gets everything sticky. In a quart tumbler, you would add 3-4 oz of grit and in a gallon one, you would add 8-10 oz. You may already see here what I meant about a larger barrel being more efficient. Next cover it all with water but leave at least an 1/8 of the barrel empty for air space. Now put the lid back on, making sure that the joint is absolutely clean, so that you get a good seal and do not scratch the joint surface.

Then put the barrel back on the tumbler and start grinding. Check it about every day to see how things are progressing. When you open the lid carefully point it away from you. This is because I have been warned that gas pressure tends to build up in them when grinding some materials and can cause the grinding sludge to spray out. I have not had this happen to me but it has to other people that I know. After about 24 hours, you will start to be able to see the effect of grinding. The sharp edges will start to be blunted and the shiny surface of the glass will start to dull. Continue for as many days as it takes to get the edges rounded to the shape that you want them. Also check the cut surface to see if it has smoothed out to your satisfaction. Never stop tumbling for more than about an hour or the grinding slurry can harden up from hydraulic compaction. If this happens, try to break up the sludge by hand before you start tumbling again or you are courting disaster.

After the first grinding step has been completed to your satisfaction, it is time to proceed on to the next grit. Start by removing all the beads and cleaning out the sludge from the barrel. Be careful in loading and unloading beads so that you do not crack or chip them. You want to drain all the sludge into a bucket because if poured down the sink or your toilet it will collect in your pipes and harden leading to some expensive plumbing bills. Rinse out the barrel and pour the rinse water into the bucket also. Rinse the beads and plastic pellets in a large bowl and pour that water into the bucket. After the sludge has settled in the bucket you can pour off the clear water on top into your flower garden

© 1996 James Kervin

212   Glass Beadmaking

and scrape out the thickened sludge into some newspaper and dispose of it in the garbage. Clean the beads and pellets again under running tap water in a strainer to get rid of any last remains of the previous grit. You have to get it all out or it can keep putting its larger scratches in the beads during the next step where it will be very visible. Cleaning the grit out of the holes is the hardest part. Try using pipe cleaners in the holes. An ultrasonic cleaner and some detergent also helps. Weed out any chipped or cracked beads as they can scratch your other beads. Then clean the barrel well. The barrel is harder to clean especially if it has been used for a while. That is why I suggest a separate barrel for each grit, especially the cerium oxide. The plastic pellets can get grit embedded in them too so you may want to set these aside for your next coarse grind and use new ones in the next step. If you do this, make sure that you mark each one and its lid as to which grit is used in it.

Now replace the beads and plastic pellets into the barrel, add the next grit, water and you are ready to roll. If for any reason you have less than 2/3 of a can of beads, you need to fill up the void somehow with glass that has been ground a similar amount of time, otherwise the sharp edges of the added glass can scratch the beads you have already spent so much time on. That is why I suggest that you start out the first grind at about 3/4 full and save graded material from previous runs for filler. More plastic pellets is not as desirable because they will cause the grind to take a lot longer, but they would work. The medium grinding step should not take more than a week at most. The way to tell when they are ready to move on to the next step is to take a bead out of the barrel, clean it off and look at it under a magnifying glass. Look to see if the pits in the surface of the glass left by the grit look pretty uniform and that the larger ones from the previous step have been wiped out. It helps to save completed samples from each step so that you have something to compare to. Also realize that you don't have to polish the beads back to a complete shine if you don't want to. The hazy look of a partially polished bead also looks good and many artists acid etch their beads to obtain that type of look.

After use of the medium grit, repeat the cleaning and refilling procedure. The fine grinding step will also take about a week. When you think that you have ground enough, take a bead out of the barrel and try seeing if it will polish up with a little cerium oxide and water on some felt. You will have to rub it for a minute or two. If you have a buffing wheel with cerium oxide, this should only take a few seconds. The beads are done if the surface has the same shiny finish wet or dry. If so, you are done with the fine grind and are ready for the final polish stage.

Try to clean the beads, the pellets and the barrel even better than before if possible. Then replace them into the barrel add water and a tablespoon of dry laundry detergent. Tumble this mixture for a couple of hours. This will help to work out any last remains of grit. Clean the beads, the pellets and the tumbler out again and rinse well. Reload the tumbler, only this time using cerium oxide and a pinch of detergent to act as a wetting agent. It also helps to add some more pellets or some other soft filler material to further cushion the tumbling of the beads this time. The most common filler material used is sawdust and woodchips. You should be able to get a good polish in about two days.

© 1996 James Kervin

Because of the higher cost of the cerium oxide you may want to save its slurry and use it again. It is probably good for three or four polishing sessions. After separating out the beads and cleaning them, do another detergent wash step to clean off the last remains of cerium oxide and to give them a brilliant shine. You should hardly be able to keep them on the shelf they will look so good.

Suggested further reading

Billeci, Andre G. Annealing Glasses, Glass Studio No. 5

Dunham, Bandhu Scott. Contemporary Lampworking A Practical Guide to Shaping Glass in the Flame, Pre-publication edition 1993

Fenton, Dan. Annealing fused work or how to be cool, Professional Stained Glass magazine, Vol. 8 No. 3 (April) 1988

Narayanaswamy, O. S. "Annealing of Glass" in Glass Science and Technology Volume 3 Viscosity and Relaxation Edited by D. R. Uhlmann and N. J. Kreidl, Academic Press Inc. 1986

Platt, Karl. Revealing Annealing, Glass Art magazine, Vol. 5 No. 5 (July/August) 1990

Scholes, Samuel R. and Greene, Charles H. Modern Glass Practice, Ceramic Book and Literature Service (CBLS), 1993

Wexler, Jerome. How to Tumble Polish Gemstones and Make Tumbled Gem Jewelry, Gem Guides Book Co., 1987

Glass Beadmaking

© 1996 James Kervin

Safety

Your safety should be your number one priority during beadmaking even above producing a quality product. The best way to stay out of trouble is to understand what you are doing and why. For this reason I have gone to great pains to try to explain to you how your equipment works and its safe use. This understanding will allow you to realize when something wrong is occurring and to take immediate action. In this chapter, I will remind you of many of the hazards of the equipment you are using and provide you general safety rules

Fires

In working with any of the high temperature processes discussed in this book, a number of general rules should be followed in order to avoid starting fires. Fires usually start because you have improperly located your equipment or have failed to maintain it properly. So check it out occasionally.

Positioning your equipment to avoid fires

1) Position your hot equipment at least 2 feet away from sheet rock walls and 3 feet from exposed wood.

2) Have a non-flammable floor surface underneath your equipment. Concrete is best, ceramic tile or brick is second best and some sort of non-asbestos fire-resistant board is the minimum requirement.

3) Use a non-flammable work surface on your work table. Sheet metal is acceptable but may conduct heat to locations where you are not expecting it to be hot and cause burns. Some other non-asbestos fire-resistant surface is better.

4) If possible equipment like kilns and glory holes should be mounted on stands to allow air circulation around them.

5) Large industrial glassworking setups or equipment may require a different type of building construction. Check into it before you expand your shop.

6) Check to see that no flammable liquids are stored near your equipment. If some are stored in the same room, provide sufficient

© 1996 James Kervin

216   Glass Beadmaking

ventilation to prevent build up of vapors and store them in a flammable liquids' storage cabinet.

7) Check all natural gas and propane sources to make sure that you have no leaks. Do this by painting all the joints in your gas system with a soapy water solution and look for bubbles.

8) If you work out of your garage, back your car out before you start working so that there are no gasoline fumes around.

9) Always keep at least one ABC rated fire extinguisher nearby. Position it so you will not have to reach over a fire to get to it – preferably near an exit.

10) Keep a clear exit from your work space at all times through which to escape in case of a fire.

Proper operation of your equipment to avoid fires

1) Never let children play around your equipment.

2) Do not allow consumables to build up in your work area.

3) Read and follow manufacturer instructions for your equipment.

4) Never leave your equipment unattended. The only exception for this might be a kiln where you can pop in and out to check on it. If you are the forgetful type, I suggest using an interval timer to remind you to check up on it.

Pressurized gas equipment

We have already discussed the hazards and most of the operational considerations for use with pressurized cylinders. But since they pose one of the biggest risks that you will be dealing with in most beadmaking situations, I believe it is prudent to list them again here in this section where they will be easy to locate for later reference. These general rules include:

1) Build a storage rack fixed to the wall for all your extra oxygen tanks and chain them into it when not in use. Have a similar rack near your workbench in which to chain your working tanks.

2) Avoid storing extra tanks anywhere near sources of heat and keep them out of the sun.

3) Use the protective covers on tank connections when not in use.

4) Make sure tanks are not overfilled.

5) Never use any grease or oils on an oxygen regulator or connection.

6) Make sure that all connections are leak tight and that your equipment is turned off when not in use. Never use leaky equipment.

© 1996 James Kervin

Keep heat, flame and sparks away from your hoses, regulators and cylinders.

7) Be sure to use flashback arrestors or at the very least check valves in your system setup.

8) Stand to one side of your oxygen regulator as you open the cylinder valve and be sure to open the valve slowly.

9) Always light the fuel gas before opening the oxygen on your torch.

What to do in case of a fire

Besides taking the safety precautions listed above, you need to learn to be able to extinguish any fire as soon as possible after it starts. This will prevent it from getting a chance to take hold and from getting near your pressurized gas equipment. To do this, you must have the right kind of fire extinguisher. For our work, this will be an ABC dry chemical extinguisher often referred to as a tri-class dry chemical fire extinguisher. These extinguishers use nonconducting chemicals (good for use around kilns) that effectively suppress the three main types of fires. These types as you may know are: (A) fires involving combustible materials like paper, wood, cardboard, cloth or other similar materials; (B) fires involving oils, paints, gasoline, chemicals or other flammable liquids; and (C) fires involving live electrical equipment, such as kilns, crock pots, etc. These ABC fire extinguishers are available in easy-to-store wall mounted units weighing between 2 1/2 to 30 pounds.

You should read over the instructions that come with your fire extinguisher and ensure that you understand how to use it. General rules for the operation and use of fire extinguishers are:

1) You should hold them upright so that the dry chemical feeds properly.

2) Most have a safety pin that you have to pull first to be able to start operation.

3) Don't get too close to the fire. Stand about 8 feet away.

4) Aim the extinguisher at the base of the fire and squeeze the handle to start flow of the dry chemical.

5) Sweep the chemical spray from side to side to completely cover the fire.

6) In order to ensure the proper functionality of your extinguisher when you need it, you should inspect it periodically, monthly or more often. They will usually have a pressure gauge which should read in the proper marked range.

7) If you have to use your extinguisher for any reason, you should have it recharged and checked out by an authorized distributor since they are more prone to leakage after once being used.

© 1996 James Kervin

218   Glass Beadmaking

8) After use, clean off all surfaces coated with the dry chemical because it is fairly corrosive.

If your fire gets near your pressurized gas tanks, evacuate the building and the nearby area. Notify the fire department and be sure to warn them about the presence of pressurized gases.

Burns

Burns can be caused by exposure to caustic chemicals, electricity, radiation or heat. In beadmaking your main concern will be heat, although we may occasionally use chemicals or be exposed to electricity. Burns, as you probably know, are classified by their severity as first, second or third degree burns. First degree burns are usually characterized by reddening of the skin and pain. This type of burn, although painful, will heal fairly quickly. Second degree burns are characterized by the development of blisters and swelling. They heal a little slower but are usually not serious enough to seek medical attention. Third degree burns involve damage to deeper skin layers and may have a charred appearance. They are often not very painful because the nerve endings in the skin may have been damaged. You should usually seek medical attention after a third degree burn because of the damage it does to the body's protective layer against infection.

In beadmaking, burns are usually a result of inappropriate attire or not paying proper attention to what you are doing. Here are some general purpose rules to help avoid receiving any.

What to wear to avoid thermal burns

1) When working, always wear natural fibers like cotton or wool, not synthetic ones like nylon or rayon. Synthetics will melt and shrink when exposed to heat.

2) Wear long pants when working, so that any hot thing that drops will not immediately land on your skin. Avoid pants with cuffs or open pockets which might catch hot items.

3) Do not wear sandals when doing any flameworking.

4) When working around very hot equipment like kilns and glory holes, protect your body parts from the heat by using gloves, long sleeve shirts, light jackets, etc.

Proper equipment operation to avoid thermal burns

1) Never reach across an open flame to grab something. Turn off the torch when not in use to reduce chances of burns.

2) Always position the hot end of equipment and glass away from you so that you will not grab the hot end. You can not see which end is hot.

© 1996 James Kervin

Safety   219

3) Put down your hot rods in such a position so that they will not roll off your workbench onto your lap. A rack helps prevent this from happening.

4) Position a dark background behind any open flames so that they become visible.

5) Turn off a kiln before you reach into it.

6) Sit in a chair which offers a quick escape backward in case you drop a hot tool or piece of glass. I do not think that one of those ergodynamically correct chairs that you kneel on is appropriate.

7) Be aware of where you have set down hot objects on your bench so that you will not touch these areas until they have cooled.

What to wear to avoid chemical burns

Whenever you are handling caustic materials you need to wear special equipment to prevent receiving chemical burns. The following is a suggested list in case you decide to work with acids especially hydrofluoric acid. Of course how much of this you wear depends on how much of the material you are handling. I would consider goggles, gloves and rubber apron the minimal protection necessary.

1) Splash goggles that seal to your face.

2) A face shield to wear over the goggles to protect the rest of your face.

3) Gloves appropriate for the material being used. Natural rubber is good for dilute acids, alkalis and alcohols. Neoprene rubber is good for dilute acids, alkalis, alcohols and ketones. Butyl rubber is good for acids, alkalis, alcohols, ketones, esters and many other solvents. Nitrile ones are good for dilute acids, alkalis, petroleum solvents, oils, grease and amino acids. You may also want the gloves long enough to roll the top down to make a cuff to prevent solvents from running down your arm

4) A rubberized laboratory apron.

5) Full length rubber overalls that fit down over your boots.

6) Rubber shirts.

7) Rubber hats.

8) Rubber boots.

9) Respirator.

What to do if you get a burn

Treatment for a burn will depend on the type of burn and its severity. In the case of very severe burns, you may also have the complication of

© 1996 James Kervin

220   Glass Beadmaking

shock. The body goes into shock as a means to reduce the demands it places on its component systems. Things that may contribute significantly to causing shock include: loss of blood or chemical balance, extreme pain or traumatic experiences. In the case of shock, you should try lie the victim down to allow better blood circulation and cover them with a blanket to preserve body heat. If requested, administer fluids in the form of sips of water or water mixed with baking soda to the ratio of 1/2 teaspoon to a quart of water. Then seek medical attention immediately.

Let's now look at the first aid treatment for the different types of burns.

Thermal burns

First-degree burns should be treated by cooling off the affected area with cold running water. Then if necessary apply a dry compress to protect the area.

Second-degree burns can also be immersed under water for up to a couple hours. Then if desired use cold compresses. After you are done cooling it, blot it dry and cover it with a sterile compress. Do not apply antiseptic preparations, ointments or sprays if the burn is severe. Also never pop blisters or intentionally remove skin. For large burns you may also want to elevate the affected limb to reduce swelling.

Third-degree burns are usually just stabilized and then medical attention is sought. Do not clean the burn, or try to remove attached clothing or other materials. Cover the burned area with a clean compress of freshly laundered material covered possibly by a clean plastic bag. Elevate the affected limb. Have the person sit down and not walk if possible. Be wary of the possibility of shock. Seek medical attention.

Chemical burns

If the burn is to the skin, wash away the chemical as much as possible with large amounts of water using a shower or hose as quickly as possible for at least 5 minutes. Remove any articles of clothing from the affected area. Do not scrub the area. If any directions for treatment of burns are present on the chemical container, follow them. Apply a bandage and get medical attention. Notify them what material you were working with. Better yet, bring the container.

If the burn is to the eyes, again wash with large volumes of water as quickly as possible for at least 5 minutes for acid burns and 15 minutes for alkali burns. (Alkali burns are more tricky because the eye might appear at first to be only slightly injured but can progress to develop deep inflammation and tissue damage.) While washing out the eye, ensure that the face and eyelids get washed also since they probably have been affected. If only one eye is affected have that eye down and wash from the nose outward when rinsing so that you are not rinsing material into the other eye. For acid burns, if a weak solution of 1 teaspoon of baking soda in 1 quart of water can be made quickly rinse

© 1996 James Kervin

Safety   221

with this solution after the water rinse. For alkali burns, check the eye for any loose particles of dry chemical and remove them with a sterile gauze or a clean handkerchief. Rinse some more, then cover the eye with dry pad or protective dressing and try to have the victim not rub their eyes. Seek immediate medical attention.

Electrical burns

Electrical burns are treated essentially like thermal burns. The only difference is that you need to be aware that shock and CPR treatment may be necessary. In order to be ready for such an emergency you should consider getting CPR training from the Red Cross.

Toxic materials

The first step in evaluating what type of material toxicity plan you need for your studio is to examine the materials that you are or will be using in your work. What are they? What is in them? Is it hazardous? How hazardous? What form does it take? How might it enter my body? The more informed you are about these materials the better you will be able to evaluate what you need to do to protect yourself, your employees and your family.

As an example, if you decide to make any Pate de Verre beads, the mold materials tend to be respiratory irritants at the very least. As an example, look at free silica which is used as a refractory additive in many mold formulations. Silica dust in your lungs can lead to a disease of a progressive nature called silicosis after heavy exposures even of only a few months duration. Of course we are talking of heavy industrial exposures here, but the same thing happens from low level exposures, it just takes more of them over a longer period of time. Thus, it is important that you observe good hygiene practices whenever working with molds and mold materials. If you mix any of your own colored glass, be aware that many of the colorants are toxic materials. They are usually heavy metals like lead that not only are poisonous but are also not easily eliminated by body. Operations like scraping kiln shelves or grinding creates dust containing silica. Other bad actors include: fiber paper that has been fired to high temperatures, overglazes since they are frequently high lead glasses, enamels and paints since they contain lead and other heavy metals, very fine frits, plaster, cements, etc. Even things that seem innocuous like vermiculite can pose a health hazard. Its chronic inhalation can cause asbestosis or cancer and ingestion can also cause cancer.

There are a number of different designations for toxins based on how this toxin works on the body. First, there are the toxins we are all familiar with, the poisons. Poisons are toxins that interfere with chemical processes in the body. These toxins may be cumulative or noncumulative depending on how fast they are eliminated by the body. Next there are mutagens which are toxins that cause changes in our genetic blueprints. Similar to these are teratogens which affect how the genes in a developing fetus become expressed by changing the

© 1996 James Kervin

222   Glass Beadmaking

background chemistry of the environment. Lastly there are the allergens which react with the body's immune system. These reactions may vary from the sniffles and watery eyes to anaphylactic shock.

The degree of toxicity of a material describes its capability to hurt you. Highly toxic materials may only need a little bit to cause problems so you can not always judge danger by how much material you are using. You also have to consider how often you use the material. Long term usage of lesser toxic materials might also lead to health consequences. As an example, cancer is now suspected to be a result of chronic exposures to low levels of many chemicals called carcinogens. In fact it is not understood if there are safe exposure limits to carcinogens.

Toxicity of materials are primarily measured by testing with animals. A material is fed to animals in increasing doses until a dose is determined that will kill one half of all the animals. This lethal dose, know as the LD 50, can be used to rank relative toxicity of different materials for ingestion. A similar type of testing is done for inhalation hazards called the LC 50 test. Based on these tests and some known levels of toxicity for certain materials in humans, threshold limit values (TLVs) can be established for safe exposures. Tables of these values are published by the American Conference of Government Industrial Hygienists. They give safe time weighted average (TWA) for chronic 8 hour workday exposures. You can use these values in two ways. First, you can use them to decide which of a number of similar materials to use for a process based on their toxicity. Second, if you do not have a choice of materials available to you, you can use the TLV-TWAs to determine how carefully you have to be with this material.

So the best practice is to minimize all possible exposures to toxic materials. To do that, you have to understand how toxic materials can get into your body. There are three main routes of entry into the body: skin contact, ingestion and inhalation. We have already discussed how to avoid skin contact with toxic materials when we discussed what to wear to avoid chemical burns. Ingestion can be avoided by restricting eating and smoking from the work place. Inhalation is harder to control because we can not restrict breathing. Let's look at what you can do to avoid problems with toxic materials in your work.

Good work practices to avoid toxicity problems

One of the best ways to avoid problems with material toxicity is to develop good work practices that incorporate a high degree of cleanliness. Examples of good work practices when dealing with powdered toxic materials are as follows:

1) Isolate a work area for mixing these materials so the dust does not get spread all around your studio. (If you do not have the space to dedicate to the mixing process create one temporarily when mixing the materials and then clean up the area right after you are done working with them.) This does not in any way mean that you should not keep an isolated work area clean. Your work area should have adequate ventilation to help remove dust from the air without at the same time tending to create it.

© 1996 James Kervin

Safety

2) Consider using restricted volumes in which to contain the handling of the materials. You could mix chemicals in a small home-made glovebox like that illustrated in Figure 101 or confine all spray painting to a paint hood.

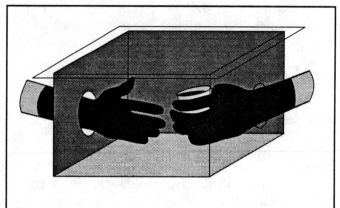

Figure 101. Small home-made glovebox.

3) If you have two processes using the same toxic material, try to collocate them so they do not spread all around the work place. Organize your work process so that both operations are done in the same area.

4) Clean your work place regularly by either wet mopping or using a HEPA vacuum cleaner. Other methods such as sweeping or using an ordinary shop vacuum will just spread the dust around into your breathing air.

5) Store all materials in covered containers to prevent dust from being spread around. This also helps in preventing some of these materials, like plasters, from absorbing water from the environment.

6) Make sure that all the materials are properly labeled as to what they are and what hazards they present.

7) Obtain and keep on file Material Safety Data Sheets for all toxic materials that you use in your work.

8) Whenever you have the choice between using one of two materials, use the least toxic one. Examples are using non asbestos gloves in kiln work or cleaning with alcohol rather than acetone.

9) Have a training program for both you and your employees so that you are sure they understand the hazards of these materials and proper work practices.

10) When working with toxic materials, you should wear a respirator rated for the type of material and process you are engaged in. Make sure that your respirator fits and that you are wearing it properly. Respirators are not 100% effective and should not be a substitute for proper ventilation

11) Acquire and have on hand at all times the proper safety clothing and equipment for handling corrosive materials that we have talked about previously. These may include the following: face shield or goggles, gloves aprons and safety shoes.

© 1996 James Kervin

224   Glass Beadmaking

12) Do not eat, drink or smoke in your studio. You shouldn't smoke anyway but don't compound the problem by having that habit result in ingesting other unintended materials at the same time.

13) Don't take your studio home with you. Wash your hands as you leave the shop or as you arrive home. (Please not in the kitchen sink.) Change your clothes before leaving the shop, or at the very least wear a long shop coat over your normal clothes that you then leave in the shop. Wash and dry work clothes separately from family clothes.

14) Dispose of all chemicals properly to avoid exposing your friends and neighbors.

Ventilation

As I discussed, the route into the body that is probably hardest to guard against is inhalation. Whenever materials are heated to the melting point and above, a mixture of particulate matter and gases is released. Inhaling large amounts of metal fumes can cause both immediate and long term effects. Acute exposures can cause flu-like symptoms within about 6 hours that last for up to 24 hours. Chronic low level exposures to metals such as lead can cause permanent neurological damage and reduced brain function. Lead fumes are released during high temperature process such as using low melting temperature lead glasses and fluxes. Some of these fumes are heavier than air, so you should ventilate your workspace both high and low. You also need to ventilate your kilns. Especially effective for this are the kiln ventilation systems that draw air out through a hole in the bottom of your kiln.

Before we discuss how to guard against inhalation problems, let's devote a little time to understand what we are guarding against. Inhalation hazards can come in a number of different forms: gases, vapors, fumes, mists and dusts. Do you know the difference between them? Gases are materials in the air that we breath that do not have a solid or liquid form at normal pressures and temperatures. Vapors are gaseous forms of solid or liquid substances that may or may not be the result of increased temperature such as steam or propane vapors. Fumes are extremely small solid particles created by heating metals to above their melting point or by chemical reactions. Mists are small droplets of liquid which are released into the air by mechanical actions such as spray, splashing or bubbling. Dusts are solid particles of many sizes and shapes that are generated by mechanical actions such as grinding, crushing, sanding. The smaller or more gaseous the material, the easier it is for the material to penetrate deep into your lungs and be absorbed by your body.

Ventilation works to solve the problem caused by these materials by either of two methods: diluting them or removing them. In dilution ventilation, the objective is to try and reduce the concentration of toxic materials in the air we breath by mixing it with large volumes of fresh air. This is accomplished by exhausting large volumes of air and replacing it with new air. This does not mean just installing a room air conditioner in a shop window. They do not exchange anywhere near the amount of air that we are talking about. Local ventilation in most cases

© 1996 James Kervin

is a better solution. Here an attempt is made to remove toxic materials from the workplace at their source by sucking them out at the point where they are generated. A simplified ventilation system that you can make for your studio would look something like that illustrated in Figure 102.

When considering ventilation plans here are some general principles to consider:

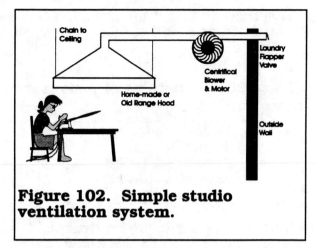

Figure 102. Simple studio ventilation system.

1) Try to remove contaminated air at its source. Pull it away from you and your employees as shown in the figure.

2) Exhaust the air outside of the shop as far from air intakes as possible.

3) Exhaust systems are more efficient if they minimize the distance and number of bends through which they have to move the air. Also air flow resistance is minimized by using circular ducting.

4) Air flow is more controllable if you avoid unwanted cross drafts and add sufficient supply make-up air through a planned intake system.

5) It is easier to control contaminated air by pulling it out of your workspace rather than by trying to push it out. Otherwise if your ducting leaks, the contaminated air will be pushed back out into your studio.

6) Discharge your effluent air in a responsible manner. Do not pollute someone else's air.

If you are really interested in installing a ventilation system, I suggest that you contact an industrial ventilation specialist or get one of reference books on this subject listed at the end of this chapter.

Carbon monoxide detectors

Carbon monoxide is a poisonous gas produced by incomplete combustion of any torch fuel and is more prevalent in torches that provide a reducing environment like the handheld torches. It is an invisible, odorless and tasteless gas that kills thousands each year. Carbon monoxide inhaled into our lungs gets dissolved into our blood. There it competes with oxygen for the hemoglobin in our red blood cells and usually wins. Once there, it clings on to the hemoglobin much more efficiently than oxygen and it takes a long period of time to get out of your system. This substantially reduces the amount of oxygen that your blood can carry to your vital organs. As the concentration of carbon monoxide increases in our blood, the symptoms as listed in Table 20 get progressively more severe. The speed with which carbon monoxide gets

226   Glass Beadmaking

absorbed and its final levels in our blood depend upon its concentration in the air we breath. At high enough concentrations, it can kill in minutes.

Table 20. Symptoms of carbon monoxide poisoning.

Symptom	CO blood level
Slight headache	15%
Severe headache	20%
Drowsiness, fatigue	30%
Nausea, vomiting	40%
Death	50%

Carbon monoxide can be removed by the ventilation systems just described. But since we know that it is an ever-present by product of our flameworking, it seems only prudent to try to determine if dangerous levels of it may be building up in our studios. Since we can not see, smell or taste it, we have to rely on sensors to warn us of its presence. Home alarms that look similar to an ordinary smoke detector are available from First Alert and Lab Safety and Supply. They cost about $40 and although not calibrated to the OSHA standard limits of 35ppm for a constant 8 hour workday exposure, they have been demonstrated by Underwriter Laboratories to provide detection capability of a wide variety of dangerous exposures listed in Table 21. OSHA level alarms are available but are more expensive. As an example, one from Lab Safety and Supply sells for about $511.

Table 21. New UL standards for carbon monoxide detectors.

Time	Carbon monoxide concentration (ppm)
15 minutes	400
35 minutes	200
90 minutes	100
30 days	15

Respirators

Sometimes when doing especially dirty operations or when doing temporary dirty operations in a general workspace, you may want more protection than is offered by your ventilation system. This is the time to use a respirator. It should be stressed that respirators are usually considered temporary measures. They should only be used as the primary protective device when no other means is possible or the contaminant is so toxic that a single control measure is not felt safe sufficient. You primary means of inhalation protection should always be your ventilation system.

If you are an employer and decide that your employees need to periodically use respirators, you should be aware that OSHA requires a written plan for their use. This plan is to acquaint your employees with respirator use and selection. It should include medical screening to look for proper respiratory system function, fit check of the respirator,

© 1996 James Kervin

training in the use of respirators as well as their limitations and setting up procedures for their maintenance.

Choosing a respirator

In choosing a respirator, you need to consider first what is the form of airborne toxic material from which you are trying to protect yourself. Is it a dust, mist, fume, vapor or gas? Next you should consider how long you may be working in that atmosphere. Longer times require larger canisters. How toxic is the material? Lastly you need to look at how they fit. They should be comfortable, leak proof, easy breathing, and non-interfering with vision. Some of these questions may be difficult for you to answer. If so, you should consult a reputable respirator consultant.

The type of respirator that most artists will use is a quarter mask respirator that covers only the mouth and nose or a half mask respirator that covers the mouth, nose and chin. Check its fit by first holding your hands over the ends of the filters and sucking in. You should feel the mask pull against your face. Next with some chemical filters in place, fan some strong smelling chemical vapors for which it is rated near your face and see if you can smell them. Be careful not to splash anything into your face. You may want to wear some splash goggles when doing this to protect your eyes. If both of those tests are successful, you should have a good seal. You guys with beards and/or long side burns should be aware that there is no way that you are going to get a good seal and that the respirator will not be completely effective for you. The fit of your respirator should be checked periodically to ensure that physical changes such as loss or gain weight have not altered it.

Once you have a good fitting respirator, you need to choose what type of filters that you will use. As should be obvious this is a function of the materials with which you are working. Dusts and fumes usually just require mechanical filtration of the air. This is provided by a filter made of folded felt or paper. Mists, vapors and gases will require cartridges incorporating chemicals that purify the air by trapping the materials. Some examples for which chemical cartridges are available include: acid gases, organic vapors, paints and ammonia.

Care of a respirator

Like any piece of safety equipment, respirators require periodic maintenance to ensure their operation when you need them. After each use they should be cleaned and checked for worn or broken parts. Look for deteriorating plastic surfaces, rusting metal and cracked glass. If okay they should be stored in plastic bags. The plastic bags ensure that chemical absorbents are not being exposed to atmospheric vapors when not in use. Not doing this can greatly reduce the useful lifetime of a respirator cartridge because they become saturated with use. For the same reason, careful records should be maintained of the amount of time that they have been used. They should be kept in a place that is out of the way but at the same time is easily accessible in the event of an

© 1996 James Kervin

228   Glass Beadmaking

emergency. This location should also protect them from sunlight and temperature extremes. You should always keep replacement cartridges and filters on hand and they should be stored similarly.

You can usually tell when filter cartridges are starting to reach the end of their useful life because they start to get harder to breath through as they get clogged up. Chemical filter life is not so easy to judge. They just stop absorbing the chemical agents without any warning. You might be able to test using aromatic but less toxic chemical agents but sometimes not. For this reason, they are usually considered to be consumed after 8 hours of use or two weeks after being unpackaged. Even if never removed from the package, some chemical cartridges may become ineffective over time. Such cartridges will usually come stamped with an expiration date. Also respirators are designed to be effective for what are considered normal exposures and will just not be effective against very high concentrations of contaminants. They will not be able to absorb all the material and will wear out quickly.

Optical considerations

In beadmaking or any process involving objects at high temperature you also have to worry about more esoteric things like exposure to non-ionizing electromagnetic radiation. This radiation has properties of both particles and waves. Its particle nature dictates that it travels as a discrete particle, called a photon, in straight lines at a fixed speed. Its wave nature dictates that the energy of each photon is inversely proportional to its wavelength (i.e. as energy increases, the wavelength decreases.) The electromagnetic radiation with which we are most familiar is caused by electrons that have been thermally excited to higher energy states falling back down to lower energy states. Each transition from a higher energy level to a lower energy level results in the release of a photon with an energy equal to that of the difference between the two energy levels. This cycle is repeated as long as heat is continued to be applied to the glowing material.

Electromagnetic spectrum

The electromagnetic spectrum is just what its name implies, a complete spectrum of radiation with wavelengths, which as illustrated in Figure 103, that go from angstroms to meters. The area of the electromagnetic spectrum of general consideration is that from about 200 to 2000 nanometers A nanometer, abbreviated as nm, is 1/1,000,000,000th of a meter (10^{-9}). The lower cutoff is 200 nm because radiation with wavelengths shorter than this is usually absorbed by air.

It is convenient to label or give names to portions of this spectrum which are usually based on some combination of properties such as wavelength, common use or biological activity. Visible light is the range of the spectrum that humans have evolved to use for sight. This familiar span ranges from the shortest wavelength of 400 nm for violet to about 700 nm for red. The exact range visible to each person varies somewhat. Radiation with wavelengths longer than this is referred to as infrared radiation (IR) and that with shorter wavelengths is referred to as

© 1996 James Kervin

ultraviolet radiation (UV). The ultraviolet region is usually further subdivided into smaller bands on the basis of phenomenological effects. Because these effects do not have sharp wavelength cutoffs, the effects may carry over somewhat between bands. The lowest band UV-C (200 to 290 nm) is not present in great quantity in nature because it is absorbed by earth's atmosphere. The band from 290 to 320 nm is called UV-B and is that band of radiation usually known for causing sunburns. Lastly the UV-A band from 320 to 400 nm is that spectral region that was used in the 60's to excite those fluorescent posters.

Electromagnetic radiation damage mechanisms

When the electromagnetic radiation in a photon is absorbed by tissue, all of that energy is transferred to the absorbing atom or molecule. This energy puts the atom or molecule into an excited state. The mode of the excitation depends upon the wavelength of the photon. The shorter the wavelength, which as may you remember equates to higher energy of the photon, the more energetic the result. In increasing order of energetics, the following may occur: molecular rotations, atomic vibrations in the molecule, changes in electronic energy state or expulsions of electrons. This highest energy result is also known as ionization and takes more energy than is available from the region of the spectrum with which we are concerned. That is why I originally said we are dealing with non-ionizing radiation.

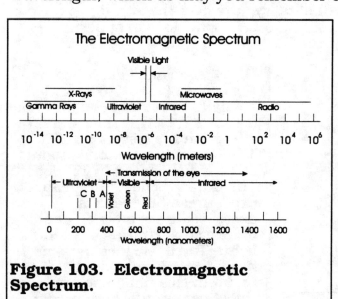

Figure 103. Electromagnetic Spectrum.

Infrared radiation may induce rotational and vibrational states in a molecule. Visible and ultraviolet radiation may induce higher vibrational states or electronic excitations. Vision and photosynthesis are two beneficial results of such an interaction. Once the energy is absorbed by molecules within a cell, any of a number of results are possible. The energy could be dissipated as heat. The molecule may be structurally altered or even break apart. The molecule may react with another molecule. The overall result to the cell from these changes may vary from changes in cell function to death. The question is how does this relate to the eye.

The eye, as illustrated in Figure 104, is essentially a near-spherical organ with a transparent window on the front called the cornea. The cornea is part of the exterior sheath of the eye called the sclera. The eye is sheltered from the outside by the brow and the eyelids of which the conjunctiva is part. The iris divides the eye into two chambers filled with clear fluids or humors. It also serves to regulate how much light enters the eye. Rays of light enter the eye and are focused first by the shape of the cornea and second by the lens onto the retina. This is where the chemical reactions that the brain interprets as sight occur. Electromagnetic radiation of different wavelengths interact differently with the eye. Let's examine how these different spectrum ranges interact with the eye to cause damage.

UV-C is essentially totally absorbed in the cornea. Its effects are cumulative over about a day long exposure because of the fast rate of growth of corneal cells. Acute effects of absorption by the cornea are essentially pain and inflammation. It may feel as if sand is in your eyes. This is usually felt sometime between 30 minutes to 24 hours after the exposure depending on the degree of the exposure. Higher exposures are felt sooner. The worst of the symptoms are usually over after about 6 to 24 hours and rarely last longer than 48 hours again because of the rapid cell growth rate. Very rarely does permanent damage result but also, unlike skin, the cornea does not develop increased tolerance with repeated exposure. The one type of permanent damage that can result to the cornea is through the growth of pterygium over the surface of the eye and some loss in sphericity of the eye.

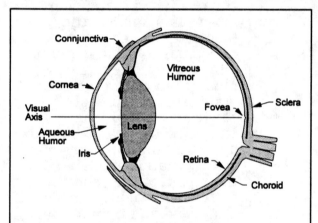

Figure 104. Cross sectional view of an eye.

UV-B is partially absorbed by the cornea (about 40%) and partially by the aqueous humor (about 10%.) This has similar effects on the cornea as UV-C. The rest of the photons (about 50%) are absorbed by the lens. The primary effect of repeated exposures of the lens is decreased transmission or increased scattering of visible light. The basic mechanisms or fundamental changes that result in this phenomenon, called cataract formation, are poorly understood. They are thought to be due to changes in cell structure, fluid imbalances, mineral buildups or protein aggregation. The damage is cumulative and permanent.

UV-A has less and less absorption by the cornea and aqueous humor as the wavelength increases toward visible light. So more and more is absorbed by the lens until the lens too starts to become transparent as the wavelength approaches visible light. This can lead to accelerated aging of the retina, but far and away the primary damage again occurs to the lens as with UV-B.

Visible light can also cause damage to the eye and this will primarily occur in the retina. Because of the eye's sensitivity to visible light, protective reactions such as iris constriction, squinting or closing of the eye will generally protect it. If you do persist in viewing bright visible light, you can suffer photochemical retinal injuries that can reduce the eye's ability to detect light.

Safety   231

Near infrared (700 to 1400 nm) is more dangerous because a good portion of it penetrates through the various ocular media and is actually focused onto the retina. This leads to heat buildup that can not be felt because there are no pain sensors there. The buildup of heat leads to denaturation of the biomolecules in the retina. In addition, absorption in the other features such as the lens and the iris can also result. Here the lens is primarily damaged by tissue peeling of the posterior surface of the lens. Damage to the iris is usually in the form of hemorrhages and inflammation.

Far infrared (1400 nm to 100 μm) is primarily absorbed in the cornea. Delivered at low power, it can again lead to itchy sore eyes. At moderate power, opacification caused by protein coagulation can result but pain felt on the skin usually causes you to close your eyes.

You have to understand that damage is actually done by ambient levels of UV, visible and IR light all the time, but that this level is such that the natural on-going cellular renewal process is able to keep up with it. Something that upsets this balance by decreasing the body's recuperative powers can only make the situation worse. Chemicals that make the eye tissue more photosensitive can do this. Tetracyline, a common antibiotic is an example of a common drug that is a photosensitizer. You may be interested to know though that individual or racial features do not seem to play as important role in eye sensitivity to light exposure as does the skin.

There are a number of factors that dictate the severity of an optical exposure that you receive. They include: the temperature of the object, its size and the distance from your eyes. The hotter an object is the more light that it emits and the wider the spectrum of the emitted light. Both of these are a result of the electrons getting raised to higher energy levels. This allows them to either have more small energy transitions as they fall to their ground state or have larger ones. More transitions means more photons although of longer wavelengths. Larger transitions means more energetic light of shorter wavelengths. The size of the hot object defines the amount of material that is heated to high temperature. This translates directly to more electrons getting excited and thus more photons released. Therefore you get a much larger dose of optical radiation from a kiln than you do from a torch at the same temperature. The last factor that effects the exposure is the distance from it. The light from a kiln seems much brighter from 3 feet away than it does from across the room. This is because the distance between photons gets greater as you get further from the light source. Thus the farther away you are, the fewer photons that hit your eye. Unfortunately knowing all this does not help too much because you can not necessarily do much about controlling these factors; you have to get the glass to a certain temperature to work it, your bead can not be too small and your arms are only so long.

Threshold limit value (TLV) standards have been set for UV, visible and IR light exposures by the American Conference of Governmental Industrial Hygienists (ACGIH). These standards give recommended limits and they are published as part of their annual booklet on TLV's for chemical materials in the workplace. These limits have been established

© 1996 James Kervin

to avoid injuries to the eye of the type listed from chronic workplace exposures 8 hours a day. To determine whether the exposure you receive is bad or not you have to first evaluate the frequency distribution of that exposure. They are weighted by the eyes sensitivity to that region and these products are then summed over the three regions. Of course if at all possible, you should always operate by the ALARA principle. Keep your exposures As Low As Reasonably Achievable.

Eye protection

There are two basic types of protection from electromagnetic radiation: absorbing and reflecting filters. One type of absorbing filter that you may already be aware of are welding filters. They are characterized by shade numbers where the higher the shade number the darker they are. The problem with using them for beadmaking is that it becomes difficult to distinguish colors when wearing them; everything looks green. Heat absorbing glass is one way to reduce the IR without losing color. Two millimeters of Shott KG5 glass will reduce the IR content by a factor of about 1000 with little appreciable color loss. Reflecting filters form the other type of eye protection and usually consists of a layer of gold or aluminum on the outer surface of your glasses. This layer reflects much of the incident radiation. This type of protective glasses suffer from a number of problems. First they can scratch easily if not handled delicately and second they change the apparent colors of your bead although not as bad as welders shades.

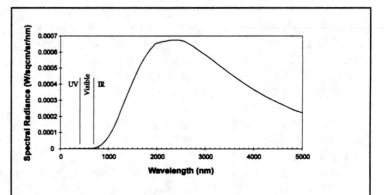

Figure 105. Blackbody model of the electromagnetic radiation from hot glass.

In order to investigate the risks of exposure to electromagnetic radiation and decide which form of protection makes sense, I developed a spreadsheet that first calculated an approximation of the electromagnetic radiation that is emitted by a hot glass object. This was done by modeling it as a black body radiator with an emmittance of one. From spectral measurements of glass irradiance that I have seen in the literature, this is not a bad assumption. It tends to under represent the UV exposure slightly as well as the visible sodium flair, while at the same time overestimating slightly the IR portion of the spectrum. From the chart in Figure 105 which depicts the spectral distribution for an object at 1700°F, it is seen that almost all of the radiation given off by such an object lies in the infrared portion of the spectrum.

The next step was to determine how much radiation passes through various different types of glasses. Bob Aurelius of Aura Lens Products, Inc. provided me with transmission curves in the UV, visible and near IR

Safety

for a variety of common glasses, but as you can see from the figure this is only a small part of the spectrum that we need to protect against. He also made me aware of Gary Meyers' study from Fusion that discusses absorption over the entire IR region. Using these and other sources I found by searching through technical libraries, I was able to estimate transmittance for various different glasses across the relevant portion of the IR spectrum (out to 5000 nm). So now I could calculate what was impinging on the eyeball.

Then to decide if that exposure was harmful or not, I compared it to the threshold limit values published by the ACGIH as discussed earlier. From this study I learned a number of things. First UV and visible light exposure do not seem to be a problem for any situation that you are likely to get into while making glass beads. Second was that for the normal beadmaker making wound glass beads, rose didymium glasses are probably sufficient. Of course there are exceptions to this rule. Figure 106 illustrates how your total IR exposure from a 2 in^2 bead heated to 1700°F changes with the distance that you hold it from your eyes. The threshold limit exposure as illustrated is 10 mW/cm^2. From the figure you see that if you were to always work with your arms outstretched to 20 inches or greater you would not even need protective glasses. Wearing protective didymium glasses allow you to work with the bead as close as 10 inches. Also if you hold the bead closer than 10 inches, your glasses will not provide you with enough protection.

Some people are more sensitive than others and may find they have to hold the bead further away to avoid that burning itching feeling that you get when you have overdone things. Alternatively they may want to wear glasses that can provide more protection than rose didymium. From examining the transmission curves that I have been provided, it appears that the AUR-92 lens does provide a little extra protection. For more even more protection, you might also want to consider using a lens that includes some heat absorbing (IR) glass such as the AGW-186. I also know that 15 nm of gold coating would provide enough reflectance to protect your eyes but do not know how much is on the glasses currently on the market. All of these glasses are more expensive than ordinary didymiums though. You could also consider using a medium welder's shade such as a #3 or #4 but you will lose your ability to see the true colors.

If you are blowing pyrex beads, the temperatures at which you are working are slightly hotter and your beads tend to be slightly larger. Also you tend to bring the bead up toward your face to inflate them. These factors

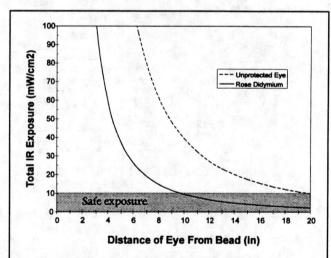

Figure 106. IR radiation reaching eye during winding of beads.

© 1996 James Kervin

will work to increase your exposure. So in this case you will want to invest in glasses with a little more protection than rose didymium. I would suggest the AGW-186 so that you still have good color rendition.

If you are making drawn glass beads, where you are working in front of a furnace and glory hole, you would be advised to read the report by Dave Gruenig on a NIOSH inspection of the Louie Glass Company, Inc. of Weston, West Virginia that was published in The Independent Glassblower. An operation such as this will expose you to considerable IR radiation both from the glass that you are handling as well as from the hot equipment. Their findings and my calculations agree that for such an operation as this didymium are not even close to being adequate. For such a situation as this, you require heavy duty protection such as a welder's shade. The problem is that to be adequate for this purpose the shade should transmit only about 1% of the incident IR radiation (about a number 5 shade). This allows your face to feel hot about the same time as your eyes are starting to receive dangerous amounts of radiation. The problem with this is that these shades are so dark that it is hard to see what you are doing.

Dave presents some good ideas on how to compromise in a way to satisfy both of these requirements. He suggests that for the general work around the shop you wear a shade that provides a good amount of protection but still allows you to see what you are doing. He suggests wearing about a #1 or 2 for this (the AGW-186 would also be a good choice and would allow good color visibility.) Then when you make a gather or reheat your work, you can flip down a darker shade like a #3 or 4 that you have mounted on a plastic face shield down over the lighter glasses. This shield should be trimmed to expose your face because if your face becomes unbearably hot, then that is an indication that you are probably getting a larger IR dose than even the shades can compensate for. Another option for getting additional protection from radiation coming off hot equipment is to permanently mount supplemental shades in front of the equipment.

During the making of kilnworked beads, you are not exposed to hot glass for long periods of time, but the physical size of the hot open kiln allows a lot of electromagnetic radiation to be emitted. For such a case, you should probably again wear at least a number 3 welders shade and try not to peek into the kiln too much.

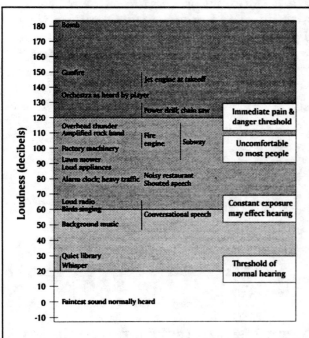

Figure 107. Loudness of common sounds.

Safety

Hearing risks

We as beadmakers are subjected to certain low level noise sources that are on almost constantly during our work. These sources include: the sound of our torch, the whir of the ventilation system, etc. We all now recognize the danger to our hearing of loud noises such as heard at the typical rock concerts, but few of us recognize the danger from day-to-day low level sound sources. Ricky Charles Dodson brought this danger to my attention because he became aware of it the hard way. He went in for a checkup one day and his doctor pointed out that he had a significant hearing loss in the high frequency range. His doctor asked him if he was exposed to a lot of loud noises in his work. When Ricky said no, the doctor next queried him about constant low-level sound exposures of some type. Ricky again could not identify anything. At least not till later when he got back to his studio and started working. He then realized that he was constantly surrounded by low-level, sound.

Sound is produced when something causes vibration waves in air. These sound waves spread out from the noise source getting weaker as they go. The measure of loudness used for sound is the bel - after Alexander Graham Bell. The term you are probably familiar with is the decibel (dB) or one tenth of a bel. Bels and decibel are logarithmic values (do not worry about what this means) of the actual loudness value such that for every 10 dB or 1 bel the sound is actually 10 times louder. For 20 dB it is 100 time louder and so on. As an example, Figure 107 illustrates the loudness levels of many common day-to-day sound conditions.

People have a responsive hearing range from about 20 to 20,000 vibration cycles per second (known as hertz or hz) but usually can discern sounds from about 500 to 4000 hz. The range of typical speech sounds is from 500 to 2000 hz. It is the upper range of about 4000 hz that is usually lost from age or constant exposure to noise. Why is this though? You might think that you would get accustomed to higher noise level with repeated exposures just like you get stronger with exercise. Unfortunately not, instead these high levels of noise damage the delicate nerves of the ear. So how loud of noises are damaging to the ear. We already alluded to this in Figure 107 with the captions in the boxes to the right but let's define it a little better. Figure 108 gives us a little better answer to this question. It gives accepted threshold limit value for daily exposures of different noise loudness levels that will not result in hearing

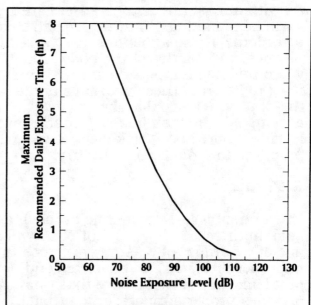

Figure 108. Maximum recommended sound exposure levels.

© 1996 James Kervin

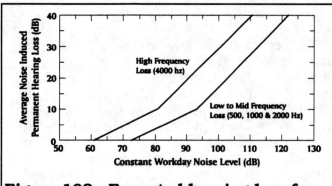

Figure 109. **Expected hearing loss from working noise exposures.**

problems as published by the ACGIH.

But if you ignore these recommendations and expose yourself to noise every day for eight hours a day, what level of hearing loss can you expect over your working lifetime (assumed to be 50 years). The answer to this question is illustrated in Figure 109. Here we see that in conditions as low 80 dB or equivalent to that of a noisy restaurant we can expect to lose 10 dB of our high frequency hearing capability. This means that a sound has to be 10 times louder before we will hear it. Similarly a 90 dB work environment, equivalent to mowing the lawn, would result in a 20 dB hearing loss. Here a sound would have to be 100 time louder before we would hear it. (Note that these values from Kryter are lower than those recommended by the ACGIH.)

So a word to the wise, you should assess your studio situation to decide if wearing some soft sponge ear plugs or those hard plastic ear muffs might not make sense to block out some of this noise. You may even find yourself more peaceful and those of you who want to can still listen to the radio or television while wearing them.

Ergonomic risks

As with almost any activity, there are ergonomic risks associated with glass beadmaking. They include strains, sprains and cumulative trauma disorders. These afflictions are the result of exceeding the normal physical capabilities of the body. The body has a way of letting us know when this has happened through pain or soreness in body parts. You need to listen to these warnings and analyze what you are doing to cause this injury. The goal is then to determine how to modify what you do to accomplish the task in a way that it matches your capabilities. Also by learning more about risk factors, you may be able to modify your work practices to reduce risk of injury.

Risk factors

One of the biggest ergonomic problem areas in the general population is back injuries. Eighty percent of us will suffer lower back pain caused by one of a number of reasons: poor posture (yes your mother was right), improper lifting or bad physical conditioning. What can you do to avoid problems? First make sure that whatever chair you use at your bench provides proper support for your back. Try to observe how you do things to ensure that you are not doing them in a way that put you in awkward positions for any period of time. Try not to bend forward, sideways or twist when lifting objects. Try to develop mechanical means of lifting heavy objects whenever possible. When lifting heavy objects, keep them close to your body. Lift from your knees whenever possible and try to have objects raised about 30" off of the floor before lifting them. Get someone to help you with heavy objects. Keep yourself in good physical condition, especially your stomach muscles which supply much of the support for your back.

A common complaint with beadmakers is of sore and tired shoulders. This is largely a result of improper positioning of the arms. Any posture where the arms are held extended from the body at angles more than 45° from the body in any direction puts strain on your shoulders. This problem is aggravated by holding this posture for long periods of time or by lifting loads on the order as little as 10 pounds. For beadmakers the primary problem comes from how they hold their arms. If they hold them pointed outward for long periods of times this will strain your shoulders. To alleviate this problem, it is suggested that you develop a means to rest your elbows on some surface during your time at the bench. This can be in the form of rests on your workbench or your chair. Also make sure that your bench is at a height such that you are comfortable when your elbows are resting on the rests.

One area that does not appear to be too much of a problem with beadmakers is elbows. One does not usually get tennis elbow from beadmaking. Elbow problems are usually the result of forearm rotations or of arm extensions with weights at the end of your arms. These types motions are not common in beadmaking.

An area of increasing concern is in the hand and the wrist. Motions of the hand which take the wrist near the ends of its motion (more than about 45° off of straight) causes compression on nerves to the hand by tendons, bones and ligaments. You need to try and hold your hands in such a manner as to keep the wrists straight when working at your bench to avoid this pitfall. The type of grasp that you use in your work also affects the stress on your wrists. Making tools with larger handles or grips up to about 1 1/4" makes them easier to handle. Padding tool grips and making them higher friction also makes it easier to work with them.

Cumulative trauma disorders

Many repetitions of an injurious body motion can increase the damaging effect of any of the above problems. This cumulative damage is increased when they are accompanied by cold, vibration or mechanical stress. Cold limits your feelings which in turn inhibits your ability to feel the natural body feedback mechanism. Vibrations require stronger gripping forces that squeeze the underlying nerves more. Mechanical stress results from any pressure on the nerves. This can be from something as simple as resting your arms against your forearms instead of on your elbows. This can obstruct blood flow and again put pressure on underlying nerves.

The most widely known of these disorders is carpal tunnel syndrome. It is the loss of feeling and dexterity to the hands and is caused by pressure on the median nerve by tendons, bones or carpal ligaments in the wrist.

© 1996 James Kervin

238   Glass Beadmaking

Repeated insults on this nerve leads to inflammation of the surrounding tissue as well as prolonged and debilitating pain. To avoid this problem, you need to keep your wrists as straight as possible while you work, avoid leaning on your forearms, take frequent rests and make sure your tools are as comfortable as possible to handle.

Suggested further reading

American Conference of Governmental Industrial Hygienists (ACGIH), Threshold Limit Values for Chemical Substances and Physical Agents and Biological Exposure Indices, 6500 Glenway Ave., Bldg. D-7, Cincinnati, OH 45211-4438, Tel (513)661-7881

ACGIH. Industrial Ventilation, 1982

The American Red Cross. Standard First Aid and Personal Safety, Doubleday & Company, Inc. 1973

Clark, Nancy; Cutter, Thomas, and McGrane, Jean-Ann. Ventilation - A Practical Guide for Artists, Craftspeople, and Others in the Arts, Lyons & Burford, 1984

Grandolfo, M. Rindi, A and Sliney, D. H., Light, Lasers, and Synchrotron Radiation A Health Risk Assessment, NATO ASI Series, 1989

Gruenig, David. "Eye Protection for Furnace Glassblower", The Independent Glassblower, Issue No. 18, (August/September), 1990

Kryter, Karl D. The Effects of Noise on Man, Academic Press, Inc, 1985

McCann, Michael. Health Hazards Manual for Artists, Nick Lyons Books, 1985

McCloskey, E. S. "Lets Make an Exhaust Hood", Glass Line, Volume 9 Number 1, (June/July), 1995

Myers, Gary E. "Optical Radiation Hazards in Glassblowing", Fusion August 1976

Rossol, Monona. The Artist's Complete Health and Safety Guide, Allworth Press, 1990

Spielholz, Peregrin. Identifying and Controlling Ergonomic Risks in Glassblowing, 1993 Journal of the Glass Art Society

© 1996 James Kervin

Appendixes

© 1996 James Kervin

240   Glass Beadmaking

© 1996 James Kervin

Glossary

annealing — process of relieving internal stress by reheating a bead and slowly cooling it back to room temperature.

aventurine — translucent glass with sparkling inclusions of copper typically gold or blue in color.

backfire — the instantanious extinguishing and reignition of a torch flame that creates an anoying sound.

blowpipe — hollow metal (usually stainless steel) tube used to gather glass and shape it by blowing into the gather.

blown beads — beads made by shaping glass tubing in a flame.

cane — a thin rod or strip of glass used to decorate beads.

canemaking — the stretching of hot glass into cane.

casing — covering all or part of the bead with a transparent color, most often clear.

COE — (coefficient of expansion) average rate of linear expansion with change in temperature of a glass measured between room temperature and 300°C. Usually expressed as a whole number with an implied multiplier of 10^{-7} in/in/°C.

colorants — materials, usually metal oxides, that are used to color glass.

dichroic — glass with a thin film of evaporative coated dielectric (non-conductive) materials. Has different colors under transmitted and reflective light.

drawn beads — beads made by drawing out a hollow bubble into tubing and then cutting this into beads.

feathering — raking through lines a number of times reversing direction of the rake after each time.

ferro — steel plate used to preheat arrange murrine slices. Traditionally done in a furnace now done in kilns.

festooning — raking through line a number of times in the same direction.

filigrana — glass rod with a solid core of a opalescent color cased in a transparent color.

flameworking — process of making glass objects in flame of a torch.

flashback — burning back of the flame into the inside of your gas system – it is very dangerous.

frit — ground glass granules.

fusing — process of melting together pieces of glass in a kiln.

gather — blob of molten glass traditionally on the end of a punty or blowpipe. In flameworking the term has been generalized to refer to glass collected on rods or tubes by partially melting them.

glory hole — gas-fired chamber used to heat glass on a punty or blowpipe to high temperatures.

hard glass — glass that melts at high temperatures - borosilicate and fused silica glasses.

iridizing — a lustrous glass surface coating usually of stannous chloride that is applied to hot glass.

kiln — an insulated chamber usually heated electrically used to precisely control high temperature exposures.

© 1996 James Kervin

242   Glass Beadmaking

kilnworking   process of working glass at high temperature in a kiln.

lampworking   same as flameworking.

latticino   literally translated from Italian as "little milk-white strands" which was made by twisting clear/white filigrana. Is often generalized to refer to any similar twisted cane.

mandrel   metal rod about which the bead is wound.

marver   surface on which hot glass can be shaped. Traditionally was made of marble now mostly steel or graphite is used.

millefiori   literally translated from Italian as "a thousand flowers." A phrase first recorded in 1827 by Heinrich Freiherr von Minutoli to characterize glass cane with cross sections depicting stylized flowers.

mosaic glass   objects made by fusing preformed elements together in a mold.

murrina   (plural - **murrine**) slice of millefiori or other complex cane used to decorate a bead.

optic mold   patterned mold used to shape gathers or parisons.

oxidizing flame a flame with an excess of oxygen.

parison   partially inflated gather on a blowpipe.

pate de verre   literally translated from French as "paste of glass." Glass process of fusing frit in a refractory mold.

point   narrowed down section of glass tubing or rod make by stretching after heating in the flame.

premixed torch   a torch where the gases are mixed inside the body of the torch.

psi   an abreviation for a measure of pressure meaning pounds per square inch.

psig   an abreviation for a measure of pressure meaning pounds per square inch gauge – that read on a gauge or over atmospheric pressure.

punty   metal (usually stainless steel) or glass rod used to hold glass object in the flame of a torch, glory hole or furnace.

raking   pulling a tool along a hot bead surface to distort it.

reducing flame   a flame deficient in oxygen. Such a flame can steel oxygen from metal oxide colorants-dulling them.

ribbon   decorative glass cane that has a thin rectangular cross section.

rods   thin cylindrical lengths of glass.

sheet glass   sheets of glass like that used in windows.

soft glass   glass that melts at a low temperature - soda-lime and lead glasses.

slumping   a kilnworking technique where glass at high temperature sags under its own weight into a different shape.

stringers   threads of glass used for decoration.

surface mixed   refers to a type of torch where the gases mix at the tip outside of the torch.

viscosity   measure of the resistance to flow of a material.

wound beads   beads formed by winding molten glass around a removable mandrel.

© 1996 James Kervin

Bead shapes

The following table gives lists the families and sub-group of regular-rounded bead shapes. These shapes are then illustrated on the following pages.

Table 22. Families and sub-groups of regular-rounded bead shapes.

Family	Class	Disc Beads	Short Beads	Standard Beads	Long Beads
Convex	Oblate	Oblate Disc	Oblate	Circular	Ellipsoid
	Barrel	Barrel Disc	Short Barrel	Standard Barrel	Long Barrel
	Convex Cone	Convex Cone Disc	Short Convex Cone	Standard Convex Cone	Long Convex Cone
	Convex Truncated Cone	Convex Truncated Cone Disc	Short Convex Truncated Cone	Standard Convex Truncated Cone	Long Convex Truncated Cone
	Convex Bicone	Convex Bicone Disc	Short Convex Bicone	Standard Convex Bicone	Long Convex Bicone
	Convex Truncated Bicone	Convex Truncated Bicone Disc	Short Convex Truncated Bicone	Standard Convex Truncated Bicone	Long Convex Truncated Bicone
	Pear Shape	Pear Shape Disc	Short Pear Shape	Standard Pear Shape	Long Pear Shape
Straight	Cylinder	Cylinder Disc	Short Cylinder	Standard Cylinder	Long Cylinder
	Cone	Cone Disc	Short Cone	Standard Cone	Long Cone
	Truncated Cone	Truncated Cone Disc	Short Truncated Cone	Standard Truncated Cone	Long Truncated Cone
	Bicone	Bicone	Short Bicone	Standard Bicone	Long Bicone
	Truncated Bicone	Truncated Bicone Disc	Short Truncated Bicone	Standard Truncated Bicone	Long Truncated Bicone
	Chamfered Cylinder	Chamfered Cylinder Disc	Short Chamfered Cylinder	Standard Chamfered Cylinder	Long Chamfered Cylinder
	Double Chamfered	Double Chamfered Disc	Short Double Chamfered	Standard Double Chamfered	Long Double Chamfered
Concave	Concave	Concave Disc	Short Concave	Standard Concave	Long Concave
	Concave Cone	Concave Cone Disc	Short Concave Cone	Standard Concave Cone	Long Concave Cone
	Concave Truncated Cone	Concave Truncated Cone Disc	Short Concave Truncated Cone	Standard Concave Truncated Cone	Long Concave Truncated Cone

© 1996 James Kervin

	Concave Bicone	Concave Bicone Disc	Short Concave Bicone	Standard Concave Bicone	Long Concave Bicone
	Concave Truncated Bicone	Concave Truncated Bicone Disc	Short Concave Truncated Bicone	Standard Concave Truncated Bicone	Long Concave Truncated Bicone
Convex & Straight	Cylinder with 1 Convex End	Cylinder Disc with 1 Convex End	Short Cylinder with 1 Convex End	Standard Cylinder with 1 Convex End	Long Cylinder with 1 Convex End
	Cylinder with 2 Convex Ends	Cylinder Disc with 2 Convex Ends	Short Cylinder with 2 Convex Ends	Standard Cylinder with 2 Convex Ends	Long Cylinder with 2 Convex Ends
Concave & Straight	Cylinder with 1 Convex End	Cylinder Disc with 1 Convex End	Short Cylinder with 1 Convex End	Standard Cylinder with 1 Convex End	Long Cylinder with 1 Convex End
	Cylinder with 2 Concave Ends	Cylinder Disc with 2 Concave Ends	Short Cylinder with 2 Concave Ends	Standard Cylinder with 2 Concave Ends	Long Cylinder with 2 Concave Ends

© 1996 James Kervin

Bead Shapes 245

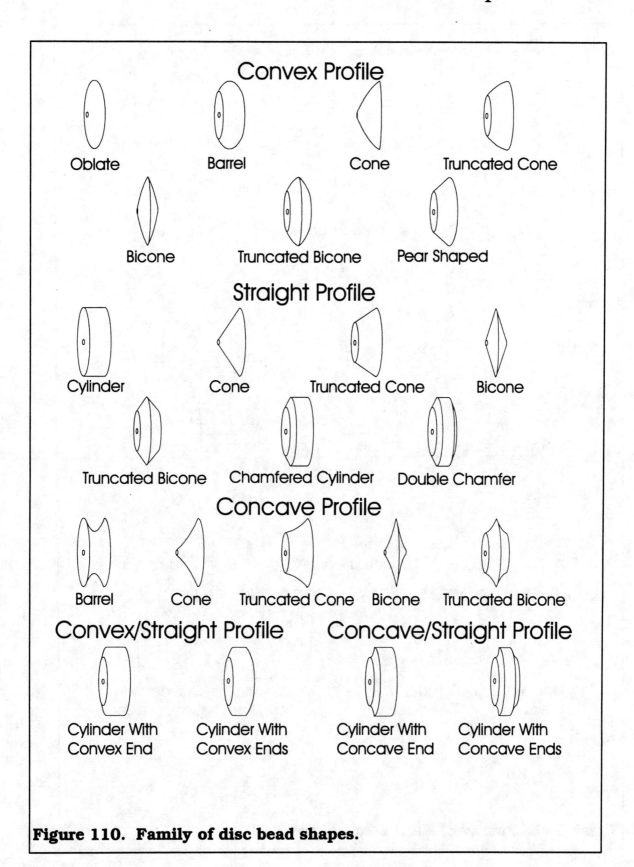

Figure 110. Family of disc bead shapes.

246 Glass Beadmaking

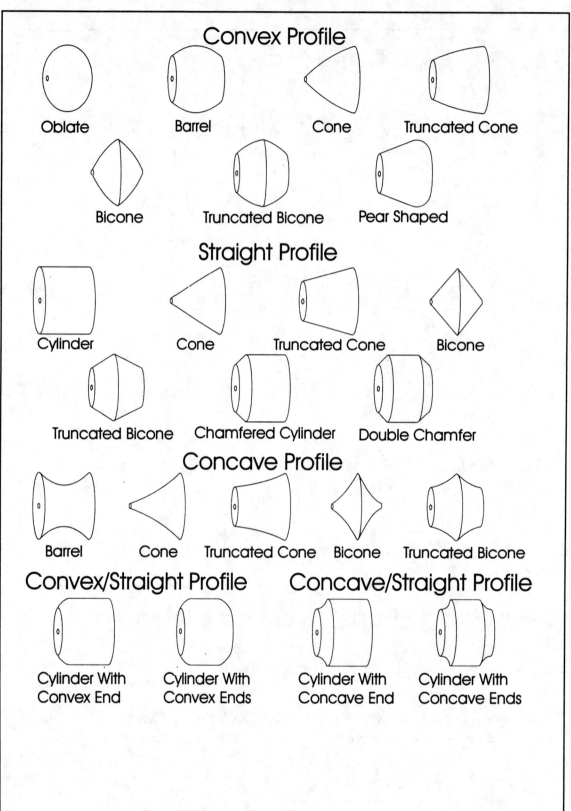

Figure 111. Family of short bead shapes.

Bead Shapes 247

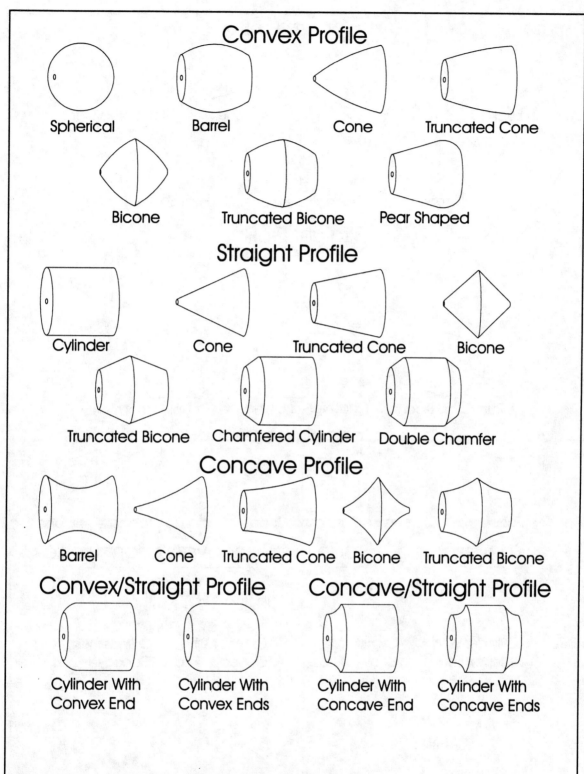

Figure 112. **Family of standard beads shapes.**

© 1996 James Kervin

248   Glass Beadmaking

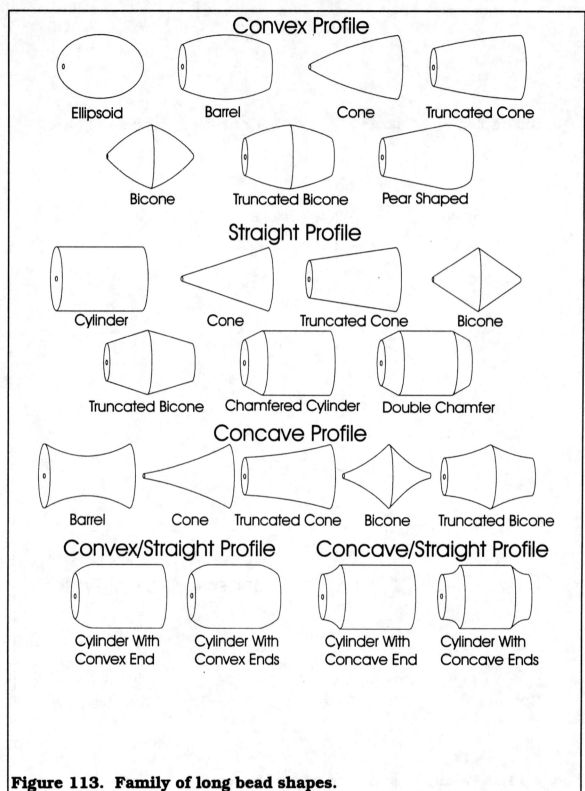

Figure 113. Family of long bead shapes.

© 1996 James Kervin

Suppliers and manufacturer sources

Alpha Supplies
1225 Holis St.
Bremerton, WA 98310
Tel (800) 257-4211   Fax (206) 377-9235
Wholesale distributor of lapidary and jewelry supplies. Includes tumblers, saws, laps, cleaners, etc.

Allen Graff
3823 E. Anaheim Street
Long Beach, CA 90804
Tel & FAX (310) 494-3823
Manufacturer of dichroic glass. Send for free catalog.

American Optical
Safety Products Division
Southbridge, MA 01550
Safety glasses

Arrow Springs
4570 Tennessee Drive
Shingle Springs, CA 95682
Tel (916)677-9482
Supplier of beadmaking equipment and supplies. Includes torches, supplies, tools, holding fingers, molds, kilns, sludge, etc.

ASG
7015 N. 58th Ave.
Glendale, AZ 85301
Tel (602) 939-7260   Fax (602) 939-8044
Wholesale manufacture of glass beadmaking supplies and tools. Instructional video and books on beadmaking.

Aura Lens Products
P.O.Box 763
St. Cloud, MN 56302-0763
Tel (612)393-3182   Fax (612)393-3188
Manufacture of protective glasses including rose didymium, AUR-92, AGW-186, and combinations of the same.

Bead Supplies International
13609 Engleman Drive
Laurel, MD 20208
Tel (301)953-1740   FAX (301)490-3099
Supplies materials for beadmaking - paddles, molds, glass etc.

C & R Loo, Inc.
1085 Essex Ave.
Richmond, CA 94801
Tel (800)227-1780   Fax (510) 232-7810
Distributor of stained glass, fusible glass, dichroic glass, hot glass tools, frits,. powders (Kugler Zimmermann, etc.), and casting glasses.

© 1996 James Kervin

250   Glass Beadmaking

Covington Engineering Corp.
P.O. Box 35
Redlands, CA 92373
Tel (714) 793-6636
Manufacturer and distributor of lapidary and cold glassworking equipment and supplies. Includes tumblers, belts, laps etc.

Crystal Myths, Inc.
3806 Cherokee Rd. N.E.
Albuquerque, NM 87110
Tel (505) 883-9295   Fax (505) 889-9556
Videotapes on glass beadmaking and sculptured glass school of lampworking.

Dichroic Fusing Source
P. O. Box 1192
Oregon City, OR 97045
Tel (503) 650-6424   (800) 827-7044
Manufacturer of dichroic glass. No minimum.

Ricky Charles Dodson
4403 Hank Ave, Dept G-1
Austin, TX 78745
Tel (512) 444-8712   (800) 624-GLAS
Distributor of Chem-o-lene.

Ed Hoy's
1620 Frontenac Rd.
Naperville, IL 60540-1762
Tel (800) 323-5668   FAX (708) 416-0448
Wholesale distributor of complete hot and cold glassworking equipment and supplies. Includes torches, regulators, tools, glass etc. $50 minimum order from the hot glass catalog.

Fenton Glass Studio
4001 San Leandro Street # 8
Oakland, CA 94601
Tel (510) 533-5515   FAX (510)
Distributor of Rueche enamels and a good place to seek instruction on all sorts of kilnworking and beadmaking instruction.

Frantz Bead Company
E. 1222 Sunset Hill Road
Shelton, WA 98584
Tel (360) 426-6712   Fax (360) 427-5866
Distributor of beadmaking equipment and supplies. Includes torches, regulators, safety glasses, tools, Moretti glass, gold leaf, millefiori, etc.

Fusion Headquarters
PO Box 69312
Portland, OR 97201
Tel (503) 245-7547

© 1996 James Kervin

Suppliers and Manufacturer Sources   251

Distributor of hot glass equipment and supplies. Include Murphy Fire Bucket, Fuse Master Products, books, videos, molds, Bullseye pattern bars, kilns, etc.

Glass Craft Inc.
626 Moss St.
Golden, CO 80401
Tel (303) 278-4670   FAX (303)278-4672
Distributor of flameworking and beadmaking supplies. Includes torches, regulators, safety glasses, tools, pyrex glass, etc.

Glass Warehouse
800 Orange Street   or   14000 183rd Street
P.O. Box 1039   La Palma, CA 90623-1010
Millville, NJ 08332-8039
Tel (800) 833-0410 in NJ call (609) 327-5228   FAX (609) 825-9014
Distributor of glass tubing, rods, blanks and sheet. Some unusual tubing shapes available.

Gypsy Dragon Bead Company
#507   2402 University Ave. W.
St. Paul, MN 55114
Tel (612) 644-9621   Fax (612) 644-0844
Importers of European glass and equipment. They have some bead presses.

Mom's Stained Glass Supplies
8740-18 Cherry Lane
Laurel, MD 20707
Tel (301) 953-1740   Fax (301) 490-3613
Distributor of stained glass and beadmaking supplies.

M-Tech Lampworking Supplies
P.O. Box 1358
Cedar Ridge, CA 95924
Tel (800) 260-2137   Fax (916) 269-2930
Flameworking equipment and supplies, torches, glass, custom graphite tools, diamond products, kilns and saws.

Pacific Glass
125 W. 157th St.
Gardena, CA 90248
Tel (310) 516-7828   Fax (310) 516-0335
Wholesale distributor of stained glass, fusing and beadmaking supplies.

Queen Beads
Distributor of Satake glass.

Spruce Pine Batch
Wholesale distributor of batching materials including colored glass powders like Kugler, Zimmermann, etc.

Steinert Industries, Inc.
1000 Mogadore Rd

© 1996 James Kervin

252   Glass Beadmaking

Kent OH 44240
Tel (216) 678-0028   (800) 727-7473   FAX (216) 678-8238
Manufacturer of glass blowing supplies many of which, like specialized marvers and optic molds which can be used in beadmaking.

The Glass Menagerie
8170 La Mesa Blvd
La Mesa, CA 91941
Tel/FAX (619)464-8323
Distributors of a full line of beadmaking and fusing supplies

Wale Apparatus Co.
400 Front St.
Hellertown, PA 18055
Tel (215) 838-7047   (800) 444-WALE   Fax (215) 838-7440
Distributor of flameworking supplies. Includes torches, regulators, safety glasses, tools, pyrex glass, etc.

© 1996 James Kervin

Related periodicals and resources

Bead & Button
Published by Conterie Press, Inc.
P.O. Box 1020
Norwalk, CT 06856
Tel (230) 857-5355
Bimonthly magazine devoted to the use of beads and buttons with occasional articles on bead artists and techniques.

Common Ground: Glass
Published by International Guild of Glass Artists, Inc.
Tonetta Lake Road
Brewster, NY 10509
Tel (914) 278-2152   Fax (914) 278-2481   CompuServe 70544,3642
Quarterly newsletter to facilitate communications among glass artists.

Fusion Journal
Published by American Scientific Glassblowers Society
1507 Hagley Rd
Toledo, OH 43612
A quarterly journal on topics of interest in scientific glassblowing.

Glass Art Magazine
Published by Travin Inc.
P.O. Box 260377
Highlands Ranch, CO 80126
Tel (303) 791-8998   FAX (303) 791-7739
Bimonthly magazine on many aspects of glassworking.

Glass Art Society
1305 4th Avenue, Suite 711
Seattle, WA 98101-2401
International nonprofit organization to advance appreciation, understanding and development of the glass arts worldwide. They have an annual convention and publish minutes of the convention.

Glass Artist Magazine
Formerly Professional Stained Glass Magazine
Published by Arts & Media Inc.
28 South State Street
Newtown, PA 18940
Tel (215) 860-9947   Fax (215)860-1812
Bimonthly magazine on many aspects of glassworking.

Glass Line Newsletter
120 South Kroeger Street
Anaheim, CA 92805
Tel (714) 520-0121   FAX (714) 520-4370
Bimonthly newsletter for lampworkers including beadmaking. It has a column on beadmaking. Also has an on-line bulletin board system.

© 1996 James Kervin

254 Glass Beadmaking

Glass Patterns Quarterly, Inc.
8300 Hidden Valley Road
Westport, KY 40077
Tel (502) 222 5631
Quarterly magazine with how to projects. Occasional articles on beads.

Lapidary Journal
Published by Lapidary Journal Inc.
Devon Office Center, Suite 201
60 Chestnut Avenue
Devon, PA 19333-1312
Tel (610) 293-0564
Monthly magazine devoted to gemstones and jewelry making. Occasional articles on glass beads and great source for information on lapidary equipment. Yearly bead issue.

Ornament Magazine
Published by Ornament Inc.
P.O. Box 2349
San Marcos, CA 92079-2349
Tel (619) 599-0222
Occasional articles on beadmaking and bead happenings with lots of color advertisements of other artists' work.

Orton Firing Line
P.O. Box 460
Westerville, OH 43081
Quarterly magazine on kiln use in glass and ceramics.

The Bead Release
4570 Tennessee Dr.
Shingle Springs, CA 95682
Newsletter for the Society of Glass Beadmakers. To join the society send $35 for individuals or $45 for family/business to:
Society of Glass Beadmakers
8170 La Mesa Blvd.
La Mesa, CA 91941

The Bead Museum
138-140 S. Montezuma Street
Prescott, Arizona 86303
Tel (602) 455-2431

The Corning Museum of Glass
Corning, NY 14830
A great place to visit and learn more about glass.

The Independent Glassblower
c/o Gruenig Glassworks
HC 30 Box 25
Barnet, VT 05821
Quarterly newsletter on glassblowing issues, equipment and practices.

© 1996 James Kervin